Vincent Colabella

About the Author

CATHERINE WHITNEY is a New York–based writer who has written or cowritten more than forty books on a wide range of topics. Whitney specializes in revealing fresh or unconventional perspectives on women's lives. She is the author of *The Calling: A Year in the Life of an Order of Nuns* and the coauthor with nine female U.S. senators of *Nine and Counting: The Women of the Senate.*

THE
WOMEN
OF WINDSOR

Their POWER, PRIVILEGE,
and PASSIONS

Her Majesty QUEEN ELIZABETH, *the Queen Mother*

Her Majesty QUEEN ELIZABETH II

Her Royal Highness the PRINCESS MARGARET

Her Royal Highness the Princess Royal, PRINCESS ANNE

Catherine Whitney

HARPER

NEW YORK · LONDON · TORONTO · SYDNEY

HARPER

FIRST HARPER PAPERBACK PUBLISHED 2007.

DESIGNED BY DEBORAH KERNER · DANCING BEARS

Family tree by Paul Whitney

The Library of Congress has catalogued the hardcover edition as follows:

Whitney, Catherine.
The women of Windsor: their power, privilege, and passions / Catherine Whitney.—1st ed.
p. cm.
Includes bibliographical references and index.
ISBN-13: 978-0-06-076584-2
ISBN-10: 0-06-076584-4
1. Windsor, House of. 2. Queens—Great Britain—Biography. 3. Princesses—Great
Britain—Biography. I. Title.

DA28.35.W54W47 2006
941.08'092'2—dc22
[B]
2005047175

ISBN: 978-0-06-076585-9 (pbk.)
ISBN-10: 0-06-076585-2 (pbk.)

08 09 10 11 ❖/QWF 10 9 8 7 6 5 4 3 2

DEDICATED TO THE WOMEN OF MY FAMILY

VERA, RUTH
RUBYE, BERTIE
BARBARA, JANET
ORPHALEE, PATTY
CATHERINE, MARY, MARGARET, JOANNE
SHERRY, MARCI, DEBORAH
MICHELLE, DEANA, MARTHA, KELLY, JESSICA
RACHAEL

CONTENTS

ACKNOWLEDGMENTS

WRITING ABOUT THE WOMEN OF WINDSOR has been like slowly unwrapping a precious and surprising gift. It is very satisfying to uncover the human element beyond the standard accounts of these fascinating historical characters. I owe this opportunity to my friend and agent, Jane Dystel, president of Dystel & Goderich Literary Management. This book has been Jane's passion for many years. She rightly noted that while volumes have been written about the Royal Family, an in-depth personal portrait of these four women and their joint roles in history had not been rendered. Were it not for Jane, this book would never have been written.

I am also grateful to Lucia Macro, my editor at HarperCollins, who has enthusiastically supported the book throughout the process. *The Women of Windsor* couldn't ask for a better home than HarperCollins.

Many people helped me along the way. In particular, I am thankful to Janet Schuler and Joanne Laha for their invaluable assistance with the research, to Paul Whitney for creating the clever family tree and for procuring a wonderful collection of photographs, to Michael Bourret for his persistence in obtaining rights, and to my friends in England, France, and the United States who vetted the most sensitive portions of the manuscript. Finally, my deepest appreciation goes to my partner, Paul Krafin, for his important input and support.

CAST OF CHARACTERS

THE FEATURED WOMEN OF WINDSOR
Queen Elizabeth, the Queen Mother

Queen Elizabeth II

Princess Margaret

Princess Anne

THEIR FATHERS AND HUSBANDS
Lord Strathmore (Bowes-Lyon)

King George VI

Prince Philip, Duke of Edinburgh

Antony Armstrong-Jones (Lord Snowdon)

Mark Phillips

Commander Timothy Laurence

THEIR PARAMOURS
Group Captain Peter Townsend

Roddy Llewellyn

Peter Cross

THEIR NEMESES
Edward, Duke of Windsor

Wallis (Simpson), Duchess of Windsor

THEIR MENTORS AND MEDDLERS
Lady Cecilia Strathmore

Queen Mary

King George V

Lady Mabell Airlie

Lord Louis Mountbatten

Winston Churchill

Sir Alan Lascelles

THEIR CARETAKERS
Clara Cooper Knight ("Allah")
Bobo MacDonald
Marion Crawford ("Crawfie")
Mabel Anderson
Helen Lightbody

THEIR CROSSES TO BEAR
Princess Andrew of Greece
Diana (Spencer), the Princess of Wales
Sarah (Ferguson), the Duchess of York
Camilla Parker Bowles, Duchess of Cornwall

THE PRINCIPAL HEIRS
Prince Charles
Prince William
Prince Henry (Harry)

THE CHATTERING CHORUS
The Corgis
The Anti-Monarchists
The Media
The Outspoken Insiders

THE HISTORICAL WALK-ONS
Prince Andrew
Prince Edward
The Archbishops of Canterbury
Prime Minister Neville Chamberlain
Franklin and Eleanor Roosevelt
Margaret Thatcher
Ronald Reagan

Introduction

AN AMERICAN AT THE PALACE

WHEN AN AMERICAN SETS OUT to write about the British Royal Family, some Brits get a little testy—perhaps justifiably so. Although the American people have a gawking fascination with the royals, our view can be somewhat jaundiced. We are unavoidably influenced by repeated exposure as children to the inspirational story of the birth of our own nation, especially that defining moment of independence from British rule. The result, unfortunately, is a tendency for ruthless irreverence reflected in tabloidesque headlines, scandalous tidbits, and anonymous snipes. Author Kitty Kelley, a prime example of this approach, considers it a point of pride that her juicy concoction, *The Royals,* is not for sale in Great Britain.

It has been observed that we Americans are so enamored of royalty that we elevate our celebrities to virtual thrones, but to make that claim is to show a fundamental misunderstanding of what royalty is. We might picture the life of royalty as a glittering façade, a lavish procession from one magnificent palace to the next, the right to never be wrong, a magical status where one is granted unconditional love and admiration.

Yet when we view the last century through the lives of the women of Windsor, a distinctly different picture emerges. These women have not been silly or irrelevant bits of fluff drifting across the public stage. The weight of duty has been the consistent theme of their lives for over a century. They have achieved true power, and it has often been hard-won.

In America we like to view ourselves as modern and progressive, as having shaken loose the bonds of a submissive past. We are subject to no one's will; we bow and curtsy to no king or queen. The underpinning of our democracy is that each citizen has an equal opportunity for greatness. Monarchies—even constitutional monarchies—are by their very nature exclusionary. Their authority is granted not by the will of the people but by the rights of succession. In contrast, our nation is founded on the notion that any boy or girl, regardless of bloodline, might grow up to sit on the highest seat of power. The reality, unfortunately, is somewhat different, especially when it comes to women. We are still stuck in centuries-old myths about women's fundamental weakness and unsuitability to lead. In the history of our nation, only one woman has ever appeared on the presidential ticket of a major party. Geraldine Ferraro's selection as Walter Mondale's running mate in 1984 briefly raised hopes of female power parity. Instead, she became a convenient scapegoat for the ticket's staggering defeat, and closed the matter for at least another twenty years.

Although Britain's monarchy is as misogynistic as any Old World institution, it offers a built-in opportunity for women to lead. When no males are in line for succession, women ascend, and for the past fifty-two years a woman has occupied the throne. Furthermore, during the last century, women have tended to play a leading role, even when they only sat on the throne as consort—the Queen Mother being a case in point. The women of Windsor have been the backbone of their nation, often a striking contrast to their weak men.

There are no parallel examples in the United States of women exerting the level of influence of either the queen or the Queen Mother. No one would dare suggest that these women are not deserving of their accrued power, or that they have not lived on an equal footing with men. The Brits have become accustomed to powerful women, and their comfort level allowed the election of Margaret Thatcher, who served as prime minister for twelve years and remains to this day the only woman to have led a Western nation.

In America we are still uneasy when strong, authoritative women take center stage, as witnessed by the uproar that follows every utterance from Hillary Clinton. No woman in America has achieved anything close to the status of the women of Windsor, and that in itself makes them a fascinating subject for our examination.

So, who are they really? The most striking fact I discovered in my research is that there isn't any one true story. Historical facts are remarkably malleable. Depending on the source, completely opposite views are taken on virtually every topic. Many key facts are in dispute. That's not altogether surprising when you consider that these are very human stories, told by those whose sympathies and biases inform their conclusions.

As an American, I don't, as the saying goes, have a dog in this fight. I don't possess what I've noticed in my British friends—the deep emotional connection, cultivated from birth, familial in nature, which manifests itself either in a reluctance to air skeletons in the family closet or in the outspoken bitterness of a neglected child. The former are jealously protective of the monarchy; the latter have had it with their dysfunctional family.

From the outside looking in with a less defensive perspective, I see a human drama filled with both flawed and noble characters. Although the women of Windsor are set apart, their experiences also have a core of universality. They are, like us, mothers, wives, sisters, and daughters. It's a simple fact that we define women more by their relationships than by their actions, even when they sit on a throne. We judge them not just by the work they do but by the character of the children they raise. So, in examining these women, we look for the ways in which they have related to others, asking:

Are royalty allowed to express love?
Can one be a royal and also a good mother?
Can compassion and duty coexist?
Do women make better monarchs than men?
Is a matriarchal society preferable to a patriarchal society?

The Women of Windsor tells the story of the past century of British history through the lives of the four women whose influence has, by both design and fate, shaped it. Frequently eclipsed in the media by the dramatic spills of lesser figures, they've remained the steady force—the continuity of a monarchy otherwise in disarray.

Individually, the women of Windsor are distinctive characters playing out predetermined roles. Yet each is more complex than she appears. *The Women of Windsor* will delve beneath the surface to reveal the human beings beneath the public image:

Her Majesty Queen Elizabeth, the Queen Mother: The
optimist and charmer, with a steely inner core, who
symbolized old-fashioned royal values.
Her Majesty Queen Elizabeth II: The stoic, dutiful ruler,
isolated by her adherence to propriety over love, obsessed
with her imperial birthright.
Her Royal Highness the Princess Margaret: The rebellious free
spirit, who never fully realized her identity, doomed by
her place in her sister's shadow.
Her Royal Highness the Princess Royal, Princess Anne: The
acerbic misfit, who walked a step behind her elder
brother yet transformed herself late in life to become an
admired figure and the queen's closest confidante.

As *The Women of Windsor* details their private and public lives, the era itself forms a dramatic backdrop. While these remarkable women have shaped the monarchy for nearly a century, they have also been shaped by the times in which they've lived. They represent the central paradox of modernity—the desire to maintain core values that stand the test of time and the need to advance humanity through reinvention. Each of the women of Windsor has been defined by how tautly she has held the tension wire of this paradox.

THE
WOMEN
OF WINDSOR

DRAMA QUEEN

LIKE SMALL TIME-RELEASED BOMBS set to detonate just when everyone has let down their guard, Princess Diana's scathing revelations keep bursting forth from the grave, more than eight years after her death. She couldn't have planned a more perfect revenge on the family she once compared to the Mafia, a family by now wishing desperately they'd never welcomed the "shy" girl with the silver-screen charisma into their midst. She has become the eternal scourge of a monarchy to which she never truly belonged.

The monarchy is still feeling the aftershocks of revelations contained in a series of videotaped interviews conducted by Diana's voice coach, Peter Settelen, in late 1992 and early 1993. Settelen sold the tapes to NBC News, and they were aired in December 2004 in the United States as part of a two-part, prime-time documentary.

Settelen has claimed that the tapes are records of voice-coaching lessons, and their intimate nature is part of a technique he used to relax the princess and help her become more comfortable with public speaking. Only the most naïve viewer could believe that. On the screen, Diana seems *quite* comfortable, curled in a chair like a devious cat. She pretends wide-eyed girlish innocence, but by 1992 she is too far down the road for that. There is cunning in the way she dips her eyes in pretended discretion after each explosive remark, then slyly peeks back up from beneath her lashes to gauge her interviewer's reaction.

Her words are anything but discreet, slicing through the dignified façade of the Royal Family. They also give lie to her well-polished image as the shy, simple young woman, dazzled by a courtship with a prince.[1]

With the practiced disdain of a girl who has always been popular with boys, she speaks of the first time Prince Charles kissed her: "He leapt upon me and started kissing me and everything. And I thought, 'Waaaaah, you know. This is not what people do.' And he was all over me for the rest of the evening, following me everywhere . . . [like] a puppy."

She rates her husband's sexual performance with a chilly indifference to his shame: "It was odd. Very odd. It was there, and then it fizzled out maybe seven years ago. It was just so odd. There was never a requirement for it . . . sort of a once-every-three-weeks look about it . . . and I kept thinking . . . and then I followed a pattern. He used to see his lady [Camilla Parker Bowles] once every three weeks before we got married."

She demands acknowledgment of her suffering, as if her position in life were the cruelest punishment: "I don't . . . when I cry . . . I can't bear people to say, 'It can't be as bad as that' or, um, 'We understand.' Nobody understands."

She talks openly about being in love with her bodyguard and at the same time berates the queen—calling her "the top lady"—for not intervening in Charles's affair with Camilla Parker Bowles.

Settelen's tapes weren't Diana's only appearance in 2004. In March, audiotapes used by Andrew Morton for his 1992 book, *Diana: Her True Story,* aired in the United States, once again presenting the princess as the hapless victim of cruel royalty.[2] As if she were a medieval virgin being sold to a lascivious monarch, she describes herself on her wedding day as "a lamb going to the slaughter." She also details her episodes of bulimia, her suicide attempts, and her paranoia.

Alas, poor girl.

Talk of a royal murder plot, which has never really abated in the years since Diana's death, has been kept alive by Mohamed Al Fayed, Dodi Fayed's father, who openly accuses Prince Philip of organizing the Paris car crash. As if to lend support to his theory, Diana's former butler, Paul Burrell, came forward in October 2004 to unveil a secret letter he claimed Diana wrote ten months before her death. In the letter, Diana states her fear of a plot by "my husband" to orchestrate a fatal car accident, thus freeing Charles to remarry.[3]

If Charles was so desperate to marry Camilla that he orchestrated Diana's death, he had a peculiar way of showing it. Nearly eight years would pass before the fifty-six-year-old prince dropped to his knee and presented his fifty-seven-year-old lover with a large heirloom diamond. By that point, even the tabloids had grown bored with them. "They're not Brad and Jennifer," sniffed one editor, referring to the couple's middle-aged dowdiness. She didn't add, but might have, that Camilla is not Diana. She will never knock a nation off its feet or put stars in the eyes of the masses. She can win points only by staying in the background, thus ceding the attention to her predecessor, whose visage is recalled in every mention of the couple's nuptials. Diana used to say that Camilla was the third party in her marriage. No doubt Camilla sensed the ghost of Diana hovering over the canapés at her wedding reception.

If Diana has a front-row seat in the afterlife, one can imagine her chortling hardily over the whole sordid mess, and enjoying her hand in it. That is precisely what distinguishes her from the queen, the Queen Mother, Princess Anne, and even Princess Margaret, who on her worst days at least tried to be loyal to her larger covenant to the Crown. Unlike these women, Diana had a clear choice in her destiny. She walked down the aisle with eyes wide open, all the while complaining that the red carpet was too rich for her tastes. She was a drama queen, unsuited for the throne. Her legacy was one of unfaithfulness, and ultimately it doomed her.

That is not to say that the monarchy is on the right path, or even that a monarchy *is* the right path. Festering beneath the surface of the current scandals are deeper tears in the fabric of the House of Windsor. The survival of the monarchy depends to a large extent on the propagation of a myth: that the Royal Family represents the ideal family, that it holds the nation together, that it makes a positive difference in the lives of the people, and that it is well worth the price. The myth of relevance is getting harder to hoist aloft. Does anyone truly believe that the dysfunctional Windsors are an ideal family? Can the monarchy, which by its very nature is exclusionary, hold an increasingly diverse society together? Does the Royal Family, whose authority is granted not by the will of the people but by the scarily random accident of birth, have the authority to guide a nation?

Not that long ago, those questions did not even rise to the surface. The queen began her reign with unprecedented goodwill, at home and abroad. It was in large part due to the immense popularity of her mother, and even through the trials of the ensuing decades, the beloved Queen Mum held the worst strife at bay. She symbolized a regal ideal—the imperial grandmother with a common touch. For many she was an antidote to harsh times, a vision of benevolence in ostrich plumes and pastel. Watching this centurion totter along on high heels, one could almost believe that a jaunty air, a warm smile, and a string of pearls could hold a nation together.

Without the Queen Mum to garner affection and provide distraction, the public has grown harsher in its scrutiny of the monarchy with each scandal. In the years since her mother's death, the queen has been like a stoic little boat rammed by the swirl of ferocious seas. Even for a woman of such staunch purpose, whose steady hand never wavers from her scepter, these are especially trying times.

The queen's biggest headache is the heir apparent himself. The Brits are resigned to Charles's marriage to Camilla, but they are less resigned to the idea of Charles as king. One would be hard-pressed to find a single example of Charles setting aside self-interest for the good of the monarchy. He is a navel-gazer extraordinaire, a poster prince for the "me first" generation. His arrogance and outdated thinking are frequently on display. He's like a dusty old shoe unpolished by life experience. In November 2004 a memo from the prince was leaked to the press, which had the prince fully on his high horse, *dissing* his own people. In his memorandum he complained that people today seem to think they are qualified for positions well beyond their abilities. The tendency, he suggested haughtily, was the result of "social utopianism."[4]

In other words, Charles to the People: *Know your place*. The memo had everyone up in arms, from the education secretary on down, and was reviled as "elitist" and downright "feudal."

It has always been said that the monarchy does not rise or fall on the actions of individuals—that the sum is far greater than its parts. But looking down the road, one is easily depressed by the plain inadequacy of those who occupy the top places in the line of succession. Perhaps if Anne, the Princess Royal, not Charles, were next in line for the throne, the nation and the world could breathe a sigh of relief, and the queen, nearly eighty, could step down with confidence that the dignity of the Crown would be maintained. But Anne is a distant number nine in the line of succession. Medieval adherence to male supremacy might yet topple the monarchy.

The burden is the queen's to bear. A lesser woman would crack, but unlike her mercurial former daughter-in-law, Elizabeth hasn't the luxury of being a drama queen. Her place in the world does not allow for temper tantrums. The royal temperament is fixed on duty. Whether that is for good or ill, history will have to judge.

1

MERRY MISCHIEF

I pity the man you marry
because you are so determined.

LADY STRATHMORE

TO HER DAUGHTER ELIZABETH

Spring 1921 ◆ ST. PAUL'S WALDEN BURY, SCOTLAND

LIZABETH'S BLUE EYES sparkled playfully as she regarded Bertie. "You spoil me," she teased. "You must know how I love proposals!" They were standing together under the giant oak at the bottom of her mother's garden, the fragrance of early-spring blossoms rising up around them.

Elizabeth's hapless suitor blushed furiously and stared at the ground. Prince Albert—Bertie—was slender bordering on frail, impeccable as always in his walking clothes. He was handsome in his own way, with a thin, kind face, and blond hair swept back to reveal a high forehead. He was sick with love for this wonderful girl, and while the warmth in her voice was unmistakable, he steeled himself for rejection.

He raised his eyes to Elizabeth's, and her face softened with regret. "I'm afraid not, Bertie," she said solemnly. "It just wouldn't do."

He couldn't ask—didn't dare ask—*why* it wouldn't do. In his mind it would do very well. In all of his twenty-five years on this earth, Bertie had never been conscious of wanting anything as much as he wanted Elizabeth Bowes-Lyon to be his wife.[1]

The second son of the King of England had been raised on a steady diet of protocol and duty, and his upbringing had never taught him to seek happiness. In his world the threads of obligation and joy were incompatible, with the former woven into his lineage. Yet here was a woman who seemed to embody both strength and cheer.

Love gave Bertie courage. This was his second proposal; Elizabeth had turned down his first. Still, he was not ready to admit defeat. To do so would be to extinguish the light from his life.

E lizabeth Angela Marguerite Bowes-Lyon, who would one day become queen, was the ninth of ten children, and her older siblings often had occasion to complain that she was spoiled. Even her most outrageous antics provoked benevolent smiles rather than frowns of disapproval from their parents. In the age-old assertion of older children, they remarked that *they* could never have gotten away with such wildness when they were young. But even her competitive siblings had to admit that Elizabeth was a very easy child to spoil. Elizabeth was a natural charmer, with a sunny disposition, wide, antic eyes, and a dimpled smile. It was a quality that would earn her the fond nickname "Merry Mischief," given her by her mother, and win her the devotion of her people for nearly a century. As one family friend gushed, "To every lover of children she had about her that indefinable charm that bears elders into fairyland."[2]

Even so, the circumstances that led this high-spirited Scottish girl to England's throne could not have been imagined at the time of her birth, on August 4, 1900. With five brothers and three sisters ahead of her to claim her parents' attention, she might easily have had her light dimmed by the defining hierarchy of birth order. But some children are just special, and Elizabeth was one of these. Instantly becoming the household favorite, she was coddled and encouraged. She was affectionately called Princess, and friends who visited the family would curtsy to her as she held out her hand to be kissed.

While Elizabeth wasn't royalty, she wasn't exactly a commoner either—at least, not in the usual understanding of the term. Her family was one of old, aristocratic Scottish lineage—not filthy rich but rich enough, especially in land.

When Elizabeth was four, her paternal grandfather died and her father became the fourteenth Earl of Strathmore and Kinghorne, inheriting Glamis Castle with its thousands of acres in the glens of Angus. Glamis Castle had been the family home of the Earls of Strathmore and Kinghorne since 1372, when Sir John Lyon was granted the thaneage of Glamis by King Robert II, and it was said to be the setting for Shakespeare's *Macbeth*.

Like any self-respecting medieval castle, Glamis was rife with turrets, spires, secret staircases, hidden passages, and ghosts. Tales abounded of the origins of these ghosts. The most famous was the Lady Glamis, whose sorry fate at the hands of the evil monarch James V was the stuff of legends. Lady Glamis was a woman of great beauty, much beloved by the people, but the king invented a charge of witchcraft and she was imprisoned and ultimately burned at the stake. Her ghost, known as the Gray Lady, was said to wander the castle corridors, never at rest.

The castle held many mysteries. For example, there was said to be a hidden room that no one had ever been able to find but that everyone believed existed deep inside a tower. Servants through the centuries claimed to have heard thuds and cries emanating through the walls, and there were rumors that the cries belonged to the "Glamis monster," a grossly deformed child born in 1700 and secreted away in the tower.

Elizabeth and her younger brother, David, her closest companion, found a magical aura along the shadowy cool passages of Glamis.

Inveterate mischief makers, they were known to collaborate on horrific pranks; their favorite was to climb the stairs to the ramparts above the castle's entryway and douse arriving guests with "boiling oil" (actually, water), then race away laughing as the drenched visitors shrieked with alarm.

The Bowes-Lyon family was boisterous and happy, thanks to its matriarch. Cecilia Strathmore, thirty-eight when Elizabeth was born, was ebullient and high-spirited. Unusual in aristocratic circles, she was a doting mother who nursed her own children and encouraged a raucous, creative atmosphere. She loved culture, art, and music and was a brilliant gardener; the Italian Garden, which she designed, still blooms at the castle today. (This love of gardening was shared by her two youngest children throughout their lives; David would go on to study at Kew Gardens.)

In spite of the tragedies of losing two of her children at young ages—her eldest daughter to diphtheria and a son to a brain injury—she wasn't an overly cautious mother. Elizabeth always remembered her early years as filled with great laughter and fun.

Lady Strathmore's large brood was a handful, however, and after Elizabeth was born she hired Clara Cooper Knight, the daughter of a tenant farmer at Glamis, to help care for the children. They called her "Allah," as they were unable to pronounce her name, and she would be a central figure in Elizabeth's life for many decades.

Lord Strathmore was a less vivid personality than his wife. A quiet, thoughtful man, he instilled in his children a sense of duty and religious rigor. He taught them an appreciation for the edict that to whom much is given much is expected.

The Bowes-Lyon family socialized in royal circles, but Elizabeth's mother was not a snob. Cecilia Strathmore once said, laughing, "Some hostesses feed royalty to their guests as zookeepers feed fish to seals." This fundamental lesson was well learned by Elizabeth; decades later, when Lady Strathmore died, she would recall her mother's great decency and what a significant model she had been.

"She had a good perspective of life," she said. "Everything was given its *true* importance."[3]

At young ages Elizabeth and David were sent for dancing lessons with Mr. Neill, a village entertainer whose long white beard gave him the appearance of a castle ghost. Under Mr. Neill's tutelage they learned the minuet, and dressed in medieval costumes created by their mother, the children would perform for guests. While they suffered through the awkward curtsies, bows, and twirls, Mr. Neill would skip in front of them playing the fiddle. The adults were charmed, and laughed and clapped indulgently. However, Elizabeth and David found the performances, and their odd teacher, embarrassing.

When the Bowes-Lyons weren't at Glamis Castle, they resided at their Hertfordshire home, St. Paul's Walden Bury. The vast, stately home, on the southern edge of the village, had been in the Bowes-Lyon family since 1725. It was surrounded by beautiful gardens and miles of countryside, and there were so many animals it might have been mistaken for a farm. These included an assortment of dogs, cats, goats, and, of course, Elizabeth's beloved miniature Shetland pony, Bobs.

Scotland ruled their hearts. Decades later, when Elizabeth as queen was touring South Africa, a veteran of the Boer Wars told her honestly, "We still feel sometimes that we cannot forgive the English." The queen replied, "I understand perfectly. We feel very much the same in Scotland."[4]

A t the turn of a bright new century, the life of an aristocratic young lady was heavily influenced by Victorian ideals. Still, there was a sense that the twentieth century heralded a new era of possibility for women. Lady Strathmore wasn't a modernist. She was more in tune with traditional values than with the women's movement that was gaining steam at that time, or with the increasingly radical suffragettes. Yet in her quiet, forceful way she ruled the family realm, making certain that her daughters and sons alike were schooled in history, language, art, and literature. French governesses were brought in while Elizabeth was still very young. Bright and curious, Elizabeth was a good student, and by the age of ten she was fluent in French and excelled in history. When David was sent off to school at age ten, Elizabeth was taught at home by a German-born tutor named Kathie Kuebler.

It was an idyllic, protected life, but harsher realities would soon come calling at the castle gate. On Elizabeth's fourteenth birthday, as she was enjoying a performance at a London music hall, Britain declared war on Germany.

Four of Elizabeth's brothers—all but twelve-year-old David—enlisted. "I'll be home for Christmas," Fergus, twenty-six, promised his little sister. She gazed into his handsome face and believed him completely. Fergus wasn't just trying to soften the blow. The common wisdom of the time was that this would be a brief combat; few could have anticipated the excruciating four-year war with its toll of four million dead.

The men fought and bled and died on the fields of France, and the women picked up the pieces. Many of the aristocracy opened their homes as hospitals and convalescent centers. One day in 1914 Lady Strathmore announced that they were turning the huge banqueting hall at Glamis Castle into a convalescent center for wounded officers. Everyone was expected to pitch in. Kathie Kuebler was sent packing; war trumped lessons, and Elizabeth's formal schooling came to an end. Elizabeth's older sister Rose left to take nurse's training, and although Elizabeth was too young to be a nurse, she was completely involved in the life of the hospice. Often her face was the first one seen by the arriving strangers with their haunted eyes and injured bodies.

They began to come in December, staring in silent discomfort as their carts traversed the mile-long driveway that led to the castle. What must they have thought, these hollow-cheeked men, when the immense castle came into view? Many lowered their gazes and tightened their jaws, probably wondering what in hell they were doing staying in a castle and being cared for by nobility. For those who only days earlier had been mired in mud, there was a surreal quality to the experience.

The sight of the kindly woman in her fifties and her smiling young daughter might have relaxed them somewhat. Cecilia Strathmore had a gift for putting people at ease. As soon as the soldiers crossed her doorstep, they became treasured guests who were never made to feel like a burden.

Cots were arranged around the perimeters of the dining hall, but Lady Strathmore gave orders that the rooms be changed as little as possible, in order to preserve their home's warm, inviting style. Easy chairs and sofas were set near the massive fireplace, where the men could relax in a homey atmosphere.

The First World War saw the advent of trench warfare, and many of the men were damaged not only by the shellfire but by the experience of living for long months in the claustrophobic gullies. Millions of rats infested the trenches, feeding off human remains and bringing disease to the living. This horror, along with the bitter cold and scarce rations, made the trenches a desperate place to be. Elizabeth tried not to imagine her own brothers suffering so, as she concocted ways to bring the light back to the soldiers' eyes. She was such a sweet and cheerful girl, in her plain white nursing shift and peaked bonnet, that even the most miserable could not suppress a smile in her presence. "My three weeks at Glamis have been the happiest I ever struck," one Scottish sergeant said, crediting Elizabeth. "She and my *fiancay* are as alike as two peas."[5]

For Elizabeth, the men's presence partially compensated for the absence of her brothers. She missed them all so much—missed, too, the way things used to be in their happy home.

There was great joy at Glamis when, almost a year after his departure, Fergus was allowed home on a short leave, following the July birth of his first child, a daughter. Elizabeth had never seen her brother look so handsome, but she secretly searched his face for traces of the haunted look she had seen in so many soldiers. If Fergus was burdened by what he had seen and experienced, he didn't show it, saving all the room in his heart and mind for his family, his young wife, and his beautiful baby.

Ten days after he returned to the front, Fergus was dead.

It was September, warm with a touch of bracing cool. Elizabeth noticed a telegram messenger cycling up the driveway to Glamis Castle. She ran to meet him, and when he handed her the telegram, she saw the pity in his eyes and was filled with dread. She raced to find her mother, who ripped open the message, read it, and collapsed onto a chair, sobbing. Her beautiful boy Fergus was dead, killed at the Battle of Loos in some godforsaken corner of France.

For the British, the Battle of Loos was a particularly devastating fight—what amounted to a suicide mission. Fought from September 25 to 28, 1915, it led to the butchery of fifty thousand British soldiers, who lacked sufficient artillery to stand against the German barrage. Captain Fergus Bowes-Lyon was one of the first casualties, and his body remained in France at the site where he had fallen. It pained the Strathmores deeply that their son would never return to Scotland for burial.

Lady Strathmore was so distraught by Fergus's death that she could not work for some time. Elizabeth picked up the slack and tried to run things as best she could. From then on, she kept a watchful eye out for telegram messengers. One more brother, Michael, would be wounded in the war and posted as missing in action. He was feared dead until 1918, when he was released from a German prisoner-of-war camp after a year and a half of captivity.

As the long years of the war dragged on, Elizabeth worked hard to keep her charges occupied and their thoughts away from the grim experiences of the battlefront. She organized cricket matches, picnics, and sing-alongs, helped them write letters home, fetched cigarettes from the village. She left an indelible impression. When Rose was married in 1916, Elizabeth took on even more responsibilities.

Everyone said that the lovely young girl with the winning smile and quick wit had a poise well beyond her years. As she swept along the drafty corridors of Glamis Castle, her carriage graceful and her head held high, she was a welcome vision of young optimism to the suffering men. She kept an autograph book, which the men gladly signed. It became one of Elizabeth's most prized mementoes, and it survives to this day.[6] One entry, teasingly scrawled by W. H. Harrop of the Eighth Seafants, read:

> *May the owner of this book be*
> *Hung, Drawn & Quartered.*
> *Yes.*
> *Hung in Diamonds, Drawn in a Carriage and Four*
> *And Quartered in the Best House in the land.*

Elizabeth grew up during those years, turning from a child into a young woman. Those who would, in the course of her life, accuse her of being frivolous simply did not understand the mettle required to bring a lighthearted pose to a period of suffering and hardship.

If Elizabeth's early life was a benevolent blend of nature and nurture, her future husband's was more a grim march to the throne. Contrast Elizabeth's upbringing with his, and you get some insight into her role as the backbone of their relationship. ●

Albert Frederick Arthur George (nicknamed Bertie) was born in 1895, fifteen years before his father ascended to the throne of England. From an early age he was overshadowed by his charismatic older brother, David. Bertie, the second son of Prince George and Princess Mary, was shy and spindly, an insecure boy with a terrible stammer that would bring his sentences to an abrupt and painful halt midword. He was left-handed but forced to write with his right hand, increasing his awkwardness. His father's cruel torments only worsened his plight. George's philosophy of child raising was once expressed this way: "I was always afraid of my father, and my children will damn well be afraid of me."

True to his word, George terrorized Bertie, mocked his stammer, and constantly made his displeasure known. As poor Bertie sweated and stuttered, his father towered over him, barking, "Get it out! Get it out!"

On his fifth birthday, Bertie received a letter from his father, which demonstrates his tyrannical parenting style:

> Now that you are five years old, I hope you will always try to be obedient & do at once what you are told, as you will find it will come much easier to you the sooner you begin.

There was no birthday gift or cake with candles. Just this stern missive.[7]

Although David did not completely escape their father's wrath, he was spoiled by comparison. Clever and handsome, dubbed "Prince Charming" by the media, David seemed to possess a visibly royal demeanor in his early years. The public swooning was amplified after his father ascended the throne as King George V and David became Edward, Prince of Wales, the heir apparent.

The children were not the only ones who trembled in the king's presence. Queen Mary appears imposing in photographs, but she was painfully shy and subservient. Some say she was as frightened of the king's wrath as were his children. Mabell, Countess of Airlie, her lifelong friend and lady-in-waiting, once observed that "she was the least self-assertive of women, essentially feminine, almost early Victorian in her attitude to her husband."[8]

Born at Kensington Palace, Her Serene Highness Princess Victoria Mary Augusta Louise Olga Pauline Claudine Agnes of Teck was semiroyal, the first cousin once removed of Queen Victoria and the great-granddaughter of King George III. Her parents were the Duke and Duchess of Teck.

Tall and slender, May, as she was called, was handsome rather than pretty, with an erect carriage, an impressive bosom, and light brown hair, which she kept wrapped tightly in a braid around her head, set off by a fringe on her forehead. Her blue eyes were intelligent, but her face was a portrait of stillness, revealing little.

She was initially engaged to Prince Albert Victor ("Prince Eddy"), the eldest son of the Prince of Wales (later King Edward VII). When Prince Eddy died of pneumonia before their marriage, Queen Victoria pressed hard for a match with her second son, Prince George, Duke of York. Why waste a suitable girl, already vetted for the throne? They were married on July 6, 1893, at St. James's Palace.

They had six children: David (who would later take the name Edward when he was made Prince of Wales), Prince Albert, Princess Mary, Prince Henry, Prince George, and Prince John. Prince John suffered from epilepsy and mental retardation, and he died at the age of thirteen. Much has been made of the fact that John was sent away from the family. A 2004 Masterpiece Theatre drama, *The Lost Prince*, essentially invents the details of his life, as nearly nothing is known or recorded.[9]

In fairness to the Royal Family, Prince John's treatment was not unusual for the time, when epilepsy, autism, and mental retardation were not well understood. The idea that these mysterious brain defects flowed through the Royal Family's blood might have been cause for alarm. The fiction still existed that royal blood was purer than common blood, and that mental illness was shameful (although, God knows, there was plenty of insanity peppered along the royal line).

George and May maintained a parenting style distinctly different from that of the Strathmores. They loved their children but were incapable of playfulness. May easily grew restless with the mundane and gloomy demands of childbearing. During one of her pregnancies she wrote to her husband, "Of course it is a great bore for me and requires a great deal of patience to endure it, but this is alas the penalty of being a woman."

Their offspring lived apart from their parents and saw them only once a day at tea. This distance became even more pronounced after they moved to the cavernous homestead of Buckingham Palace.

Queen Mary's glacial, imperious air was off-putting, and she could show the maddening insensitivity of the aristocracy. Once, viewing London's East End slums, she cried out to a group of residents, "Why, why do you live here?" as if they had chosen pauperdom above pearls.[10] In truth, Queen Mary wasn't that unusual for a royal of her era, appearing grand, larger than life, and bestowed with unfailing direction if not wisdom or charm. She cherished her role and threw herself into innumerable projects and charities.

In 1909, at the age of fourteen, Bertie entered the Royal Naval College, Osborne, where he struggled academically, often placing at the bottom of his class. His teachers complained to his parents that he was bright enough but lacked interest in his studies. Even so, he was promoted after two years to Dartmouth Royal Naval College, where Edward was studying. During this period, both of the brothers contracted measles and mumps.

It was an unpromising start for the sickly young Bertie, but he was determined to become a naval officer. He joined the navy at the start of the war and was assigned to a ship, the *Collingwood,* but again ill health plagued him, keeping him landlocked. He had his appendix removed but continued to suffer from chronic stomach pain.

Finally, in May 1916, he got his wish and was returned to his ship. Soon he saw his first action in the Battle of Jutland. Bertie learned something about himself then. Battle enthralled him. He was able to achieve mentally what he struggled to accomplish physically. He wrote to his brother Edward of his experience in battle: "When I was on top of the turret, I never felt any fear of shells or anything else. It seems curious but all sense of danger and everything else goes except the one longing to deal death in every possible way to the enemy."[11]

Shortly afterward, a duodenal ulcer was diagnosed, and surgery once again took Bertie out of action. He spent the remainder of the war at a desk, but he never forgot what it felt like to be in battle, and this knowledge gave him great empathy for the common soldier and sailor for the remainder of his life.

The final days of the First World War were precarious times for the British Royal Family. Anti-German sentiment was at a fever pitch, and German blood coursed through the family's veins. The royals' German connection was extensive, dating back hundreds of years. King George I, who reigned from 1714 to 1727, was German by birth, and many royals had married Germans. Most were raised bilingually. When Queen Victoria married Prince Albert of Saxe-Coburg and Gotha, she took her husband's name, making the British throne the House of Saxe-Coburg and Gotha.

Queen Mary was born in London, but her parents came from the German province of Teck, and she spent much of her youth in Germany. Kaiser Wilhelm, now England's enemy, was the king's first cousin, and the king was even godfather to one of the kaiser's sons.[12]

The War Propaganda Bureau, headed by Charles Masterman, had spent the war churning out organized hatred for the Germans. At its inception, Masterman had invited twenty-five leading British authors—including Arthur Conan Doyle, G. K. Chesterton, and Rudyard Kipling—to Wellington House, the bureau's headquarters, to discuss ways of best promoting Britain's interests during the war. All the writers at the conference agreed to the utmost secrecy, and it was not until 1935 that the activities of the bureau became known to the general public. Several of the men attending the meeting agreed to write pamphlets and books that would promote the anti-German sentiment. The bureau persuaded commercial publishers to print and publish the material. In words and pictures, Germans were portrayed as bloodthirsty Huns whose goal was nothing short of the destruction of civilization.

Those with German roots or German-sounding names were treated with undisguised prejudice, and there were reports of dachshunds being stoned in the streets. It was considered unpatriotic to play music by great German composers such as Beethoven and Bach. There was real fear at the palace that the Royal Family's own German roots could bring the monarchy crashing down amid a sea of public outrage. Saxe-Coburg and Gotha was not a name upon which to take a stand in 1917 Britain.

While the king could not wash the stain of German blood from his lineage, he could invent a new façade. On July 17, 1917, a proclamation was issued, "declaring that the Name of Windsor is to be borne by His Royal House and Family and relinquishing the use of all German Titles and Dignities."

Thus the twentieth-century House of Windsor was born. The reintroduction of the monarchy was in fact a cleansing of its Germanic soul. *Saxe-Coburg and Gotha is dead . . . long live Windsor.*

The king made other declarations as well, in part to assure that stray German royals would not soon marry into his newly packaged family. It had long been the custom for royals to marry royals, and the only practical way to accomplish this was for royal families to look outside their own kingdoms. Now the king conceded that royals might choose their mates from the aristocracy of their own lands. It had the practical effect of setting the stage for a world-altering match.

The second son of King George V and Queen Mary wasn't exactly a hit with the ladies. Bertie's public shyness and stammer made him an awkward suitor, a fact only partially compensated for by his being the king's son.

The rosy-cheeked Scottish lass Elizabeth, with her dark brown hair and laughing blue eyes, was, on the other hand, perfectly at home in every social situation. Elizabeth had come of age at a very special time for a young woman. Her war service, undertaken while she was still technically a child, made her part of a class of women who had earned respect and independence, including the right to vote.[13] She was formally introduced to society at the age of nineteen, and her confident air in the company of men made her immediately popular.

Elizabeth and Bertie met in the summer of 1920, at a Royal Air Force ball at the Ritz Hotel in London. Elizabeth's escort was Bertie's equerry, James Stuart (Jamie), a handsome war hero for whom she was feeling the first stirrings of love. Bertie watched Elizabeth from across the ballroom as she danced with Jamie. Her laughter floated merrily in his direction, and it was immediately apparent to him that his eyes were not the only ones admiring her. There was something quite remarkable about this woman. For while she was pretty and flirtatious, and loved to dance, she was somehow proper. Elizabeth Bowes-Lyon was not among the ultramodern flapper set, influenced by loose Americanized standards, flaunting their independence with long nights of drinking, gambling, and even promiscuity. Neither was she dreary and pretentious, or coolly regal in the manner of his mother. Laughter had been in short supply in Bertie's life, and he was drawn to it as a moth to a flame.

As Lady Mabell Airlie, who had known Elizabeth all her life, would observe, "Lady Elizabeth was very unlike the cocktail-drinking, chain-smoking girls who came to be regarded as typical of the 1920s. Her radiant vitality and blending of gaiety, kindness and sincerity made her irresistible to men."[14]

Bertie immediately set out to woo this fascinating woman, undaunted by the fact that her brightest smiles seemed reserved for others. By some accounts, these others included Bertie's elder brother. Elizabeth had a core of ambition in her young soul, and for a time she might have set her sights on the Prince of Wales. Not only was he more appealing than Bertie (superficially, at least), he was also in direct line for the throne. There is some dispute about this, but many years later when he was Duke of Windsor, Edward would tell royal biographer, Michael Thornton, "Elizabeth Bowes-Lyon was determined to marry into the royal family, so . . . she settled for 'the runt of the litter.'"[15]

Most likely, this version of the story is nothing more than irresistible speculation, too delicious to pass up. One cannot help imagining the dramatically different turn history might have taken had Edward married Elizabeth and never started an affair with Wallis Simpson. Given the rumors, never disproved, that the Prince of Wales was sterile, this marriage would have set the monarchy on an entirely different course.

Whatever Elizabeth's true motivations, she found it hard to take the besotted Bertie seriously. Frankly, it is difficult to imagine the popular, charismatic Elizabeth being the least bit infatuated with a man who blushed and stumbled over his words.

Bertie first proposed to Elizabeth on a chilly December day in 1921, as they walked the gardens of St. Paul's Walden Bury. He would later tell Edward, "Waiting for her answer was worse than Jutland, waiting for the German shells to arrive." Elizabeth sweetly turned him down.

A few months later he proposed again, and again she turned him down, gently trying to spare his feelings with kind words expressing her fondness for him.

There was at least one other man in Elizabeth's life, the prince's equerry, Jamie Stuart, who had introduced them in the first place. He was devilishly handsome and worldly, a real ladies' man, and Elizabeth and Jamie were often seen together. As time went on, Bertie had reason to despair that he would ever win Elizabeth's heart.

Others, however, were busily knitting a plot to bring the two together. Cecilia thought Bertie would make a good match for her youngest daughter, and King George V and Queen Mary agreed. "You will be a lucky fellow if she accepts you," the king told his son.

As that didn't seem to be in the cards, some stealthy intervention was needed. In early 1922, Jamie suddenly left England for a post working in the oil fields of Oklahoma. It has often been suggested that his leave-taking was arranged by Queen Mary and Lady Strathmore. If so, it was an unnecessary precaution. Elizabeth was no longer serious about Jamie; she'd learned of his wandering eye and had decided he simply wasn't husband material.[16]

In January 1923, Elizabeth visited Lady Airlie and poured her heart out to the older woman.[17] Her entire life had been directed toward marriage, and she had no fear of its obligations. Indeed, she welcomed them. But marrying into the Royal Family was another matter. On one hand, she was ambitious enough to be intrigued by the idea of a royal match. On the other hand, if she married Bertie, she would never have another moment of true freedom, and she was hesitant about living under the yoke of protocol and public scrutiny.

She spoke, too, of her deepest emotions, asking Lady Airlie, a war widow who had been deeply in love with her husband, how she could know if she truly loved Bertie. She had feelings for him, but was it love? Lady Airlie gently counseled her that love would grow with marriage—not the kind of guidance one might hear today, but fitting advice in royal circles of the time. Bertie's mother had received much the same advice before she married his father.

Shortly after this conversation, Elizabeth accepted Bertie's third proposal of marriage, made as the couple took another nature walk. "If you're going to keep this up forever, I might as well say yes now," she told the stunned Bertie. "And so I do."

Was the union forged by desire or will? It is the rare commoner who achieves royalty without possessing an iron will and ambition. Perhaps, too, Elizabeth recognized Bertie's substance as a man, qualities that went beyond his shy, somewhat awkward demeanor. She believed that the dear man who wore his heart on his sleeve would make a good husband and father—and it turned out she was right. She might have known something else as well—an idea picked up from her mother, who said of Bertie, "He is a man who will be made or marred by his wife." Perhaps she decided to "make" him.

Elizabeth was very conscious of propriety and tradition; however, shortly after her engagement, she innocently gave the press an interview. *The Star* had sent a reporter named H. T. Cozens-Hardy to the Strathmores' Bruton Street home in London, where he received a cool reception from Lady Strathmore. But just as she was about to turn him away, Elizabeth appeared in the doorway. Cozens-Hardy would write that she had "the most radiant face that the purloins of Bond Street had ever seen," and this glorious girl gaily invited him into the breakfast room for a chat. "I am *so* happy, as you can see for yourself," she told him.

When Cozens-Hardy asked about the rumors that she had rejected Bertie before finally accepting his proposal, Elizabeth laughed. "The story that he asked me two or three times amused me," she said. "It was just news. Now look at me. Do you think I am the sort of person Bertie would have to ask twice?"[18]

The king was furious that Elizabeth allowed the press to speak to her, and he soon dispatched an equerry from the palace, stating that "by order of the King" no further interviews were to be given. It made an impression on Elizabeth, who went to her death at 101 years having never given another interview. (That is not to say that she didn't privately contribute details and give the palace stamp of approval to many authorized writings.)

Elizabeth might have regretted the publicity herself. "I feel very happy, but quite dazed," she wrote to a friend after the interview. "We hoped we were going to have a few days' peace at first, but the cat is now completely out of the bag and there is no possibility of stuffing him back."

There were many disappointed suitors, as diarist Chips Channon wrote: "There is not a man in England today who doesn't envy him [Bertie]. . . . The clubs are in doom."

The wedding of Elizabeth Bowes-Lyon and the Duke of York took place at Westminster Abbey on April 26, 1923, the first time a royal son had been married there since the thirteenth century. Upon her marriage Elizabeth became Her Royal Highness the Duchess of York.

It was a lavish affair, and more than one million people lined the streets of London as they would do some sixty years later when the

Prince of Wales married Lady Diana Spencer. Elizabeth wore a gown of antique ivory lace and chiffon moiré, embroidered with silver thread and pearls, created by court dressmaker Madame Handley Seymour. Her long train of antique Nottingham lace was borrowed from Queen Mary.

The public was wild for the couple, and weeks before the wedding, gifts began arriving by the truckload from all over the world. Most of them had to be returned, as gifts from persons unknown to them were not to be accepted by members of the Royal Family. The newspapers printed every detail. The BBC applied to the palace for permission to do a radio broadcast of the wedding. It would have been quite a media event, but the idea was rejected by church authorities who feared that "disrespectful people wearing hats might listen in public houses."

The morning of the wedding, Elizabeth's mother helped her dress at the Strathmores' Bruton Street home. It was a bittersweet moment for Cecilia—her last daughter to marry. She knew that Elizabeth was taking on a monumental challenge, but she had confidence that this special girl, of all her children, was up to the task.

As Elizabeth emerged from the house for the carriage ride to Westminster Abbey, she breathed in the damp, clean air. It had rained steadily during the night, but now it was beginning to clear. She stepped into the carriage and into a new life.

In his wedding sermon, Archbishop Cosmo Lang's voice boomed from the rafters with words that bespoke the gravity of the occasion. He challenged the couple: "Will you take and keep this gift of wedded life as a sacred trust? With all our hearts we wish that it may be happy. But you cannot resolve that it shall be happy. You can and will resolve that it shall be noble. You will not think so much of enjoyment as of achievement. You will have a great ambition to make this one life now given to you something rich, true and beautiful."

No flowery prose for the new couple! However, the archbishop's words were appropriate to the moment, and they resonated down the span of the decades.

Here is the simple truth, confirmed by history: If Elizabeth had not married Bertie, he might never have been king. Not only was she his anchor, but she would become the stabilizing force of the monarchy. The first bride of Windsor, she set a course that would change England and the world.

CHAPTER

2

WE FOUR

The whole continent is in love with her.
GOVERNOR OF SOUTH AUSTRALIA,
REFERRING TO ELIZABETH AFTER
THE ROYAL COUPLE'S 1927 TOUR

Winter 1924 ◆ LONDON

ELIZABETH WOULD NOT HAVE dreamed she could be so happy. The uncertainties of her courtship melted away once she settled into married life with Bertie. She could see the core of goodness and responsibility at the heart of her shy husband, and she longed for the world to see it, too. His dashing older brother, the Prince of Wales, may have captured most of the attention, but Bertie was the real thing.

True, she might not have been ravished by love for Bertie in the romantic ways that she'd heard about, but she accepted that love was something one nurtured into bloom over time. In addition, she realized that she had much to bring to this union. In her presence Bertie grew more confident, and she loved the way she was able to enhance his image.

Looking back across the century's landscape, it is easy to picture the new Duchess of York as the Lady Diana of the 1920s. Her arrival in the Royal Family had an instantaneously brightening effect, shaking some of the dust off and giving a good airing to the dark rooms.

In other ways, however, she was as different from Diana as night from day. Elizabeth stood behind her husband; she didn't stride out in front of him. She was disinterested in the limelight. Theirs was a partnership. She pulled Bertie out of his shyness, whispering reminders to him that improved his social graces. "Wave, Bertie, wave!" she'd instruct as they left public occasions. He followed her advice and felt better for it.

Married to Bertie, Elizabeth had little expectation of ever being queen, but she was determined to be a proper duchess. Life was good. The couple enjoyed a luxurious and privileged life as minor royals, and the early years of their marriage were happy. They were well liked by the British people; Elizabeth's sunny nature made the House of Windsor a more cheerful place, and the press was soon calling her "the smiling duchess."

One drawback, however, was Bertie and Elizabeth's first home in London, White Lodge in Richmond Park, formerly the home of Queen Mary. (Today it houses the Royal Ballet School.) Elizabeth hated the large, drafty house. She could never get warm there, and developed severe bronchitis her first winter in residence. During those early years she also suffered a miscarriage and began to worry about whether she would be able to have a child. News of a second pregnancy in 1925 was greeted with guarded happiness.[1]

The heir apparent, Edward, the Prince of Wales, didn't think his father did a particularly good job of easing the fears of his people after the war. The nation was in economic ruin, and the public was becoming increasingly vocal in its growing discontent. "Where is this land fit for heroes?" became the rallying cry of discharged soldiers,

9540 0001393

0001393 9540

**Sell your books at
sellbackyourBook.com!**
Go to sellbackyourBook.com
and get an instant price
quote. We even pay the
shipping - see what your old
books are worth today!

who had banked on the promise of prosperity in offering their lives for service.

The desperate plight of the citizenry focused a bright light of scrutiny on the Royal Family. Then, as today, their majestic lifestyle seemed unaffected by harsh economic realities. Many people believed that the royals should be more in touch with ordinary people, and that sacrifices endured by the masses should be borne to some extent by the palace. Edward enthusiastically shared that belief, but any small effort to change the royal manners and customs were rebuffed by his father with an abrupt "Well, we never did that in the olden days."[2]

Edward was endlessly frustrated by his father's resistance to change. "My life had become one of contrast and commotion," he wrote later, "whereas order and perfection ruled my father's."[3]

Although Edward and Bertie were close, Edward thought Bertie was too much of a homebody and a traditionalist—"withdrawn from the hurly-burly of life that I relished."[4]

The Prince of Wales fancied himself a shepherd to the poor and the outcast, but although he talked the talk, he did not walk the walk. In the midst of the nation's deepest financial crisis, Edward petitioned the government to exempt him from paying taxes on revenue from the Duchy of Cornwall—land that is traditionally bequeathed to the Prince of Wales.[5] He worked out an arrangement whereby he would voluntarily donate a fraction of the proposed tax bill to the Treasury.

Indeed, if the public thought the Royal Family immune to sacrifice, they had good reason. When at the height of the Great Depression the population endured hardship, including a 10 percent cut in unemployment benefits, the king offered to cut 10 percent off the Civil List—the monies paid to support the operation of the Royal Family. The practical effect of this seemingly generous offer was not to reduce the King's own wealth but to slash the staff and salaries of people working in the royal household, thus increasing unemployment. Meanwhile, the king gave himself what amounted to a huge tax cut when he made the unilateral decision to cease paying taxes on his income from the Duchy of Lancaster.

On April 21, 1926, the day Elizabeth Alexandra Mary made her entrance into the world, the nation was preparing to stop dead in its tracks—literally. The duke and duchess's first child was born eleven days before the greatest labor strike in British history. An estimated three million workers in various occupations walked off their jobs. The trains and buses halted, power plants grew dark, factories ceased production, and even the newspapers were silent. However, according to Lady Airlie, the trauma of the country barely made a ripple at the palace, where "there were few obvious repercussions of the strike beyond the fact that the sentries at the gate had exchanged their red coats and bearskins for khaki and forage caps."[6]

Nor was the nation's plight foremost in anyone's mind at the Strathmores' home on Bruton Street. As rain pelted against the windows throughout the long night, doctors worked furiously with their exhausted patient to safely deliver the baby, who was in a breech position. Finally, more than twenty-four hours after Elizabeth had begun labor, they were forced to do a cesarean section. •

In 1926, a cesarean was far riskier than it is today, especially when performed outside of a hospital. It was a measure of last resort, taken only after a lengthy and complex labor.

In addition to the family and medical staff, a secretary from the Home Office was present during the delivery to certify the baby's lineage. This necessary intrusion stemmed from the Warming-Pan Plot of 1688, when it was alleged that a substitute baby had been placed in the bed of James II's wife. Though the allegations were false, a senior government official had attended every royal confinement since. This was, of course, only a partial validation of royal lineage, as no Home Office representative was present at conception.

Bertie did not witness the delivery. Like all fathers of the day, he was relegated to the sidelines, where he paced and chain-smoked through the long hours, in a state of high anxiety.

The child was instantly embraced by the public. Bertie's family was male-heavy, and everyone was delighted to have a girl. Officially, the child was third in line for the throne, but at the time that didn't have much practical meaning. The chance of her actually becoming queen was rather slim. It would have to mean that Edward, Prince of Wales, first in line, would not succeed his father, and that no sons were born to him or Bertie in the intervening years.

Elizabeth's former nanny, Allah, was called into service, in the tradition of passing nannies from one generation to the next.

Bertie and Elizabeth were blissfully happy with their beautiful daughter, and rapturous about her perfectly composed little face and tufts of blond hair. "You don't know what a tremendous joy it is to Elizabeth and me to have our little girl," Bertie wrote to his mother. "We always wanted a child to make our happiness complete and now that it has happened, it seems so wonderful and strange."[7]

Indeed, he would have been quite content to stay at home in the nurturing embrace of his little family. But duty called. In the fall of that year the king approached Bertie and Elizabeth with a serious request: He wanted them to represent him on a seven-month tour of the Commonwealth.

Bertie had become closer to his father in adulthood. The king recognized qualities in his second son that he had never fully appreciated until contrasted with the eldest. While Edward was impetuous and outspoken, Bertie was thoughtful and measured. Both he and his wife had a strong respect for tradition and ritual. With Elizabeth at Bertie's side, the king felt he was a fitting representative of the throne.

There was just one problem. Bertie's damnable stammer—what he referred to as "the curse that God has put upon me." It wasn't very noticeable in private conversation, but it appeared like a wild rash whenever Bertie had to make a public address. The world tour would require many such speeches, so something had to be done.

The king arranged for Bertie to work with Dr. Lionel Logue, an Australian specialist who treated speech disorders.[8] He taught Bertie to breathe from the diaphragm, and made him slowly repeat long sentences. Elizabeth sat with her husband daily, patiently practicing the tongue twisters designed to wrest Bertie's words from his vocal cords:

> Let's go gathering heathy heather with the
> gay brigade of grand dragoons.

By the time of the trip, Bertie's practice had paid off to the extent that he was able to calmly give a toast each evening on board ship and address the crowds without fear.

Elizabeth had been busy working with her husband and making preparations for the long journey, but as the trip grew closer, she frequently teared up at the immeasurable sacrifice it would entail. Her baby was nine months old, at an age where each day brought a new accomplishment. Seven months seemed like a lifetime to be away from her, and she would never be able to retrieve the moments she missed. The day of their departure, Elizabeth could not take her eyes off her daughter until the last second their car pulled away, and then they had to circle Grosvenor Square several times so she could compose herself for the departure ceremonies.[9]

Bertie and Elizabeth were a hit on the road. At the end of the trip, Sir Tom Bridges, governor of South Australia, reported to the king that almost everywhere the people liked the Duke of York better than his older brother, the Prince of Wales. "His Royal Highness has touched people profoundly by his youth, his simplicity and natural bearing," he wrote, "while the Duchess has left us with the responsibility of having a continent in love with her."[10]

By this time Elizabeth had even won over the king, and in her presence his hard demeanor softened. He once called her a "gleam of sunshine," and the two developed a warm relationship. "Unlike his own children, I was never afraid of him," Elizabeth would say later.

While she was in Australia, the king wrote her a message that was un-characteristically doting: "Your sweet little daughter has 4 teeth now, which is quite good for 11 months."[11]

It was time that Bertie and Elizabeth owned a home of their own, and after they returned from their tour they purchased a five-story stone house at 145 Piccadilly, with a terrace in back that overlooked Hyde Park and Buckingham Palace. The king also gave them a gift of a country house, the Royal Lodge in Windsor Great Park, which was dilapidated but charming, with land for gardening. The prince soon adopted his wife's love of gardening and actually became a gifted horticulturalist, his specialty being rhododendrons.

During the summers, they vacationed at Glamis Castle, a time Elizabeth cherished so much that she refused to give it up in 1930 when she was more than eight months into her second pregnancy. This created high drama for the home secretary, who was required to be present at the birth. What if the child arrived before he could reach Glamis? What if the child was male, in direct line for the throne? If the birth was not properly witnessed, there might be a challenge to the order of succession.

The hand-wringing might have seemed extreme, but these were grave matters then. As a result, the home secretary, J. R. Clynes, arrived at Glamis nearly a month before the birth, cooling his heels at Lady Airlie's neighboring castle.

Also waiting eagerly for the birth was Princess Elizabeth, nick-named "Lilibet" after her own unsuccessful attempts to say her name. At four, Lilibet was a precocious busybody.

On August 21, Elizabeth gave birth to a second daughter, Margaret Rose, at Glamis Castle. Although Bertie and Elizabeth were pleased to have another girl, they knew that the king would be disappointed. He had expected—almost demanded—that the second child be a boy. Afraid to tangle with his father, Bertie sent a note to his mother. "I do hope that you and Papa are as delighted as we are to have a grand-daughter," he wrote, adding nervously, "or would you sooner had a grandson?"

As the first new princesses of the century, Lilibet and Margaret were the objects of intense interest and love from the public. While Allah attended to baby Margaret, her assistant, the redheaded twenty-three-year-old Bobo MacDonald, cared for Lilibet.

For the next six years the family lived a relatively quiet existence, dividing their time between 145 Piccadilly, the Royal Lodge, and magical vacations in Scotland. They were "we four," a team united against the outside, as close as any family could be.

Bertie's sole ambition for his children was that they be happy. He seemed to be constantly trying to rewrite the story of his own childhood by giving his daughters lives of love and laughter. He was particularly besotted with Margaret, a child brimming with affection, who would throw herself into his arms and hang on, showering him with kisses.

The girls adored their mother's parents and enjoyed the complete absence of protocol on their summer visits to Glamis Castle. Lord Strathmore was an old-fashioned country squire, with a long handle-bar mustache that tickled the girls' faces when they kissed him. They loved to tramp across the land with him, clearing brush and pruning trees. Their grandmother was cheerful and warm, always ready with a pot of cocoa after a chilly excursion. The girls listened breathlessly to her stories about Glamis Castle, and she encouraged them to explore and to dress up in period costumes she kept stored in trunks.

The Duchess of York believed the girls' education should be spontaneous, playful, and fun, and they were educated at home by a governess in line with the new ways of teaching introduced by reformers such as Maria Montessori. In 1932, when Lilibet was six, Elizabeth hired Marion Crawford as their governess. "Crawfie," as the children nicknamed her, was a strong and vigorous young Scot with a direct, no-nonsense approach to life. She was an adequate teacher, but the princess had very little formal education. The duchess herself had a limited education, cut short at age fourteen, and she believed her girls were destined for marriage and lives of aristocratic service to good causes.

Crawfie was concerned about the high level of confidence the duke and duchess had in her teaching abilities, and she often consulted with Queen Mary, who had strong opinions about the girls' studies. In particular, Queen Mary pressed for changes in the curriculum that would advance Lilibet's knowledge of history and geography at the expense of arithmetic, which she deemed of little use to women who would never be asked to balance their own household accounts.

Considering their privilege and position in society, it is quite shocking how undereducated the princesses were. Their studies were not at all well rounded; history and geography largely focused on the British Empire, and most of their lessons were of the finishing-school variety—dancing, art, riding, and preparation for traditional domestic roles.

Lilibet always loved horses. She'd started her riding lessons before she was six. She learned to ride well and was instructed in the care, feeding, and training of the horses, as well as how the stables were managed. Margaret wasn't an animal lover like her sister. Her passion was for music. She was a more than competent pianist, and she loved to sing.

Lilibet was an obedient child, undemonstrative and naturally reserved, although her temper, usually controlled, exploded from time to time. She could be exceedingly bossy with her younger sister, often remarking disapprovingly about her "childish" behavior. Tattling on Margaret, she would haughtily say to their governess, "I really don't know what we are going to do with Margaret, Crawfie."[12] Although Lilibet often was sympathetic and aware of others' needs and comforts, she also had a cool, observant side. If she showed coldness or impudence, she was rebuked, usually by Queen Mary.

Their grandmother did not hesitate to chide the children, and she could be harsh. She could not abide any signs of bigheadedness. She believed in royal dignity but emphasized that it was quite different from snobbishness. On one occasion Lilibet, eleven, had been out for a ride with her grandmother. As the footman was helping her down from the carriage, he said, "Down you come, young lady."

"I am not a young lady," Lilibet replied tartly. "I am a *Princess.*"

Queen Mary, regarding her granddaughter with frank disapproval, added, "And one day we hope you will be a lady, too."[13]

But it was Margaret who bore the brunt of her grandmother's chiding. Queen Mary had her lady-in-waiting, Mabell Airlie, write to Crawfie of the nine-year-old princess: "Her Majesty is rather sorry to hear that Princess Margaret is so spoilt, though perhaps it is hardly surprising. I dare say, too, she has a more difficult and complicated character, and one that will require a great deal of skill and insight in dealing with."[14]

Her grandmother's sternness left an impression on Margaret. "I detested Queen Mary," she told a friend many years later. "She was rude to all of us except Lilibet who was going to be Queen. Of course," she added rather snippily, "she had an inferiority complex. We were royal and she was not."[15]

Bertie's older brother, Edward, the Prince of Wales and future King Edward VIII, remained unmarried, and his colorful nightlife generated much gossip. He had many affairs, often with older, married women, and as he approached the age of forty his parents worried that he might never settle down.

Although he was heir to the throne, the prince was not a man of somber duty like his brother. A dubious tribute in *Vanity Fair* read, "Hats off to the indestructible Dancing Drinking Tumbling Kissing Walking Talking and Sleeping—but not Marrying—Idol of the British Empire."

He was often joined on the party circuit by his brother George, Duke of Kent, a gorgeous blue-eyed blond who was a favorite subject of the rumor mill. George was said to have had many affairs, with both men and women, and there were whispers that he had a cocaine problem. His unfettered existence would end in 1934 with his marriage to the stunning Princess Marina of Greece.[16]

Their other brother, Henry, the Duke of Gloucester, was also settling down. Good-natured and unpretentious, Henry was a popular cavalry officer who married the wealthy Scottish socialite Lady Alice Montagu-Douglas-Scott in 1935. Now all of the brothers were married except the one who needed it most.

Despite their strikingly different lives—one led in domestic bliss at home with his wife and two daughters, the other out on the town in silken evening wear—Bertie and Edward were close. Edward was a frequent visitor who adored his little nieces, and they him. But all of that was to change. *

CHAPTER

3

CLASH OF
THE TITANESSES

A thoroughly immoral woman.

ELIZABETH'S VERDICT ON WALLIS SIMPSON

1933 ◆ LONDON

OMETHING WAS WRONG with the
Prince of Wales. He seldom visited Bertie, Elizabeth, and the children, and when he did he was distracted and aloof. One might have chalked it up to the
natural concerns of a royal heir whose father's health was failing. But
Edward wasn't behaving like a future king who held the weight of the
world on his shoulders. He was erratic and defiant. He didn't even attend church—unheard-of for the next head of the Church of England.

One explanation: He was in love.

Wallis Warfield Simpson, an American from Baltimore, Maryland,
currently married to her second husband, had become the mistress of
the Prince of Wales. The two met in 1931 at a dinner party hosted by
common friends. Edward was enchanted by the sharp, witty American.

She was, he thought, the most independent woman he had ever known. In vast contrast to his mother, who had never been known to disagree with his father, even politely, Wallis was fierce and argumentative. Edward found it an engaging quality. The sycophantic tendencies of his friends and colleagues, male and female alike, were a bore. He enjoyed a woman who spoke her mind, without a care in the world that he was the Prince of Wales.[1]

The prince and Wallis became social friends, but as the years passed, he found himself facing a startling reality: He was falling in love with her, and it was possible she felt the same way.

Only the blind could fail to see that an intimate relationship was developing. When King George V bluntly asked his son if he was having an affair with Mrs. Simpson, Edward lied and said they were just good friends.[2] But the rumors persisted, and the bold American woman was seen with him everywhere he went.

Edward did not seem to mind her dominating ways, although the servants resented her bossiness. Elizabeth despised Wallis. She considered her "the lowest of the low, a thoroughly immoral woman."[3] Wallis, for her part, felt contempt for Elizabeth; she mimicked her and openly joked about "the dowdy duchess" and "the monster of Glamis." Herself svelte and stylish, Wallis (who famously said, "You can't be too rich, or too thin") took special glee in remarking on Elizabeth's more rounded form, calling her "Cookie"—short for "fat Scottish cook."

Wallis Simpson was anathema to Elizabeth, a woman bred in the old-fashioned values of duty and decorum. The monarchy meant something to her as a source of pride and identity. This coarse American with designs on the heir respected neither the sanctity of the family nor the sanctity of the throne. Elizabeth disapproved of the way her brother-in-law showered his mistress with diamonds, rubies, and emeralds; she was literally dripping with jewels. With a keen woman's eye, Elizabeth further doubted that the fierce love Edward felt for this American interloper was fully reciprocated. This judgment would be confirmed for her but not shared with the world until after the Queen Mother's death. Secret documents, which had been sealed in Windsor Castle vaults, prove an investigation by the Special Branch into Wallis's life, and give evidence that she had a secret lover, even as her relationship with the prince was heating up. One document, signed by Albert Canning, read, "The identity of Mrs. Simpson's secret lover has now been ascertained." The letter went on to identify the man as Guy Marcus Trundle, although the accuracy of this identification has been disputed by virtually everyone who knew Trundle.

For a romantic lead, Wallis Simpson seemed poorly cast. Her narrow, calculating eyes, square masculine jaw, slightly bulbous nose, and cheerless smile gave her neither beauty nor charm, although she was always impeccably and expensively clad in the latest couture. What was her power over the Prince of Wales, who in her presence seemed more hapless fool than Prince Charming? There are different kinds of love and different reasons for obsession. The undying romance might have been more the obsession of two needy souls than the connection between blissful soul mates.

There is evidence that the Prince of Wales was sexually immature and that he craved dominance—perhaps from a need to re-create the role of the cowed little boy he had been in his father's presence. He was the product of a cold mother and a brutal father, and these joint influences made a lasting imprint on him. Today we have a fuller understanding of the cycle of abuse. We know that abused children often grow up to follow one of two paths—either becoming abusers themselves or seeking relationships that serve as a perverse comfort zone, mirroring the abusive experiences of their youth. In his relationship with Wallis, the prince chose the latter.[4]

According to Freda Dudley Ward, one of his early girlfriends, "He made himself the slave of whomever he loved . . . it was his nature; he was a masochist. He liked being humbled, degraded. He *begged* for it."[5] By the accounts of those who witnessed the couple in more private moments, Wallis happily obliged.

In 2003, the grandchildren of Freda Dudley Ward put up for sale at

Sotheby's more than three hundred letters written to her by the prince of Wales between 1921 and 1923. Edward is revealed as an obsessed, clinging lover, who sometimes wrote his mistress several times a day. According to Marsha Malinowski, head of Sotheby's books and manuscripts department, "I was absolutely shocked that this was a twenty-seven-year-old man writing. These are the letters of an adolescent. It was almost like puppy love. It seems as though his emotional growth was stunted. He was pining and pining for her."

For Wallis, the goal might not have had anything to do with sex or even love. Her ambition was barely masked, and she clearly expected to be queen. Imagine the thrill for an American socialite and double divorcée.

E dward's personal fate was hopelessly entangled in the melodrama that was brewing in Europe. The Great Depression had given rise to a new force in Germany—Adolf Hitler's National Socialist German Workers' Party. Hitler's promise to restore Germany to the vitality it enjoyed before the First World War was enthusiastically embraced by his people.

In the early days of the Third Reich, the British monarchy was not averse to appeasement. (One of the chapters in Hitler's *Mein Kampf* is titled "England as an Ally.") The reasons were complex, including the family's own German roots. But the primary appeal of appeasement was avoidance of war. The palace feared, with good reason, that another war so close on the heels of the last would destroy the European monarchies. Better, many thought, to align Britain with the emerging power of Germany, against the looming threat of the Soviet Union. George V is quoted as declaring to David Lloyd George in 1935, "I will not have another war. *I will not.* The last one was none of my doing and if there is another one and we are threatened with being brought into it, I will go to Trafalgar Square and wave a red flag myself sooner than allow this country to be brought in."[6] Although the king's interest in avoiding war with Germany was motivated more by his desire to protect the constitutional monarchy than by support of Hitler's ideology, the Royal Family did seem to share, if only to a mild degree, the anti-Semitism of the aristocracy. Even the Duchess of York was not free of this prejudice, describing Edwina Mountbatten as "only partly English," since "her mother was half-Jewish."[7]

It was at best a cautious stance, and Edward's problem was that he was the soul of incaution. His growing contempt for parliamentary government and old-fashioned constitutional methods, led him, more than any other royal, to admire the fascist regimes in Germany and Italy. Fearing that he was too much of a Nazi sympathizer, the Foreign Office took the drastic step of excluding secret information from the prince's briefings.

In 1935 the prince gave a speech at the annual conference of the British Legion—an organization of retired military who desired peace with Germany—in which he declared, "The best way to ensure the peace of the world is for the British veterans of the Great War to stretch forth the hand of friendship to the Germans." When he learned about his son's speech, the king was furious. The prince had failed to seek authorization from the Foreign Office before making his controversial remarks and had crossed the line separating the Royal Family from political questions. Even though the views expressed in Edward's speech were not very different from his own, the king warned the prince that he was never to discuss political questions again. At the heart of the constitutional monarchy was the principle of the king's neutrality.

"Monarchy and government are like two inebriated men leaning against each other," historian Lynn Picknett once wrote. "If one should lose his footing, the other comes crashing down too." This tension is held voluntarily in a necessary check and balance of the other's power, and political neutrality is the cornerstone of the monarchy. By openly voicing political positions, Edward was carelessly wandering into a danger zone. Many viewed his imminent reign with apprehension.

Toward the end of his life, the king bitterly expressed doubt that his eldest son could fill his shoes. A lady-in-waiting once heard him declare, "I pray to God that my eldest son will never marry and have children, and that nothing will come between Bertie and Lilibet and the throne." He mournfully predicted to Prime Minister Stanley Baldwin, "After I am dead the boy will ruin himself within a year."[8]

The king's health was declining by the summer of 1935, and some observers said that Prince Edward's activities were a contributing factor. Bertie witnessed with concern Edward's obstinacy and withdrawal from his family. Elizabeth shared his worries, and was quick to point the finger of blame at Wallis Simpson. It angered her that Wallis had pushed herself so deeply into Edward's life, forcing everyone else into the background. The animosity between the two women grew.

In January 1936 King George V died, and his eldest son ascended the throne as King Edward VIII. Although he would immediately assume the crown, in keeping with custom the official coronation would not occur until a year after his father's death.[9]

The Duchess of York watched as her little family shifted position, like chess pieces moving ever closer to their fate. She was appalled to read the sensational headline in the *Daily Express* before the king was even laid to rest: "Nine-year-old Princess Elizabeth, eldest daughter of the Duke and Duchess of York, is now second in line of succession to the throne. One day she may be Queen of England." Such speculation worried Elizabeth enormously, adding to her concern about the obsessive attention the public gave her eldest daughter.

As the months passed, Elizabeth could not deny that George V's death had uprooted the entire family. The loss of the strong, certain patriarch had created a fault line, and the rift was most apparent in the relationship between the new king and Bertie. Increasingly, Edward was keeping a distance from his brother, no longer calling upon him for advice or including him in his plans. He continued his relationship with Wallis Simpson, who had rented a small house at Felixstowe, a port town north of London. Wallis had not yet secured a divorce from husband number two, the cuckolded Ernest Simpson, and she had now developed serious doubts about whether the relationship could survive Edward's coronation. "It's impossible for us to marry," she told the king, but he shrugged off her concerns with the confidence of a man who had always had everything he wanted. "Don't worry," he told her. "I will manage it somehow."[10]

He most certainly believed it. His reliance on his great popularity clouded all judgment of what was truly possible. And the people *did* love him, even if the palace insiders and government officials did not.

From the beginning of his reign, the new king showed a lack of interest in protocol and routine. He was determined to herald in a new era, more modern and open than his father's. He challenged the old ways, suggesting a more democratic flavor to palace life—less ceremony and fewer airs. His outspokenness about both domestic and international affairs, as well as his willingness to intervene in state matters, troubled many in government.

By the summer, with the official mourning period for King George V drawing to an end, Edward became more open about his illicit relationship. When he took a vacation cruise with Wallis, the world's paparazzi descended on the couple, and in major newspapers outside Britain photographs appeared showing the king and Wallis partying, swimming, and cuddling. The pictures never made it into the British press, which was still keeping its distance from the rumors.

The Duke and Duchess of York were seldom included in the king's gatherings at that time, and Elizabeth was sure she knew why. Where Wallis was, she was not to be. However, in September she and Bertie were invited to a dinner at Balmoral Castle, one of the family's favorite properties, in Aberdeenshire, Scotland. Elizabeth had already heard talk of Wallis's imperious behavior at the castle and was horrified to learn that she was staying in the bedroom always used by Queen Mary, and strutting around the place like, well, like a queen!

When the duke and duchess entered Balmoral, Wallis regally approached them with her hand outstretched, clearly acting as the official hostess. In a rare moment of ungraciousness, Elizabeth ignored Wallis, pointedly saying as she strode past her, "I came to dine with the King."[11] If Wallis was hurt by the rebuff, she didn't show it. The two strong women were faced off—one as sleek as a racehorse, the other plump and deceptively soft. In this quiet battle of the titanesses, Wallis clearly felt herself to have the upper hand. At her insistence, Elizabeth and her husband were banned from future guest lists. But she underestimated Elizabeth's influence.

Bertie and Elizabeth might have been out of the king's loop, but they had their sources at the palace and in the government. Reports that the king was talking about marrying his mistress filled Bertie with dread.

The private drama became a government matter when Wallis petitioned for a divorce. Realizing there could be no other reason for the petition but her determination to marry the king, Prime Minister Baldwin reluctantly broached the subject with Edward, urging him to convince Wallis to withdraw her petition. The king refused, saying it was not his place to tell her anything.

The king could not understand the big fuss about Wallis. He merely wished to be given the same rights his subjects enjoyed, including the right to be with the woman he loved. Edward held no religious beliefs—was, in fact, indifferent to religion, which he thought was for old fogies—so he couldn't take seriously his role as Defender of the Faith and head of the Church of England, nor did he care about the church's attitude regarding divorce.

For the most part, the people of England were blissfully unaware of the emerging scandal, as it was not reported in the press. But newspapers in Europe and America were spiking the story with scandalous innuendos, including speculation about Wallis being a nymphomaniac, a Nazi sympathizer, and, most bizarrely, not even a "real" woman but a hermaphrodite.[12]

The silence on the part of the British press couldn't last forever. With news that Wallis had been granted permission to divorce her husband, pending a six-month waiting period, the prime minister informed the king that senior members of the government would be meeting to discuss "the serious situation which is developing."

Later, the king would tell Wallis, "To use a good American expression, they are about to give me the works."

The king made one last attempt to state his case to Baldwin. "I intend to marry Mrs. Simpson as soon as she is free to marry," he told the prime minister. He went on to say that he would be most happy if he could marry her as king—and might be a better king for being happy. But he stated firmly that if the government opposed the marriage, he would abdicate.

In a tense conversation with his mother, the king told her the same thing. Queen Mary was terribly distressed by the news, but her son urged her to see it his way. "Please won't you let me bring Wallis Simpson to see you?" he begged her. "If you were to meet her you would then understand what she means to me and why I cannot give her up."[13]

Queen Mary stiffly refused. Later, she would chastise her son harshly in a letter, writing, "I do not think you have ever realized the shock which the attitude you took up caused your family and the whole Nation. It seemed inconceivable to those who had made such sacrifices during the war that you, as their King, refused a lesser sacrifice."[14]

Bertie sat slumped in his chair, smoking furiously. His brother, the king, was slouched on a couch across from him, nervously shoving tobacco into his pipe. It had been a long time since the two had met privately to speak of what was really going on. Bertie had tried in recent weeks to contact his brother, to talk to him and lend support, but his calls had been ignored. Now, at last, Edward was leveling with him, and he could hardly believe what he was hearing. Edward repeated his assertion that he would abdicate rather than give up Wallis.

Bertie paled. "Oh, that's a dreadful thing to hear," he said miserably. "None of us wants that, least of all I."

"I'm afraid there's no other way," Edward replied. "My mind's made up."

Bertie felt as if the gloom settling around him would never be lifted. To make matters worse, his wife was in bed with a severe case of influenza. He did not want this burden, and frantically scoured his mind for another solution.

Was Edward serious about abdicating? Perhaps it was a bluff. If so, Edward was playing a dangerous game.

On the face of it, the marriage he proposed was impossible. The king, as head of the Church of England, could not marry a divorced woman. There was some discussion of a morganatic marriage, a European tradition that had never been tried in England. A morganatic marriage was between a royal and a woman of lesser status, and precluded the nonroyal partner and her offspring from any claims on titles or property.[15] It is hard to imagine Wallis agreeing to such an arrangement; in any case, it was never seriously considered.

Throughout, Edward must have believed that the people would take his side, and surely Wallis encouraged him in this belief. As an American, Wallis was somewhat naïve about the extent of Edward's power to control their destiny. Although at times she wavered, she most likely *did* believe it would all be sorted out. In *Gone with the Windsors*, Iles Brody writes of Wallis:

> She had imagined that the mere wish of the King would marshal her
> on her way to a third marriage and to the Throne. The power of the
> Government, the advice of Ministers, simply had not entered into
> her calculations. She had equally failed to reckon with public opin-
> ion and with the views of the masses. So that when harsh reality

crashed into her fairy-tale view of the near future, "she was stunned"!
Cinderella, discovering that the fairy godmother's wand would not
work, could not have been more dismayed. . . . In her words: "There
must be some other way," came out, too, that naive romanticism of so
many Americans, who seem to picture the King as a demigod who
can control all things in England (excepting the weather)."[16]

But when the story finally broke in the British press in the first
week of December 1938, the public delivered a harsh verdict.

Edward was stunned by the swell of public opinion against him. He
had failed to grasp an essential truth about the British people. While
they loved the king's common touch, they did not really want him to
be like them. They wanted to look up to their king, not sideways, and
certainly not *down*.

In this conflict between love and duty, the king and the government
could not agree, and after many meetings and discussions with the
prime minister and the Archbishop of Canterbury, the king, defeated,
decided that he must step down.

Elizabeth would always speak of these as terrible days for the monarchy, and she would imply that the burden of the throne was not one she
or her husband accepted gladly. She called it an "intolerable honor."
This doesn't seem entirely plausible. At worst, Elizabeth might have had
mixed feelings about assuming such a grave role, though surely she realized that her stalwart husband, with her at his side, would make a sound
ruler. In her own heart she must have relished the opportunity to restore
the dignity and strength of the monarchy. Besides, what is rarely noted
is that Albert's ascension wasn't by any means automatic. Although the
line of succession is clearly established in the event of death, Parliament
must approve the successor in cases of abdication. There was a brief flirtation with making the popular cavalry officer Prince Henry the king,
but it didn't gather steam.

It is at least possible that Edward might have had his way if he had
generated less fear about his abilities to lead the monarchy in such dif-

ficult times. Many believed that the king's unconstitutional intervention in the politics of the country, and his friendly relations with Hitler, sealed his fate more than an inconvenient romance. He was, in effect, constitutionally unsuited to rule.

Edward VIII signed the Instrument of Abdication on December 10, 1936. The event was witnessed by his three younger brothers, Albert, Henry, and George. The document read:

> I, Edward the Eighth, of Great Britain, Ireland, and
> the British Dominions beyond the Seas, King, Emperor
> of India, do hereby declare My irrevocable determination
> to renounce the Throne for Myself and for My descendents,
> and My desire that effect should be given to this
> Instrument of Abdication immediately.
>
> In token whereof I have hereunto set My hand this
> Tenth day of December, nineteen hundred and thirty six,
> in the presence of the witnesses whose signatures are
> subscribed
>> SIGNED AT FORT BELVEDERE
>>
>> IN THE PRESENCE OF
>> Edward RI
>> Albert
>> Henry
>> George

The mood at 145 Piccadilly was somber, but the princesses were going about their normal day's activities when they heard crowds outside shouting their father's name and cheering. Lilibet ran downstairs and asked a footman what all the ruckus was about. He told her that her father was now the king, and she ran back upstairs and breathlessly told Margaret the news.

At six, Margaret did not understand the concept of abdication, but it sounded ominous. "Are they going to chop off his head?" she asked with alarm. Lilibet patiently explained that, no, their uncle would just stop being king, and their father would take his place.

"Does that mean you will have to be the next Queen?" Margaret asked.

"Yes, someday," Lilibet replied.

"Poor you," said Margaret.[17]

Marion Crawford wrote of a revealing conversation with Margaret. When told that the family was moving to Buckingham Palace and that she would no longer be titled Margaret of York, Margaret asked, "Then who am I?" Crawfie responded, "You are just Margaret." The child complained, "But I have only just learned to write York. Now I am nobody."[18]

The next day the princesses listened along with a worldwide audience while their uncle gave his final radio address:

> A few hours ago I discharged my last duty as King
> and Emperor, and now that I have been succeeded
> by my brother, the Duke of York, my first words must
> be to declare my allegiance to him. This I do with all
> my heart. You all know the reasons which have impelled
> me to renounce the throne. But you must believe me
> when I tell you that I have found it impossible to carry
> the heavy burden of responsibility and to discharge my
> duties as King as I would wish to do without the help
> and support of the woman I love.

In spite of the finality of the abdication, there was some small corner of doubt that it was truly intended as permanent. In his memoirs, *A King's Story,* Edward wrote that the timing of events left a small opening that might restore him to the throne. The coronation of Bertie as King George VI would not occur until May 1937, and Wallis's divorce would be official in April. The duke wrote that he felt confident there would still be time to "work things out."[19] This illusion was supported in the American press, where it all seemed just a matter of ironing out a few insignificant disagreements. Maybe Edward took this press too seriously. It was an unthinkable scenario.

Edward never got it. In scorning the old-fashioned Victorian ideals that prevented him from having his heart's desire, he failed to recognize that the ideal of duty was not a plastic overlay to an authentic life. Duty was the core of the monarchy, a transcendent characteristic possessed by those who would hope to lead during the turbulent times ahead.

Edward was blinded, too, to the true significance of his abdication. In abdicating he had agreed to a voluntary exile of two years to avoid the appearance of there being two kings vying for the throne. But Edward assumed that he would return after that time, his new wife in tow, to play a significant part in the monarchy—with a ceremonial and advisory role suitable for the Duke of Windsor. He didn't understand that leaving the throne would change his relationship to his family and to the monarchy forever. He was deeply offended that none of his family would attend his wedding to Wallis; nor would they acknowledge her by giving her the respect he felt she was due—the coveted title Her Royal Highness.

Queen Mary was distraught by her eldest son's betrayal. Confiding her distress to Lady Airlie, she asked about her lady-in-waiting's sons. "Tell me, have they ever disappointed you?"

Lady Airlie later recalled the conversation and her reply. "I answered that I thought all sons—and daughters too—disappointed their parents at some time or other, and that when this had happened in the case of my children I had always tried not to be possessive, and to remember that their lives were their own and not mine."

Excellent advice, but the queen responded sadly, "Yes, one can apply that to individuals, but not to a Sovereign."[20]

Elizabeth pulled herself together to greet the dawn of the new regime. Although her illness had made her weak, she called upon reserves of strength, knowing that she was the center relied upon by all others: her dear husband, so devastated by events that his stammer had reappeared; Queen Mary, angry and depressed by Edward's betrayal; and her precious daughters, whose carefree lives would be irrevocably altered. It was Elizabeth's role to protect them and to do what she could to mend their broken spirits.

M oving from 145 Piccadilly to Buckingham Palace was like going from a lovingly tended nest to a public building. As Crawfie put it, "Life in a palace rather resembles camping in a museum." Buckingham Palace was immense. With six hundred rooms and hundreds of staff, it was difficult to find a corner of privacy. The sounds of mice scurrying in the drafty corridors and tapping from inside the walls were constant, and there was always a chill in the air, no matter how modern the heating.[21]

Elizabeth worried that her little family would never feel comfortable in this awful place, but Bertie tried to reassure her. "It's not so bad," he said. "I lived here for thirteen years. You get used to it."

But it *was* so bad. Too vast for intimacy, too public for a real family life, it was a monstrous prison. More than that, it was leaving a home where they had been happy to live in the eye of the storm. The children were nervous about the move. When Elizabeth gently told the girls they would be living in Buckingham Palace, Lilibet furrowed her brow and asked, "Do you mean for*ever*?"

For the family, coronation day started before dawn. As she wrote in an account of the day, titled "To Mummy and Papa in Memory of Their Coronation From Lilibet By Herself," Lilibet was awakened at five o'clock in the morning by the Royal Marine band striking up outside her window. She and Bobo put on dressing gowns and shoes and crouched at the window, watching with excitement as the crowds gathered in the early morning cold.[22]

Looking at the official coronation photograph, one gets the impression that the little family is playing royal dress-up. Bertie and Elizabeth seem consumed by the voluminous robes, their large crowns balanced on slightly bowed heads. The little girls, in cream-colored lace gowns with ermine-trimmed cloaks and gold coronets pressed into their curls, might be mistaken for wax-museum statues were it not for the hint of a toothless smile coming from six-year-old Margaret.

It was the end of family as they knew it, and the beginning of history's cascade. They no longer belonged to themselves alone as "we four." They belonged to England.

4

THE MOST DANGEROUS WOMAN IN EUROPE

Sometimes one's heart seems
near breaking under the stress
of so much sorrow and anxiety.

QUEEN ELIZABETH, IN A LETTER TO

ELEANOR ROOSEVELT, JUNE 11, 1940

June 7, 1939 ✦ NIAGARA FALLS, NEW YORK

HE KING'S TRAIN, specially outfitted by Royal Canadian Pacific and painted royal blue and silver for the occasion, rumbled across the Niagara Falls suspension bridge, which had been built in the mid-1800s to foster commerce between the United States and Canada. Swaying above the stunning vista, it served as a powerful symbol of the ability of nations to reach across the roiling chasms of their differences and find common purpose. The symbol was not lost on King George VI and Queen Elizabeth, as their trip to America had been arranged for just this reason. In this journey of humility and hope, the lines from Henry Austin's poem "Niagara" resonated, sobering and true:

> O perilous bridge 'mid gusts of dazzling pearl,
> Or where a diamond storm enshrouds the way.
> Thou seem'st like Life a span 'twixt Day and Night;
> For tho' eternal rainbows crown the rocks,
> Halos of Hope, charmed circles of high Faith,
> Commanding entrance through the chasms of Doubt,
> To deeps of nobler knowledge and soul-strength,
> Yet all this beauty overwhelms the mind
> By clash of contrast with our littleness.[1]

This pioneering visit of England's king and queen was both noble and desperate, and its purpose was clear: England now found itself dependent upon the goodwill of its former colonies—the very nation that it had met twice on the battlefield. If the king and queen were not exactly going to America with hat—or crown—in hand, they were well aware of the stakes.

Straining to see through windows sprayed with a fine mist from the falls, Elizabeth let a small thrill break through her sobering occupations. They were to be the first British monarchs to step foot on American soil in the history of this young nation. Her father-in-law had never considered such a visit, even though he valued the collaboration the two countries had formed during World War I. Her chest swelled with the pride of the moment.

She was not wary of Americans. In many ways she enjoyed their open, friendly smiles and warm spirits. She felt confident that she could win them over. In this land, she knew, friendliness was matched with welcoming arms. She had despised Wallis Simpson not, as many people assumed, for her American roots but rather for the evil fruit that nestled in the greedy branches of her soul. She believed that Americans would come to embrace the new monarchs with the same enthusiasm they had once given Edward VIII and Wallis.[2]

Elizabeth glanced at her husband, whose face was pensive. He had the burden of the crown, and his task was larger than hers. He despised crowds, and was fearful of stumbling over his words or appearing inept. His brother had been—still was—a great favorite in this nation. She had faith in him, though. One of the things she admired most about Bertie was that he never tried to be anything other than the man he was. Pretense was foreign to him. And in his simple, noble way, he, too, won people over. She knew the trip would be a success.

When the train chugged to a stop on the American side of the bridge, a delegation headed by Secretary of State Cordell Hull stood to greet them. A brilliant strip of red carpet was rolled out, and the king and queen disembarked to the roar of an enthusiastic crowd, which blended with the ever-present roar of the falls.

As the train continued on to Washington, D.C., the king and queen must have contemplated the difficult year behind them and the troubling specter that brought this trip into being. A year earlier they had favored appeasement efforts with Germany, and had encouraged Prime Minister Neville Chamberlain to make overtures and to seek peace at almost any price. The memories of the suffering of war and its terrible price were still fresh in their minds. In September 1938, when the prime minister returned from the Munich conference with a peace agreement signed by Hitler—paid for by Czechoslovakia, which was forced to cede the Sudetenland to Germany—there was briefly reason for hope.[3] The statement Chamberlain carried read optimistically:

> We, the German Führer and Chancellor, and the
> British Prime Minister, have had a further meeting
> today and are agreed in recognizing that the question
> of Anglo-German relations is of the first importance
> for our two countries and for Europe. We regard the
> agreement signed last night and the Anglo-German
> Naval Agreement as symbolic of the desire of our
> two peoples never to go to war with one another again.

We are resolved that the method of consultation shall
be the method adopted to deal with any other questions
that may concern our two countries, and we are determined
to continue our efforts to remove possible sources of
difference, and thus to contribute to assure the peace
of Europe.

By this time, the idea of collaboration with Germany had gained favor in England. The City of London's Crown bankers backed Hitler,
confident that Britain and Germany could form a strong European alliance that would keep the Russians in check.

Buoyed by Chamberlain's successful negotiations, the king and
queen invited him to wave to cheering crowds from a balcony at Buckingham Palace, and Chamberlain announced to the people, "My good
friends, for the second time in our history, a British Prime Minister
has returned from Germany bringing peace with honor. I believe it is
peace for our time. . . . Go home and get a nice quiet sleep."

It was a short-lived rest. Hitler had broken the Munich Agreement
and seized the rest of Czechoslovakia in March. Now they seemed on
the brink of war.

There was also the matter of the king's brother, whose relentless
harassment of Bertie angered Elizabeth. Her husband, she thought,
was too forgiving by half, and he had encouraged Edward in the belief
that all could somehow be normal between them. But reality inter-
vened when it came to the question of titles. While Wallis was allowed
the title Duchess of Windsor, she would be refused the more precious
title Her Royal Highness, and without those three letters, HRH, up
front, her status would not be truly royal.[4] The outrage over this slight
burned up the phone lines, but Elizabeth encouraged her husband
not to relent. In Elizabeth's opinion, the behavior of the Duke and
Duchess of Windsor warranted permanent exile. Shortly after they
were married, the couple visited Hitler, and they'd behaved as allies,
although they were in no position to do so. A sycophant to the point of

embarrassment, Edward was seen giving the Nazi salute several times, defending it later as simply "good manners."[5]

The Nazi high command believed that Edward had been forced to abdicate for his pro-German views, and it laid out the red carpet for the couple. The duke and duchess even took tea with Hitler. There were rumors of the duke's willingness to consider returning to the British throne under German dictation, along with his pro-German wife, in the event of a German victory over Britain. Secret papers, locked away until recently, reveal a plot by Hitler to overthrow England and return Edward to the throne with Wallis as queen. As Rudolf Hess wrote to Hitler: "There is no need to lose a single German life invading Britain. The Duke and his clever wife will deliver the goods."[6]

The Duke of Windsor was lobbying hard to secure a return to England, using friends like Neville Chamberlain and Winston Churchill to convince the king.

There is probably no better example of the influence Elizabeth exerted over her husband than this crucial moment in history. George VI was inclined to proffer an olive branch to his brother, but Elizabeth was adamant. She believed the warnings of Sir Horace Wilson, a savvy politico who had been advisor to former Prime Minister Stanley Baldwin. Wilson wrote of Wallis: "It is clear to me that it is [her] intention not only to come back here but to set up a 'court' of her own—and there can be little doubt to do her best to make things uncomfortable for the new occupants of the throne. It must not be assumed that she has abandoned hope of becoming Queen of England."[7]

At one point Chamberlain actually tried to persuade the king to let the Duke and Duchess of Windsor return to England and perform the normal duties of royals. Bertie wavered, but he could not crack the united iron front presented by his wife and mother opposing the idea. In December 1938 the king wrote to Chamberlain, letting him know that a return was impossible, even for the purpose of a visit: "I think you know that neither the Queen nor Queen Mary have any desire to meet the Duchess of Windsor and therefore any visit made for the purpose of introducing her to members of the Royal Family obviously becomes impossible."[8]

The king informed his brother that if he returned to England without an invitation, he would be stripped of his royal allowance. When the duke started to protest, the king angrily countered, "How do you think I like taking on a rocking throne and making it steady again?"[9]

Edward was enraged. Wallis was apoplectic. Elizabeth didn't care.

By the time President Franklin D. Roosevelt invited the king and queen to visit the United States, all hope of appeasement with Germany had been dashed. Now the future of Europe and the world seemed to rest on a strong alliance against fascism.

The President and Mrs. Roosevelt personally met the train at Union Station in Washington, D.C., where the royals disembarked into the steamy southern heat. The king strode forward and clasped Roosevelt's hand in a firm shake. "Well, at last I greet you," Roosevelt said, beaming.

Six hundred thousand people stood along the motorcade route, everyone straining to catch a glimpse of the queen. The moment was captured in *Time* magazine: "She was the perfect Queen: eyes a snapping blue, chin tilted confidently, two fingers raised as a greeting, as girlish as she was regal. Her long-handled parasol seemed out of a storybook."

She was an instant hit. The American infatuation with Edward and Wallis was fading into memory. In no time at all, Elizabeth and Bertie had won their hearts.

There were some issues with Congress. Americans were holding their full support of an alliance with Britain in abeyance, unwilling to offer complete commitment to Europe's approaching war. Some members of Congress were urging the president to confront the king about the small matter of five billion dollars that England still owed the

United States for World War I. (In King George VI's private notes of a discussion with Roosevelt, it seems this matter was discussed and the president willingly waived the debt for the time being.)[10]

At a state dinner, the American legislators were disarmed by the queen and were ebullient and friendly. Too friendly, perhaps. A Texas congressman slobbered, "Cousin Elizabeth, you're a thousand times prettier than your pictures." Another besotted member suggested canceling England's war debt if the United States could keep the queen.

Some members of the royal party found them crude, but Elizabeth was an old hand at gracefully deflecting the attentions of rude males. She won them over with a wink and a smile.

President Roosevelt's powerful assistant, Harry Hopkins, had never had much use for the British or their Royal Family, but the queen converted him with an endearing gesture. She had learned that Hopkins's small daughter was disappointed upon meeting the queen because she wore ordinary clothing, just like everybody else. She had expected a "Fairy Queen." Before the White House banquet, the queen dressed up in an elaborate ball gown and tiara and snuck upstairs to the room where the little girl was sleeping. The enchanted girl got her "Fairy Queen," and the queen gained Hopkins's admiration for life.[11]

"The British sovereigns have conquered Washington, where they have not put a foot wrong and where they have left a better impression than even their most optimistic advisors could have expected," the *New York Times* enthused.

After two days in Washington, the king and queen headed to New York City, where they would dedicate the British Pavilion at the 1939 World's Fair.[12] They were met by exuberant crowds along the way; an estimated 3.5 million people lined the route on the West Side Highway, cheering, waving, and calling out hellos.

As Elizabeth had anticipated, the Americans were ready to embrace them. The people admired the king, who appeared both gentle and resolute, and they adored his wife.

The queen clearly appreciated the easy warmth of the American people, and she especially enjoyed her time at Hyde Park, the president's private residence, where she could relax and let her royal hair down. "They are such a charming and united family," she raved in a letter to her mother-in-law, Queen Mary, "and living so like English people when they come to their country house." One feature that was decidedly *not* like the English was a family picnic where hot dogs were served—a culinary choice that horrified many but delighted the royal couple. A *New York Times* headline the following day read, KING EATS HOT DOGS, ASKS FOR MORE.

The next evening, as the king and queen prepared to leave on a train for Quebec, many eyes were tearful. "Good luck to you," Roosevelt said with heartfelt emotion. "All the luck in the world." Everyone knew how desperately they would need it.

As the train departed, someone in the crowd began singing "Auld Lang Syne," and soon everyone was singing. "It seemed to me," Eleanor Roosevelt would later write, "that there was something of our friendship and our sadness and something of the uncertainty of our futures in that song that could not have been said as well in any other words."[13]

The king and queen returned to England to face the inevitable march to war. The failure of Neville Chamberlain's appeasement of Adolf Hitler (who dismissed George VI as "a simpleton") was complete when, on Sunday, September 3, 1939, he declared in the House of Commons, "This country is now at war with Germany. We are ready." The new king was, like his father before him, a war leader, although it would be another year before Luftwaffe bombs began to fall on London's East End.[14]

Chamberlain's failure was punished. He was unseated and replaced by Winston Churchill, who had once been a close ally of King Edward VIII. At first King George VI and Churchill did not hit it off. Churchill was a man of great physical and intellectual charisma, who liked being in charge and hoarding all the publicity. The king missed his old friend Chamberlain, with whom he saw eye-to-eye and in whose company he felt comfortable.

The question of what to do with the Duke and Duchess of Windsor remained much on everyone's minds during this period. Probably to get the couple out of Europe, the decision was made to appoint the duke Governor of the Bahamas. In August 1940, the duke reluctantly accepted the position, and they would spend the rest of the war in a distant land, awaiting a return to the throne that would never come. Instrumental in cementing the couple's fate was the woman Hitler called "the most dangerous woman in Europe"—the queen herself.

With war upon them, many British families were seeking temporary shelter in Canada, and there was a great deal of pressure for the queen to send her children overseas. She was unwavering in her refusal. "The children will not leave unless I do," she said. "I shall not leave unless their father does, and the King will not leave the country in any circumstances whatever."[15]

Instead, on May 12, 1940, the day after Winston Churchill took office, the children were sent with Crawfie to the heavily fortified Windsor Castle, an imposing circular fortress more than nine hundred years old, which was once used by William the Conqueror. Its huge medieval walls were virtually impenetrable, encasing more than one thousand rooms. With hundreds of people working there, it was practically a small city.

Windsor Castle was damp and cold under normal circumstances, but war rationing of fuel rendered it frigid. The dungeons, reconstituted for use as fallout shelters, evoked nightmarish images of distant horrors. It was a gloomy but safe place for the girls to be. Wandering through the dark, icy rooms, their windows blackened, Margaret grumbled, "Who is this Hitler spoiling everything?"[16]

Queen Mary was also persuaded to leave her London residence,

Marlborough House, for the country, along with sixty-three servants. She was unhappy upon leaving, but her sojourn at Badminton in Gloucestershire proved to be an active time for her. She personally "adopted" the 120 men from the Gloucestershire regiment stationed there, organized campaigns to collect scrap metal, joined the locals in their efforts, and boldly carried a small pearl-handled revolver in her parasol, stating that if the Nazis tried to kidnap her, she wouldn't go without a fight.

She was so invigorated by her active life and her first taste of freedom from protocol in more than fifty years that at the end of the war when she was ready to return to London, she cried as she told the people who had meant so much to her, "Here I have been anybody to everybody. In London I shall have to begin being Queen Mother all over again."[17]

Beginning September 7, 1940, London suffered fifty-seven straight nights of bombing. By the war's end, a third of the city, including the House of Commons, Buckingham Palace, and most of the East End, had been damaged or destroyed. The destruction of the East End, a blighted area immortalized by Charles Dickens, was particularly disastrous for the thousands left homeless.

To this day, the British people speak admiringly of the courage and compassion displayed by King George VI and Queen Elizabeth during the Nazi campaign, as bombs nightly lit up the skies of London. Throughout this period the king and queen were a constant presence, paying daily visits to the bombed neighborhoods. The queen wanted it known that the Royal Family shared the plight of its people, although this took some convincing. The first time the king and queen visited the victims of a bombing, they were booed. It must have been a surreal sight—the sedan pulling up to the rubble and the queen stepping out in her finest attire, with feather-plumed hat and pearls, as if she were going to a dinner party. During those early days the queen was scathingly criticized for appearing amidst the rubble in bright outfits, hats, and pearls, instead of more somber attire that would fit the mood. She paid no attention. She intended for her colorful visage to lift the spirits of those in despair, and to show a measure of respect. As she liked to remind her critics, the people would not have visited her home in anything but their Sunday best; how could she do otherwise?

It seemed to work, thanks to the queen's genuine feeling for her people and her perfect common pitch. One day in London, the royal couple came upon a woman trying to coax her terrified dog out of her bombed home. Laying a sympathetic hand on the woman's shoulder, Elizabeth said, "Perhaps I can try. I am rather good with dogs."[18]

On another occasion, while the king and queen visited a bombed-out area, someone in the crowd shouted out, "Thank God for a good King!"

The king replied, "Thank God for a good people."[19]

The royal walkabouts came to symbolize the monarchy's solidarity with the population, memorialized by a popular song:

> The King is still in London town
> with Mr. Jones and Mr. Brown . . .

The connection grew stronger after Buckingham Palace was bombed for the first time.[20] The king and queen were upstairs in the king's sitting room, which overlooked the quadrangle, when they heard the unmistakable roar of an aircraft overhead. Then, as they watched frozen in horror, they saw a bomb dislodge itself and fall on the other side of the palace. It was followed by more bombs; several hit the quadrangle below, a mere thirty yards from where they were standing.

Uninjured but shaken, the king and queen hurried to the makeshift bomb shelter. Later, when they surveyed the extent of the damage, they were amazed to be alive. The king was enraged. He believed the bombing of Buckingham Palace, so boldly undertaken, could have but one goal—to kill him and restore Edward to a Nazi-run throne. Elizabeth agreed, but she tried to make light of the near miss. Always sensitive to the agonies of the people, she quipped, "I'm glad we were bombed. Now

I can look the East End in the face." At last she was able to commiserate from firsthand experience with other victims in her nation's capital. To put Hitler and his Nazi regime on notice, she let the palace information officer announce that she was practicing shooting a revolver.

The king grew in stature during the war, becoming for his people a symbol of resistance. He was more forceful and eloquent in his public declarations, showing a capacity to pull the emotional strings of a nation. "There will always be an England," he declared in one radio broadcast, "to stand before the world as the . . . citadel of hope and freedom."[21]

The icy relationship between the king and Churchill had melted in the heat of their joint resolve. Radically different in personality and demeanor, the two men found that they shared common values, and Churchill's prior disdain for the monarchy dissolved completely. "This war," he wrote the king, "has drawn the Throne and the people more closely together than was ever before recorded and Your Majesties are more beloved by all classes and conditions than any of the princes of the past."[22]

Churchill, who had once been solidly in Edward's corner, even over the question of whether he should marry Wallis, had shifted allegiance, although Edward didn't fully understand this until he appealed to Churchill to "restore the Duchess's rank." Churchill passed on the request to the king, who scoffed at the idea and explained the family's position to Churchill: "When he abdicated he renounced all the rights and privileges of succession for himself and his children—including the title 'Royal Highness.' In respect to him and his wife, there is, therefore, no question of his title being 'restored' to the Duchess—because she never had it."

Churchill fully supported the king. In any case, he felt there were far more important matters to be concerned about. This was war. Who had time for such silliness?

As the destruction grew and the casualties mounted, Elizabeth received a message from her newfound friend Eleanor Roosevelt:

Dear Queen Elizabeth,

Ever since England was forced into the war I have wanted to write and tell you how constantly you and the King are in my thoughts.

Since meeting you, I think I can understand a little better what a weight of sorrow and anxiety must be yours.

We can but pray for a just peace and my warm sympathy is with you.

Sincerely yours,
Eleanor Roosevelt[23]

In her lengthy, emotional reply, Queen Elizabeth poured her heart out to her new friend and colleague across the ocean.

My Dear Mrs. Roosevelt,

I was deeply touched by your kind thought in writing me such a charming and sympathetic letter. I do appreciate what you said, and send my heartfelt thanks. Sometimes one's heart seems near breaking under the stress of so much sorrow and anxiety. When we think of the gallant young men being sacrificed to the terrible machine that Germany has created, I think that anger perhaps predominates. But when we think of their valour, their determination & their grave spirit, their pride and joy are uppermost.

We are all prepared to sacrifice everything in the fight to save freedom, and the curious thing is, that already many false values are going, & life is becoming simpler and greater every day. It is encouraging to know that the United States is gradually beginning to realize the terrible menace of the Nazi way of living. We who have lived near it for some years, to some degree understand the danger, but it is all far worse than our simple peace loving people could ever take in, until faced with the awful reality.

I must tell you how moved I have been by the many charming, sympathetic, and understanding letters which I have received from kind people in the United States. Quite poor people have enclosed little sums of money to be used for our wounded, our sailors, or mine sweepers. It really has helped us, to feel such warmth of human kindness & goodness . . .

Sometimes, during the last terrible months, we have felt rather lonely in our fight against evil things, but I can honestly say that our hearts have been lightened by the knowledge that friends in America understand what we are fighting for.

We look back with such great pleasure to those lovely days we spent with you last June. We often talk of them, and of your & the President's welcome & hospitality. The picnic was great fun, and our children were so thrilled with the descriptions of the Indian singing & marvelous clothes—not to mention the hot dogs!

The most wonderful relays of hospital comforts and clothes have been arriving here from the United States—we are so deeply grateful for such invaluable help.

Now that the Germans have started their bombing and destruction here, the clothes will be doubly welcome in the many little homes where all personal belongings are lost—blown sky-high. It is so terrible to think that all the things we have worked for these last twenty years are being lost or destroyed in the madness of such a cruel war—better housing, education, nursery schools, low cost of living, & many others. But perhaps we have all gone too hard for material benefits, & ignored the spiritual side of life. I do believe that there is a gradual awakening to the needs of the spirit, and that, combined with adversity and sorrow overcome, will lay the seeds of a far better world.

In one of the nice letters I have had recently from America, a lady wrote of the sorrows of "your world." It seems such a curious distinction, her world and our world are apparently different! I did not feel that at all when I was with you all last year.

Please give many kind messages to the President, we do so

*admire his great work & wise statements, and I hope with all my
heart that we may meet again someday.*

*With all good wishes to you both,
I am,
Yours very sincerely,
Elizabeth R.*

In pouring out her heart to Mrs. Roosevelt, the queen had a political as well as a personal aim. She hoped to create a vivid enough picture of Britain's circumstances to move America from the sidelines of
the war. She and Bertie had been encouraged by their budding friendship with the Roosevelts and had felt optimistic that their efforts
would pay off in American support. The king had taken it as a firm
promise when Roosevelt said to him during their 1939 United States
visit that "if London was bombed, the U.S.A. would come in," but that
had not happened.[24]

On the question of the war, Roosevelt was facing a divided population. Isolationist forces, mostly in the Midwest, were staunchly
against United States involvement. Although a Gallup Poll found
that 84 percent of the population was opposed to Hitler, there was a
fierce debate about whether the nation should send its own forces to
the European theater. Roosevelt was inclined to be an international-
ist, but he didn't believe he had the public support needed to go
to war.

For many Americans, the battlefield was far removed from their
lives and concerns, but others felt the crisis in a more personal way. In
1940, the poem "There Are No Islands, Any More," by Edna St. Vincent Millay, was published in the *New York Times*. Subtitled "Lines
Written in Passion and in Deep Concern for England, France and My
Own Country," the poem was a call for unity between free nations
across the ocean, and its final lines were a warning to America of the
cost of doing nothing:

Lest French and British fighters, deep
In battle, needing guns and sleep,
For lack of aid be overthrown
And we be left to fight alone.

It took the Japanese attack on Pearl Harbor on December 7, 1941, for America's isolationist mood to disappear. The United States was ready to fully engage, now on two fronts, in Europe and the Pacific.

In 1942 Queen Elizabeth invited Mrs. Roosevelt to visit England and observe firsthand the remarkable war effort being waged by the women of the country. With the enthusiastic support of her husband, who was prevented by health and obligation from making the trip, Mrs. Roosevelt came to Buckingham Palace for a three-week visit, traveling under the code name Rover.

Her most vivid first impression of Buckingham Palace was how *cold* it was. Central heating had been turned off due to war economies, and only a small fire burned in her vast suite of rooms. (She later learned it was the queen's own suite, which she had given up for the First Lady.)

Food rationing produced some peculiar meals—not at all the elegant fare one might expect at the palace. Mrs. Roosevelt was amused to see the meager tinned foods being served on gold and silver platters.

Recalling her experiences accompanying the king and queen to bombed areas, Eleanor wrote, "The people would gather almost everywhere they went, standing outside the ruins of their houses and waiting until Their Majesties had tramped through the rubble. Often the King or Queen spoke to them quietly and on other occasions the people would address their monarch, but these exchanges of words were always in a tone of sympathetic understanding. The people suffered stoically and I never heard them complain or speak bitterly."[25]

It was a busy three weeks. The First Lady was interested in seeing as many of the blitzed areas as possible, and she was taken around by the royal couple and by Churchill's wife, Clementine. The courage and determination of the people brought tears to her eyes. "We talked with people like the old couple, who still slept nightly in an underground shelter in London, though they could easily have been evacuated to a country area," she wrote. "They told us they had lived so long in the shelter that, while they liked to go out in the daytime and sit in their old home—even though there was not enough of it left so that they could sleep there—they preferred to return to the shelter at night rather than move away. We visited Red Cross clubs of all kinds and went to American and British Service camps."

The visit was meaningful in that it placed on full public display the grit of three strong women: the Queen, Clementine Churchill, and Eleanor Roosevelt. During her stay Mrs. Roosevelt had the opportunity to observe another strong woman in the making. Lilibet impressed the First Lady. "She was quite serious," she said with admiration, "and with a great deal of character and personality."[26]

5

HEIR PRESUMPTIVE

Oh dear, Crawfie, I hope
he doesn't come over here.

LILIBET, SPEAKING OF HITLER

Autumn 1940 ♦ WINDSOR CASTLE

THE QUEEN REGARDED her eldest daughter thoughtfully. Lilibet was so poised for a girl of fourteen, so solemn. Her status as heir presumptive weighed on her.[1] She would most certainly follow her father to the throne, and with the constant danger and uncertainty of war, that might happen sooner rather than later. Her mother, remembering the carefree laughter of her own girlhood, would have loved nothing more than to rub the cloud of destiny from Lilibet's somber eyes.

Elizabeth longed for her children's lives to be normal, or what passed for normal in a time of war, but although Margaret could be silly and delightful, more was required of Lilibet. The king's relationship with his eldest daughter had changed after the coronation; his every word and action seemed designed to prepare her for a time when the weight of the crown would be on her head.

Now Lilibet stood before her, straight-backed and determined to make her case. She hated being holed up at Windsor Castle, she told her mother. Others her age were helping the war effort. Every night she lay awake in her bed behind the fortress walls and listened to the distant rumble and thud of bombs, hating the helpless way she felt. Hadn't her mother herself often talked about how proud she'd been to do her part helping to tend to the soldiers at Glamis Castle? Why, she was the same age as Lilibet when the First World War broke out. Lilibet merely wanted a chance to contribute something more substantial than the children's work of the Girl Guides.[2]

But it wasn't the same at all. For one thing, bombs were not falling on Scotland during the First World War. For another thing, Elizabeth Bowes-Lyon had not been singled out—at least, not yet—to play a leading role in the continuation of the monarchy.

Worried though she was, Elizabeth couldn't help feeling a sense of pride in her daughter. She realized that Lilibet was emulating her parents' example—and isn't that what any mother would want? After all, she had often repeated to her daughters the lesson her mother had taught her: "Your work is the rent you pay for the room you occupy on earth."

Lilibet was stubborn. She would not be dissuaded, and so at last it was decided that she would make a radio address to the children of the nation. In October the equipment was set up at the castle and she delivered the speech with moving force, her high, sweet voice strong and clear through the microphone. Her address was listened to by hundreds of thousands of families, adults and children alike, but it resonated most with the children, who huddled night after night behind blackout curtains, shaken to the core by the thundering raids. Lilibet wanted to reach out to them across the radio waves and comfort them. "Thousands of you in this country have had to leave your homes and be separated from mothers and fathers," she told them. "Margaret

Rose and I feel so much for you, as we know from experience what it means to be away from those we love most of all. We know, every one of us, that in the end all will be well."

Lilibet was pleased with her performance, and the letters poured in to show that she had made a difference. But she wanted more. "I ought to do as other girls my age do," she insisted. She didn't want to be a princess in a gilded cage.

If Lilibet demonstrated a gift for empathy, her sister was showing that her gift was the ability to inspire laughter. A high-spirited ten-year-old, Margaret was a real cutup and a natural performer. She wanted to take singing lessons, and when her father said no, she sang anyway. At her instigation the children were allowed to produce elaborate Christmas pantomime programs, which were strikingly professional and showcased Margaret's talent. She hungrily accepted the accolades after each performance.[3]

From birth, it seemed, Margaret had instinctively differentiated herself from Lilibet, as if her designated role was to go against the grain. Her parents were indulgent, especially the king, who adored his sparkling youngest, but no one really knew what to do with her. Lilibet's role was cast by history, but who was Margaret to become?

During the war years Lilibet's thoughts strayed, as any teenage girl's might, to romance. She pined for one young man in particular, a handsome naval officer whom she'd first met when she was only thirteen.

In July 1939, before the start of the war, she had joined her parents on the royal yacht *Victoria & Albert* for a visit to the Royal Naval College at Dartmouth. Dining with them on board was a naval cadet, Prince Philip of Greece, who had been given a special dispensation to join the Royal Navy as a foreign national. Philip was the nephew of Lord Louis Mountbatten, a member of Churchill's inner circle who was currently serving as head of the Combined Operations Command.

Philip was a handsome young man, whom Crawfie would later describe as "a fair-haired boy, rather like a Viking, with a sharp face and piercing blue eyes."[4] Lilibet thought he was funny and charming, and she sat blushing throughout the meal. But Lilibet was a mere child of thirteen, and Philip was an eighteen-year-old man of the world, currently wooing (among others) the American model Cobina Wright.

Philip's lineage and personal history were something of a tangle. Although he had the title Prince Philip of Greece, he was only marginally pedigreed, from a family of destitute royals, and his lineage was a mixed bag of Greek, German, Dutch, Russian, and British. His grandfather was Danish by birth, the son of King Christian IX and Queen Louise. In 1863 the Greeks, who were without a monarch after years of Turkish rule, invited the eighteen-year-old Prince William to become their king. He married Olga, the granddaughter of Tsar Nicholas I of Russia, and they had seven children. Philip's father, Prince Andrew, was the second-youngest. He married Alice of Battenberg, the daughter of Prince Louis of Battenberg and a great-granddaughter of Queen Victoria.

When Philip was a young boy, his father was forced into exile, and the strain of her husband's dispossession was too much for Philip's mother. She separated from his father, also gradually removing herself from reality. In 1930 she was institutionalized for a time with a diagnosis of paranoid schizophrenia after exhibiting alarming behavior—remaining prostate on the floor for long periods, and claiming to receive instructions from Jesus Christ. She once declared that Christ was married to her alone.[5]

Philip spent his childhood being shuttled among relatives and was eventually taken under the wing of Lord Louis Mountbatten, his mother's younger brother. Mountbatten had always favored the British side of the family, and he served in the Royal Navy during the First World War. In 1917, the year the Saxe-Coburg and Gothas became the Windsors, the Battenbergs became the Mountbattens. They were similarly inclined to downplay their German roots, in name if not always in loyalty.

It is doubtful that Philip took much notice of the young girl who would be queen, but the same could not be said of his uncle. Uncle Dickie, as the girls called him, was relentlessly ambitious for his nephew, and he made no secret of the fact that he wanted to see Philip marry into a *real* royal family.

Given his rocky beginnings, Philip had grown into a remarkably poised and accomplished young man. His uncle had seen to it that he received a fine education and was introduced in all the right circles. He was also close to his cousin Marina, the beautiful wife of the king's brother, Prince George of Kent.

Lilibet's grandmother, Queen Mary, obsessed with matchmaking, took note. As soon as it became clear that Lilibet would someday be queen, she'd started thinking about a husband for the girl, which infuriated Bertie and Elizabeth. Lilibet was only thirteen, a mere child. It was far too early to be considering such matters. The Queen Mother didn't agree. It was never too early to lay the groundwork for a successful marriage.[6]

Any hope of normal teen life was overshadowed by the war and by Lilibet's position. In adolescence Lilibet was a striking combination of maturity and naïveté. She had never had anything approaching an easy, casual relationship with her peers, male or female.

In 1941, when Lilibet was fifteen, Philip visited Windsor Castle on leave. Tall, slender, and dashing in his naval uniform, he was an impressive young man, although Crawfie watched him somewhat askance. She thought Philip a show-off, and she noticed that Lilibet never took her eyes off him, flattering him by hanging on his every word.

Philip was well aware of Mountbatten's plan. He once grumbled to a friend, "My uncle has ideas for me. He thinks I could marry Princess Elizabeth."[7] The manipulation made Philip uncomfortable. Lilibet was still a child, as far as he was concerned. His uncle's overt angling for position was embarrassing, and he cringed at Mountbatten's embellishments.

Still, throughout the war Lilibet and Philip wrote letters back and forth, and she knit him woolen scarves and sweaters, daydreaming about her handsome hero. Once she took her governess aside. "What, Crawfie, makes a person fall in love?" she asked, with shining, hopeful eyes.

Crawfie spoke about strong common interests and shared goals, but she couldn't explain the helpless fluttering heart or the hypnotic effect of being in the other's presence—feelings that cannot be described and when experienced for the first time are overwhelming and confusing.

Crawfie felt protective of Lilibet and was troubled by her fervor. Yet here was a girl whose head was squarely attached to her shoulders. She might have been more worried if Margaret gave her heart away. Lilibet, however, "was reserved and quiet about her feelings. If you once gained her love and affection you had it forever, but she never gave it easily."[8]

On the outside, Lilibet was almost compulsively orderly—in her demeanor, in the way she kept her room, in the careful way she spoke. Unlike her untidy sister, she didn't wear her heart on her sleeve. On the inside, she was bursting with incomparable emotion that she didn't know how to fully express. Toward the close of 1943, Lilibet told Crawfie that Philip was "the one."[9]

George VI didn't relish "the damned red carpet" aspects of being king. For him it was a burden whose sole purpose was to keep him away from fully participating in the real drama of the war. Although throughout the war he wore a uniform, he had no military role or authority, and his wife was much better at interacting with the people. An American newspaper dubbed her "Minister of Morale."

"How I hate being King!" he had once exploded, his famous temper boiling over. "Sometimes at ceremonies I want to stand up and scream and scream."[10]

The king's only pleasure during those long war years was the opportunity to spend time with his girls. How striking the difference in his two daughters! He marveled at their distinct personalities, although the differences could not be accounted for by personality alone. As the future queen, Lilibet was treated in adult ways even as a child. Her life stretched ahead of her as one with serious purpose. Margaret was allowed to be a child—and a free-spirited one at that. She had the ability to collapse the king into laughter, no matter how deep his worries. Her infectious spirit lightened his load, and he allowed her to sit at the piano and play and sing the songs of the day, her high, sweet voice acting as a salve on his mind.

On some occasions during the war the family gathered at Balmoral Castle in Scotland. It was there on August 25, 1942, that they received terrible news. Bertie's brother George, the Duke of Kent, had been killed in a flying accident in the Scottish mountains as he headed to Iceland to inspect RAF bases. The family was devastated, and Marina, his wife, was inconsolable. Only seven weeks earlier, on July 4, she had given birth to their third child. Prince George, who was on friendly terms with Franklin Roosevelt, had asked him to be the child's godfather. The president of the United States had happily agreed, and Prince Michael had been given the middle name Franklin.[11] Now Marina, only thirty-five, was a widow with a brood of young children. It was a terrible tragedy and the Royal Family's first loss of the war.

His brother's death hardened Bertie's resolve to defeat the Germans. To mitigate his feelings of impotence, he traveled 52,000 miles by rail during the war so he could visit the troops. He loved being in their company and longed to be among them in the heat of action.

As D Day approached, he thought he might have an opportunity. The king had heard that Churchill planned to watch the first day's action from a cruiser off the coast. The king wanted to join him on board, and he excitedly told Elizabeth of his plan. The queen couldn't have relished the thought of her husband putting himself in such danger, but knowing how much it meant to him, she kept her fears to herself and praised his courage.

It was not to be. Members of the government wisely determined that the very idea of the king and the prime minister being sitting ducks so close to the action was suicidal.[12]

The king couldn't hide his disappointment when he wrote to Churchill, "The right thing to do is what normally falls to those at the top on such occasions, namely to remain at home and wait."

The king did not recognize his own longings in the persistent efforts of his daughter Lilibet to participate in the war effort. Although she had been allowed to register under the wartime youth service organization at the Local Labor Exchange, the act had no practical significance, as her father was adamant that she remain out of the fray.

Finally, in March 1945, with the end of the war only weeks away, he agreed that eighteen-year-old Lilibet could join one of the women's services. Lilibet was elated, and loved flashing her identification card as evidence that she was a real woman making a real contribution. The card read:

No. 230873 Second Subaltern Elizabeth Alexandra Mary Windsor. Age 18. Eyes blue. Hair brown. Height 5'3"

Lilibet was issued a khaki uniform, and she delved into her training with enthusiasm. She loved being among "ordinary" girls, although she couldn't exactly have ordinary relationships with them. At the end of her training she could negotiate London's jammed streets in a Red Cross van, change tires, and repair carburetors. There was a satisfaction to be found under the hood of a car that wasn't available at the palace.

It was a short-lived adventure, as the war was soon over. On April 19 the blackouts ended and the lights went on across London. Big Ben was illuminated for the first time in years. On V-E Day, May 8, Lilibet traded her greasy overalls for celebration attire and stood with her parents and Margaret on the balcony of Buckingham Palace as a crowd of ten thousand cheered and danced and hugged in the street below.

The girls begged to be allowed to join the festivities, and to their delight their parents agreed. The king was eager for them to enjoy themselves. "Poor darlings, they've never had any fun yet," he wrote in his diary.

They snuck out the side door of the palace, accompanied by Elizabeth's brother, David Bowes-Lyon, and a group of friends. Unrecognized, they joined the crowds cheering their parents, then danced the night away. Fifty years later, Margaret would recall the end of the war in vivid terms:

> What was very exciting was when the floodlights came on, because it was the complete antithesis to the blackout. And you can't imagine how awful the blackout had been; everything was dark and everything was gloomy. Suddenly the lights came on and lit up the poor old battle-scarred palace. My mother was wearing a white dress with a tiara . . . and it all sparkled, and there was a great roar from the crowd which was very exciting. VE Day was a wonderful sunburst of glory. I don't think I'll ever forget it as long as I live.[13]

The exhilaration that followed victory over Hitler was soon displaced by the bitter realities of the postwar years. The king, recalling how his father, George V, faced near revolt from the impoverished classes after World War I, had reason to fear the same. The British people were waking up after the war, emerging from fallout shelters and brushing the dust from their eyes to see a society in ruins—figuratively and literally. Entire neighborhoods had been reduced to cavernous pits. Homelessness, disease, and hunger were at crisis proportions. The people now turned expectantly toward the palace and the House of Commons to reward them for the extreme sacrifices they'd made during the war.

They had adored the unflinching Churchill in times of war, but when the issue changed from bombs to butter, they turned him and his party out of office, replacing him with Clement Attlee, the Labour Party's decidedly uncharismatic favorite.

The loss of his friend and confidant was an enormous blow for the king, who could have used Churchill's solid presence. The world was still threatening. His friend Roosevelt was in the grave, having died on the eve of victory. Japan had yet to be defeated, and Stalin was rising in the East. There was little time for celebration.

6

LILIBET'S
PRINCE CHARMING

It was wonderful, magical.

LILIBET'S DESCRIPTION OF PHILIP'S PROPOSAL

Summer 1946 ◆ BUCKINGHAM PALACE

*L*ILIBET WAS FURIOUS with her father. Why couldn't he accept her decision to marry Philip, and stop filling their dinner table with alternative candidates from the ranks of available military officers? She didn't care a whit about those men, and her father's stubborn indifference to her choice was maddening. Why was he so intent on thwarting her love?

The king was not being entirely unreasonable. Like any father, he only wanted what was best for Lilibet, and hers had been a sheltered life. Although she was twenty, he worried about her inexperience with men. She was old enough to take the throne but too young, he thought, to marry.

But his deepest concern—one Elizabeth shared wholeheartedly— was the German problem. Philip's strong German family ties were bound to cause problems for the monarchy. In 1917 the king's father had dramatically attempted to sever the Royal Family from its German lineage. This union would bring up old wounds and perhaps create new ones. It wasn't only Philip's German heritage that was an issue, it was his family's Nazi ties.

Philip's immediate family had been thick with the Nazi Party since its beginnings, and Philip himself had been schooled in its philosophy. As a child, while under the care of his older sister Theodora, whose husband would later become an officer in the German army, Philip had been sent to a "progressive" German school founded by her husband's father, which was considered a virtual petri dish for Nazi views. The husband of Philip's sister Sophie was the head of Göring's intelligence office during the war, and his sister Margarita's husband had been a corps commander.[1]

Queen Elizabeth did not like or trust Louis Mountbatten, the sly puppeteer who was promoting the match. He was too cozy with the Duke of Windsor for her taste. They were old friends, and Edward had been best man at Mountbatten's wedding. Furthermore, Mountbatten's transparent ambition offended her sensibilities. Uncle Dickie had been orchestrating this match for years. When Elizabeth was eighteen, Mountbatten had asked his cousin, King George of Greece, to broach with King George VI the subject of his nephew marrying Lilibet.[2] The king and Queen Elizabeth had not taken kindly to the matchmaking, George gruffly responding that their daughter was far too young for any such discussion.

That hadn't stopped Mountbatten, who had been busy behind the scenes working to burnish Philip's profile and make him more royally palatable. He'd convinced his nephew to apply for naturalization as a British citizen and to forsake the Greek Orthodox Church for the Church of England.

To further bury his inconvenient Germanic roots, Philip was persuaded to revoke his family name—Schleswig-Holstein-Sonderburg-

Glucksburg—and take his uncle's name as his own. He also renounced his title, Prince of Greece, and became, simply, Philip Mountbatten.

Although Philip agreed to these adaptations, he also bristled at his uncle's interference. "Please, I beg of you," he wrote Mountbatten at one point, "not too much advice in an affair of the heart or I shall be forced to do the wooing by proxy." He had feelings for Lilibet, but he hated being pushed. Mountbatten was making the design of his life all too inevitable.[3]

Even without the German ties, Lilibet's parents had strong reservations regarding Philip's suitability as a son-in-law and husband for their daughter. They had to be pragmatic about the future. They liked Philip, but it was difficult to imagine this brash young man willingly assuming the mantle of consort to the queen. Philip's nature could be summed up in a word: *reckless*. He was reckless in his words, often speaking his mind in ways that shocked people. He was reckless in his behavior—a sower of wild oats and a dangerous driver. Indeed, he drove so fast that the very idea of Lilibet riding with him made her parents cringe. Philip was a worldly naval officer, who had been linked with a number of glamorous women. Their daughter was a virgin, inexperienced with men and as protected as a hothouse flower.

The king's advisors made it clear that they weren't pleased with this penniless foreign prince as a match for Lilibet. They stressed to him that the changes his father had made were intended to foster the survival of the monarchy through homegrown nobility.

While all of this hand wringing was going on at the palace, Lilibet was quietly following her heart, often meeting Philip at his cousin Marina's. By now the press had picked up the scent of romance, and public curiosity was high. When Lilibet was out on public engagements, she was constantly barraged with questions about her boyfriend, and people would call out rudely, "Where's Philip?" Observing her sister's frustration, Margaret said to Crawfie that being royal meant "nothing is your own, not even your love affair."[4]

In the late summer of 1946, Lilibet invited Philip to Balmoral, and he proposed to her there. Without seeking her father's permission, as she was required to do, Lilibet happily said yes.

King George VI wasn't feeling well, and the battle of wills with Lilibet did not improve his mood. He drank and smoked heavily, lost his temper frequently, and could not be soothed by the gentlest ministrations of his wife. On the whole, the king was a sweet, charming, even humorous man, but he could erupt into fits of temper over nothing—his "gnashes," as they were called. These worsened when he was ill or overly stressed.

The end of the war had brought ceaseless strain. No sooner had the victory celebrations ended than one crisis after another had sprung up like brushfires. The British Empire had lost India to independence; relationships with the Soviet Union were not going well; and economic hardship and public unrest had grown.

An additional headache reappeared in the guise of the Duke and Duchess of Windsor. By the end of the war, it was very clear that they had lost the minds and hearts of the people. Bertie and Elizabeth had proved their moral fiber, and the contrast with the disgraced Edward and his faux-regal bride could not have been more plain, as *Time* magazine would report after the war:

While the Duke of Windsor spent the war years in the Bahamas, sinecure with the woman for whom he had abandoned the throne, the King held the fort in London, and endured like other Londoners. Like theirs, his home was bombed. His children, like theirs, were sent to the country; his relations, like theirs, died in the line of duty. He shared with his people the sweat and tears of war. A memorable wartime newsreel depicted on one side of the Channel a ranting, raving Hitler, surrounded by tanks and planes, and on the other side, all alone, the quiet figure of the steadfast King. . . . Two

nights a week George slipped into overalls, and stood at a bench in
a nearby arms plant, turning out precision parts for R.A.F. guns.

However, in Edward's view the end of the war signaled a new
chance for inclusion, and he returned to England, sans Wallis, to discuss his postwar role with the king. The palace was especially chilly on
the day of his arrival, and Elizabeth flatly refused to see him. It was
the king's miserable task to inform his brother that there would be no
official role for him; furthermore, he must not think about returning
for good, as Wallis would not be allowed to live in England.

Edward left the meeting feeling humiliated and disgusted. "What a
smug, stinking lot my relations are," he raved. "You've never seen such
a seedy, worn out bunch of old hags most of them have become."[5]

The king, who had been busy mopping up the traces of scandal
from the duke's wartime flirtation with the Nazis, could only shake his
head at his brother's bravado. "He didn't seem to think he had done
anything wrong," he told Mountbatten.

Then, on top of all this, the king learned that Philip and Lilibet had
become engaged behind his back. He was furious. He recognized his
daughter's steely will and knew she would not be denied in this matter,
but perhaps she could be delayed. Finally, the two struck a compro-
mise. Lilibet would wait a year, until after her twenty-first birthday, to
announce her engagement. Also, she would accompany the family on
a three-month tour of South Africa.

Queen Mary was in full support of the union, but she saw no harm
in the delay requested by her son. "After all," she reminded Lady Airlie, "he had to wait long enough for *his* wife, and you can see what a
success their marriage is."[6]

On February 1, 1947, the family set sail for South Africa on the
HMS *Vanguard,* for the final voyage of "we four." On board, the
queen tried gamely to reprise her role as head mood lifter, once even

leading a conga line around the deck.[7] Margaret joined in happily; she was having a wonderful time. Not so for the king and Lilibet. Bertie was restless and frustrated. He complained often that he had no business taking such an extended trip when he was needed back home. Lilibet was the soul of courtesy, as always, but her smiles lacked sparkle. She didn't relish this time spent away from Philip. She couldn't sleep, and she suffered terrible seasickness on the choppy seas, writing to Crawfie, "I for one would willingly have died, I was so miserable."[8]

Although the king complained that he should be back in Britain, the journey was not a vacation. Indeed, it had an important political aim. With the loss of India, Great Britain was in danger of becoming a diminishing power in the world. For all practical purposes the British Empire was dead. Now it had become a voluntary association of fifty countries, requiring an effort to keep appeased. South Africa was like a vast, undeveloped jewel in the Commonwealth's crown, with the potential for adding riches and power to its flagging fortunes.

Lilibet's twenty-first birthday came toward the end of the trip, while they were visiting Cape Town. A wonderful party was held, and Lilibet broadcast a speech to the Commonwealth, declaring her fealty in a ringing, unwavering voice: "I declare before you all that my whole life, whether it be long or short, shall be devoted to your service and the service of our great imperial family to which we all belong."

To Lilibet's joy, her parents announced her engagement to Philip as soon as they returned, and preparations began for a November wedding. The king grumbled about spending so much on frivolity during a time of such economic deprivation, but excitement about the wedding seemed to infect the gloomy citizenry with an enthusiasm that had been missing from public life. In that respect it served a positive purpose. Winston Churchill declared it "a flash of color on the hard road we have to travel."

The couple's first home would be Clarence House, a large stucco building next to St. James's Palace, which had been in the Royal Family for more than a hundred years. The house was a mess. During the war it had been turned over to the British Red Cross and the Order of Saint John of Jerusalem, and offices had been cobbled together to accommodate two hundred staff of the Foreign Relations Department. It would need a great deal of renovation to make it habitable for the princess and her new husband. The king persuaded Attlee to petition the House of Commons for the funds.[9]

The Royal Family, whose sensitivities about spending weren't always so finely tuned, was surprised when the renovation became a matter of public debate. They didn't consider it at all inappropriate that a lavish residence would be prepared for the princess while the country was in a dire economic state. In the end the money was approved, but it would be more than a year before Clarence House was ready. In the interim Lilibet and Philip would live with her parents at Buckingham Palace.

The plans for Lilibet's wedding intersected with the king and queen's silver wedding anniversary. In a broadcast, Elizabeth expressed heartfelt and meaningful sentiments that she must have hoped her daughter would adopt as her own: "The world in our day is longing to find the secret of community, and all married lives are, in a sense, communities in miniature. There must be so many who feel as we do that the sacrifices of married life are in some way the highest form of human fellowship, affording a rock-like foundation on which all the best in the life of the nation is built."

It was a perfectly pitched note. Once, so long ago, her family had been "we four" against the world. Now they were at the service of the world. Elizabeth recognized that her marriage was not diminished but enhanced by this intrusion—that marital love could be strengthened in the face of a common mission.

Wedding preparations proceeded cautiously, although Lilibet would not have to skimp on her dress. Fabric and clothing were still being rationed, but the government allowed every bride two hundred extra clothing coupons. (Many women sent their coupons to Lilibet, but they had to be sent back, as it was illegal to give them away.)[10]

Her wedding dress was designed by the queen's favorite dressmaker, Norman Hartnell—a glorious gown of ivory satin embroidered with more than ten thousand seed pearls and a fifteen-foot train. A veil of diaphanous white silk and tulle was arranged beneath a diamond tiara.

Although the young couple was mindful of appearances during these times of hardship, not much could be done to stem the flow of gifts. There were thousands of them—Steuben crystal (President and Mrs. Truman), a fully equipped movie studio (Lord Mountbatten), an Arabian horse (Aga Khan), a grand piano (the Royal Air Force), a hunting lodge in Kenya (the Kenyan people), Persian rugs, fine china, four full-length mink coats, and, of course, jewels. Queen Mary literally presented her granddaughter with a chest of jewels, which included a priceless diamond brooch given her by Queen Victoria. The king gave Lilibet a sapphire-and-diamond necklace and earrings. The king and queen together gave her a ruby-and-diamond necklace, diamond drop earrings, and two strands of pearls.[11] It was a stunning display of opulence. The family was fond of commiserating with the public, but royalty was royalty. In effect their attitude was *We feel your pain—just not too much.*

One delicate issue that had to be resolved was what to do about Philip's family.[12] It wouldn't be seemly to have the groom's pews filled with Nazi sympathizers, so it was decided that his sisters and their families would not be asked to the wedding. Nor would the Duke and Duchess of Windsor be invited.

As for Philip's mother, the queen found her "pleasant but odd . . . definitely odd."[13] After being marginally cured of schizophrenia in the 1930s, Alice had retained her religious fervor and started a religious order, the Christian Sisterhood of Martha and Mary, and now dressed entirely in gray. Odd though she might have been, Alice was a good woman with strong moral convictions. During the German occupation of Greece, she courageously hid a Jewish family in her Athens home, and her life was devoted to charitable works.[14] She was proud of her son and was planning to attend his wedding. At the gentle suggestion of the queen, she agreed to forego her gray robes for more suitable attire, just for that day.

Typically, the groom is something of an outsider during the frenzy of wedding preparations, and Philip was no different. At loose ends, he delved wholeheartedly into his last days of freedom, often accompanied by his good friend and comrade in night crawling, Mike Parker. (After the wedding, Philip would make Parker his private secretary.) His recklessness was in evidence. He crashed his car twice during this period, once badly, to the alarm of Lilibet and the horror of the palace. And he relied on his pals from the Thursday Club to see him through his final days of being single.

The Thursday Club was a ribald stag club that met every week in a third-floor room of Wheeler's Restaurant in Soho. Among its eclectic membership were Peter Ustinov, Larry Adler, screenwriter Donald Ogden Stewart, the photographer Baron Nahum (known simply as Baron), and the actor David Niven. Also a member was Stephen Ward, who, among other endeavors, was involved in procuring women. (Ward's call girl, Christine Keeler, would later be cited in a sex-spy scandal with Harold Macmillan's war minister, John Profumo.) Baron was known to give wild parties at his personal residence, and Philip, who had joined the club in 1946, was often in attendance.[15] The Thursday Club allowed Philip a small bit of manly independence—a pleasure he figured would be in short supply once he was married.

On November 20, 1947, the king walked his eldest daughter down the aisle at Westminster Abbey, as the nation cheered. Philip, with his best man, Mike Parker, beside him, watched nervously.

With the wedding Philip was created His Royal Highness Philip, Duke of Edinburgh.

The king sent Lilibet an emotional letter on her honeymoon, and it shows how deeply felt her transition from daughter to wife was for this man who treasured having his family around him.

> *I was so proud of you and thrilled at having you so close to me on your long walk in Westminster Abbey. But when I handed your hand to the Archbishop I felt I had lost something very precious.*
>
> *I have watched you grow up all these years with pride under the skillful direction of Mummy who, as you know, is the most marvelous person in the world in my eyes, and I can, I know, always count on you, and now Philip, to help us in our work. Your leaving has left a great blank in our lives, but do remember that your old home is still yours and do come back to it as much and as often as possible. I can see that you are sublimely happy with Philip, which is your right, but don't forget us is the wish of*
>
> *Your ever loving and devoted*
> *Papa*[16]

Her parents might have worried that she would feel left out with all the spectacle surrounding her sister, but Margaret, now turning eighteen, had managed to carve out a life for herself as a separate individual. The catalyst for Margaret's postwar social life was the arrival of a new American ambassador, Lewis W. Douglas, whose lovely blond daughter, Sharman, was an adept socialite. Two years older than Margaret, Sharman quickly pulled her into her crowd of glamorous and fascinating friends. It was Margaret's first opportunity to spread her wings in the world beyond the palace, and she shined. For once she, not Lilibet, was the center of attention—popular, pretty, free-spirited—a girl every camera loved. There were many parties after the war; some weeks Margaret was out every night, her relatively innocent exploits covered in the papers. The media followed her like a pack of drooling hounds. Because she was so glamorous and so different from her buttoned-up family, everything she did was gossip-worthy. A photo of Margaret dancing the cancan at an American Embassy party made front pages worldwide.

Her parents indulged her, glad to see her having fun. When Crawfie worriedly mentioned to the queen that Margaret wasn't getting enough sleep, the queen (perhaps remembering her own postwar partying days) brushed her off. "We are only young once, Crawfie," she said. "We want her to have a good time. With Lilibet gone, it is lonely for her here."[17]

Everyone believed that after Margaret had experienced a period of freedom and fun she'd settle down with an acceptable aristocrat and fade into the royal scenery. They didn't appreciate Margaret's complexity—the multitude of vying urges that drove her behavior.

Philip was not the kind of man who could easily tolerate the idea of walking a step behind his wife. He knew, of course, that Lilibet would someday be queen, and at that point he would have little independence. But even with his father-in-law's rocky health, he must have figured on a good ten years before that happened. In that time he planned to establish his naval career and cement himself as head of his household. He started by impregnating his wife within three months of the wedding.

Lilibet was deliriously happy and deeply in love. By all accounts, including those indiscreetly made by Philip, they had a robust sex life.[18]

With his daughter carrying a future heir apparent or heir presumptive, the king had to make a couple of key decisions before the birth. The first was the matter of the home secretary's attendance. In an uncharacteristic bow to modernity, the king decided to end the practice. No doubt he and the queen retained dismal memories of Home Secretary J. R. Clynes lurking around Glamis for weeks before Margaret's birth.

It was also determined that any offspring of Lilibet's would be titled Royal Highnesses. Neglected in the discussion was the issue of a last name. Lilibet's married name was Mountbatten, and any children would assumedly be Mountbattens as well. No one thought to ask what then would become of the House of Windsor, an issue that would soon rise again.

Charles Philip Arthur George was born November 14, 1948, and Elizabeth breast-fed him for two months before turning him over to his nurse, Helen Lightbody. When the family moved to Clarence House a few months later, Elizabeth began a practice she would continue throughout Charles's young life, scheduling time with him as if he were a standing appointment—an hour after breakfast and a half hour before supper.

In October 1949 Philip was granted his wish to resume his naval career. He was posted as first lieutenant of HMS *Chequers,* on the Mediterranean island of Malta. Lilibet joined him there, but Charles remained in London, in the care of two nannies, Mabel Anderson and Helen Lightbody, and his grandparents.

On Malta Lilibet lived for a time with Lord Mountbatten, who was posted there as well. She was exhilarated by the freedom and the grand social life among the other young married couples. For a brief, carefree period, she tasted the normalcy she craved. Yet, how normal was it, really, for the mother of an infant to so casually abandon him to the care of others?

Later that year Lilibet found that she was pregnant again, and she returned to London for the birth of her second child, Anne, on August 15, 1950. However, when she finished breast-feeding four months later, she again joined her husband on Malta, leaving both children behind.

Much has been made of the way royal duty means long absences from one's children. But there was nothing duty-bound about Lilibet's decision to spend such extended periods as a "normal wife" sans children on Malta. However, when the press gently scolded the couple for spending so much time away from their children, Philip tartly replied, "They're quite well enough without being fussed over by their parents."[19]

When Philip and Lilibet returned from Malta in July 1951 to take on a greater public role on behalf of the ailing king, Charles was nearly three and Anne almost one.

The forced return was not a happy development for Philip, and it would have been even more traumatic had he realized it would signal the end of his naval career. But there really wasn't any choice. During the previous two years, the king's health had been declining steadily. An operation in 1948 to relieve the effects of arteriosclerosis and improve his circulation had only temporary effects. In 1950, around the time of Anne's birth, he had developed a severe cough and was being treated for a lung infection. He was heartened by the election, which returned his old comrade Winston Churchill, now seventy-six, to power.

Almost immediately after their return to London, Lilibet and Philip left for a tour of Canada and the United States. It wasn't the roaring success of Bertie and Elizabeth's 1939 tour. The Canadians expected a younger version of the warm, smiling queen, and in that respect Lilibet was not her mother's daughter. The Canadian press was critical, grumbling that the princess never smiled. She fared somewhat better in the United States, where Harry Truman greeted her with great enthusiasm and affection—more like a daughter than a distant royal.

Upon their return the king and queen met them at Victoria Station. Standing beside his grandmother was the stiff little figure of Charles, a four-year-old tin soldier, solemn and erect. Lilibet's reaction to seeing her son for the first time in months was memorialized in newsreels, which show her giving him an absentminded pat on the head as she strode past him to greet others in the party. Charles didn't quite seem to know who she was.

No sooner were Lilibet and Philip back in London than they began preparations for a five-month tour of Africa, India, and Australia. It was a trip the king had planned but was now too ill to undertake.

The king and queen came to see them off on their journey. As Elizabeth waved to them, her heart lurched. Her father looked tiny and impossibly frail as he smiled up at her wanly from the tarmac. He waved and waved as if his hand in the air could hold her to him. It was the last time she would see him alive.

The couple were at their hunting lodge in Kenya enjoying a weekend break from official appearances when Philip, who'd been given the news by Mike Parker, took his wife aside and told her that her father had died quietly in his sleep the night before. Later she'd think it odd but also sweet that Philip had been told first so he could break the news to his wife in the most gentle and private way. They walked the grounds as Lilibet wept against Philip's shoulder, feeling for all the world like a distraught young girl and wanting to be that, if only for a moment.

This was always the way it was and would be with them. She was Queen of the Commonwealth; Philip was head of the family. But this moment stood out for both of them. In grieving for the king, they were also grieving for their lost identities. Their lives, and their marriage, would never be the same. Each deep in private thought, they boarded the plane for home.

Back in London, Winston Churchill's rumbling voice broke through the regularly scheduled radio programming to speak to the people about the man they had come to love and admire. With the king's death, Churchill said, "there struck a deep and solemn note in our lives which as it resounded far and wide, stilled the clatter and traffic of twentieth century life in many lands and made countless millions of human beings pause and look around."

When their plane landed in London, Lilibet looked out to see the small round figure of Churchill, waiting to declare his allegiance. Behind him was a long line of Daimler sedans. "My God," she said with a sigh, "they've brought the hearses."

When she reached Clarence House, her eighty-four-year-old grand-mother, Queen Mary, was the first to greet her. Lilibet began her usual curtsy, but Queen Mary stopped her and instead dropped into a deep curtsy herself. She was no longer Lilibet; she was Queen Eliza-beth II.

7

MRS. MOUNTBATTEN
ASCENDS

How small and selfish is sorrow.
But it bangs one about until one is senseless.

ELIZABETH, THE QUEEN MOTHER,

TO A FRIEND AFTER THE KING'S DEATH

January 1952 ◆ LONDON

HAT A DIFFERENCE a death makes. Elizabeth, now the Queen Mother, might have had cause
to reflect, as she had at the death of Bertie's father,
that the abrupt severing of a family's head leaves the body in
shambles.

As the newly ascended queen, Elizabeth II drew on a lifetime of
practiced composure to coolly perform her duties, but her mother and
sister were in a state of paralyzing grief. Margaret refused to leave her
room and sobbed to her mother, "It seems that life has stopped forever.
I wonder how it can go on."[1]

During this period Margaret was the odd woman out. It was as if she did not exist. Condolences poured into the palace, addressed to her mother, her grandmother, and her sister. Parliament sent a formal note of sympathy to the three women, never mentioning Margaret.

The Queen Mother, normally the source of warmth and comfort in times of crisis, had temporarily lost her way, and she could do little to help Margaret. She felt her own life was destroyed. At the young age of fifty-one, her status, her identity, and her role had been shattered as completely as wartime bombs had once shattered the palace windows. She was stunned by Bertie's death, as she had been convinced in his last months that he was improving. It was unlikely that she knew the doctors suspected lung cancer. "He was so much better," she wrote to a friend. "I really thought he was going to have some years perhaps less anguished than the last fifteen."

Casting about for blame, she bitterly concluded that the Duke and Duchess of Windsor were directly responsible for her husband's early demise. "If only he hadn't had to carry the weight of the world on his shoulders," she said, her husband would be alive.[2] She publicly referred to Wallis as "the woman who killed my husband."

Her inner ambivalence on this matter must have been great, however, because she also realized that this supreme sacrifice might have saved England and the world. If Edward had been king, especially with Wallis by his side, who knew what the ultimate course would have been? Besides, she had thrived as queen.

She burned with disappointment and envy. It seemed ludicrous that she, a successful, experienced monarch, still young, should be relegated to mothballs. Here, then, was yet another example of the impracticality of the rules of succession. Although the Queen Mother was in her prime, beloved by her people, respected by world leaders, and well versed in the multitude of duties that went with her title, she was not a Windsor by birth and thus could not continue to sit on the throne after her husband died. Royal lineage dictated that her daughter Elizabeth, a young woman of twenty-five, ascend to the throne. The tables were now turned, and she would be required to curtsy to her daughter.

The new queen was aware of the difficulty of this transition, and she tiptoed around her mother, not wanting to assume imperial airs, although she now had imperial obligations. "Mummy and Margaret have the biggest grief to bear for their future must seem very blank, while I have a job and a family to think of," she wrote to a friend.[3]

Summoning a stoic strength, the Queen Mother held herself together for the king's funeral ceremonies. Shrouded in black, the women of Windsor walked behind the coffin of King George VI as it was carried into Westminster Hall. Elizabeth laid a wreath on his coffin, with an inscription, "Darling Bertie from his always loving Elizabeth." A second wreath from Churchill was inscribed with a single word: "Valour." More than 300,000 people filed through Westminster Hall to pay final respects to the king.

Among the mourners was the king's brother, the Duke of Windsor. Hopeful that a change in regime might mean rapprochement, Wallis had sent him off with the words "I'm sure you can win her [the new queen] over to a more friendly attitude."

The family was cordial to Edward, but in this matter Lilibet was her mother's daughter. No sooner had Edward arrived than he received word that his ten-thousand-pound-a-year allowance would be discontinued, since it was a private gift from the king. He was livid at this slap in the face, but all appeals were in vain. Even though the Queen Mother reluctantly agreed to a meeting, she spent the time reminiscing about Bertie and completely avoided any discussion of his status. Wallis was never mentioned. Leaving the palace after this charm offensive, worse off than he had been before, Edward muttered angrily, "Those ice-veined bitches."[4]

The king was not cold in his grave before Lord Mountbatten began plotting the destiny of the new monarchy, privately telling friends that the House of Windsor would soon become the House of

Mountbatten. After all, the queen's married name was Mountbatten, not Windsor.[5]

Queen Mary caught wind of Mountbatten's bragging and was extremely upset. After a bit of high-level meddling, she was satisfied that Churchill and the cabinet were firmly of the opinion that the royal house should remain Windsor, and set out to nip Mountbatten's plans in the bud.

Although Philip always kept a certain distance from his uncle's blatant ambition, this was a matter that engaged him fully. He fought vigorously for his name—if not his adopted name, Mountbatten, then his adopted title, Edinburgh. He would not sit quietly while the palace and government insiders publicly emasculated him.

Behind the scenes, working to extinguish any deal, was Sir Alan Lascelles, the enormously powerful private secretary the queen inherited from her father. Lascelles had never liked Philip and had been against Lilibet marrying him. Philip thought Lascelles was an old stuffed shirt with outdated opinions. He chafed at the man's smug power plays but could do little about his influence with the queen. And now Lascelles was advising her in no uncertain terms that for the good of the monarchy, the Mountbatten name must be put in mothballs.[6]

What was the queen's true position on the matter? It's certainly possible that she would have sided with Philip were it not for the impassioned intervention of her mother and her grandmother, who convinced her that it would not have been the will of her father or grandfather to see the House of Windsor end so prematurely, and the behind-the-scenes machinations of Lascelles. She sought the advice of Churchill, who was both prime minister and father figure to her now. He agreed with the others. The House of Windsor must be maintained.

A formal declaration by the queen, crafted with the advice of government officials, put the matter to rest: "I hereby declare My Will and Pleasure that I and My children shall be styled and known as the House and Family of Windsor, and that my descendents who marry and their descendents, shall bear the name of Windsor."

Almost pathologically averse to confrontation, Lilibet must have suffered mightily at the choice she had been forced to make. But in a world where blood is thicker than love or loyalty or lifetime service, Philip could not be appeased. He was sophisticated and worldly, his wife inexperienced and dependent. She looked up to him and relied upon him. Now he was forced to abandon his thriving military career to support his wife in her royal duties, but without any authority of his own. "I'm just a bloody amoeba," he complained to Mountbatten—suggesting that his sperm had a place in the monarchy, but he did not.

Early on, Philip lobbied for a role; perhaps he could take care of some of the details his wife didn't have time for. Lascelles shut the door firmly on any such idea. He didn't want to give Philip an inch for fear he'd take a mile.[7]

Philip was also bitter about having to give up the only real home he had known since he was a small child. He loved Clarence House, whose renovation he had personally supervised. Moving to the hulking mausoleum of Buckingham Palace would further diminish his stature as head of the family.

Once again he fought—this time for his home. Why couldn't the family continue to live there, while the queen went to work at the "office" every day? The palace hierarchy met the suggestion with utter bafflement. It could not be. It had never been done. In the end, Churchill himself put the kibosh on the idea. The queen belonged in Buckingham Palace.

Not to worry, though. Clarence House would be put to good use. The Queen Mother and Margaret would be moving there as soon as it could be redone to their taste.

Philip's dismay aside, it had taken some doing to convince the Queen Mother to make this move. The death of her husband had defeated her. She couldn't picture what role she could play on her own, for as she said sadly, "It wasn't me, it was us together." She spoke of returning to Scotland and fading into retirement. During that period of desperate grief, she was obsessed with her husband, unable to let go. According to some accounts, she consulted the famous medium Lilian Bailey in an effort to reach out to Bertie beyond the grave. Bailey would later say that in a deep trance state she was able to channel the late king on many occasions, and he spoke to his widow through her.[8]

When Winston Churchill visited the Queen Mother at the palace and listened to her speak of retirement, the wily old soldier gauged the situation exactly right. Everyone around the Queen Mother had coddled her in her grief, out of respect and sympathy. No one, least of all her daughter, had wanted to pressure her, and as a result she'd been left to think of herself as useless. All her life Elizabeth Bowes-Lyon had responded with grit and devotion to every challenge, and Churchill saw that what she needed now was a call to arms. As she spoke of her plan to retire, he broke in. "Absolutely not," he said in his most commanding voice. "This young Queen is going to need you by her side an awful lot. And this is no time for you to go and sit in Scotland."[9]

In his gruff, direct way, Churchill broke through the Queen Mother's shell by reminding her of her duty and reassuring her of her importance to the monarchy. Determined to craft a new role for herself, she issued a public statement: "My only wish now is that I may be allowed to continue the work we sought to do together."

Three months after the king's death, the Queen Mother performed her first official duty, flying to Scotland to inspect the First Battalion of the Black Watch, the Scottish force in which three of her brothers had served during the First World War, before it headed for Korea.

Philip had one thing in common with his mother-in-law. At the peak of his life he was left without any official position. Although King George VI had bestowed the title His Royal Highness on Philip before his marriage to Lilibet, Philip had renounced his title Prince of Greece, and would not be a prince until the queen made him one in 1957. He was certainly not a consort, in the manner of his predecessor Prince Albert, husband of Queen Victoria. The queen was desperate to offer her husband a role, a salve to his bruised manhood. She also wanted him by her side, as her mother had been by her father's side.

To offset the awkward ceremonial inequality, the queen gave Philip an official seat by her side by making him regent. This role, established by the Regency Act of 1937, determined that in the event the sovereign became indisposed or died before her heir reached his eighteenth birthday, the next in line to the throne would be appointed regent and make all of the critical decisions for the throne. By rights this role belonged to Margaret, but the queen chose to disrespect her sister to soothe her husband. The revised Regency Act of 1953 stated, "In the event of a regent becoming necessary in my lifetime, my husband should be the Regent and charged with the guardianship of the person of the Sovereign."

The palace courtiers, imagining a catastrophe that would elevate the Mountbattens, disapproved, but on this point the queen held firm. She also appointed Philip to head the Coronation Committee, and that raised a few eyebrows. Of all the ceremonies of the Crown, the coronation was the most elaborate, steeped in layer upon layer of symbolism. It was feared that Philip, an unabashed modernist who despised palace snobbery, would try to update the ceremony with disastrous results.

Philip struck a blow to tradition when he suggested that the coronation be televised. Gasps of revulsion echoed throughout the palace and Parliament. How gauche! How vulgar! Churchill and his cabinet were firmly against the idea. Television was in its infancy, and there was still an inherent distrust of the medium that could bring the most elevated occasion into the common folks' living rooms while they guzzled beer and ate greasy chips.

However, on this matter Philip was able to persuade the queen, who agreed with her husband that the image of the monarchy would benefit from exposure to the masses. Televising her coronation would be a remarkable feat—a worldwide transmission that blended the medieval and the modern in an inspiring historical occasion.[10]

A sad note was struck when Queen Mary died a little more than two months before the coronation. She had never quite recovered her strength after Bertie's death, and for months she'd been suffering from a serious intestinal condition. Doctors wanted to operate on her colon, but she waved them off, saying she was prepared to die and "did not wish to go on living as an old crock."

She had but one request, that the coronation not be delayed by her death. She insisted that the queen promise her it would not, and Lilibet, taking her grandmother's hand, promised. The old woman smiled. "I had so wanted to see you crowned," she said.[11]

She fell into a coma and died peacefully on March 24, at the age of eighty-five. The Duke of Windsor, by now fully embittered, remarked on her death without sentimentality, saying, "I'm afraid the fluids in her veins have always been as icy cold as they now are in death."[12]

Coronation day, June 2, 1953, brought a driving rain—the standard English weather for important events—but that did not deter one million people from lining the route the queen's carriage would take.

Thanks to the wonders of television, more than three hundred million people worldwide viewed the coronation for seven and a half hours of live reporting. Press from all over the world was in attendance. One of them, a reporter from the *Washington Times-Herald,* would play a future role in world events. Her name was Jacqueline Bouvier.

The coronation ceremony was dramatic pageantry, following a form that hadn't changed in more than a thousand years. The assembly at Westminster Abbey included representatives of Parliament, the church, and the state. Prime ministers and leading citizens from the Commonwealth and dignitaries from around the world attended. The Duke of Windsor was not invited to this occasion, but Philip's mother was there. Mother Superior Alice Elizabeth even had a special, quite stylish, gray habit made for the occasion.

All eyes were riveted on the slight figure of the queen as she entered, stunningly clothed in a crimson velvet robe trimmed with ermine and gold lace, lavishly decked out in jewelry. As she took her place before the Archbishop of Canterbury, the luxurious robe was removed and she began to take off each piece of jewelry, symbolically divesting herself of wealth. Finally, she stood humbly, dressed only in a simple white garment. The gold royal robe was placed around her shoulders, and she took her seat in St. Edward's Chair, a throne that had been in use by sovereigns since 1620.[13] One by one the archbishop presented her with the symbols of authority. Placing the scepter in her right hand and the rod in her left, he prayed: "Be so merciful that you be not too remiss, so execute justice that you forget not mercy. Punish the wicked, protect and cherish the just, and lead your people in the way wherein they should go."

They were beautiful words, full of meaning and promise. They had been said to her father before her, and he had taken them to heart. It was up to her, she knew, to do the same.

Finally, the archbishop approached, holding St. Edward's Crown made of solid gold and encrusted with rubies and pearls. Its weight as he placed it on the queen's head foretold the burdens and glories of her office.

And then the crowd roared, "God save the queen!" as trumpets blared and the great guns of the Tower and Hyde Park boomed. Philip rose, the first of the queen's subjects to swear allegiance. He knelt at her feet, his eyes alight with emotion as he spoke the ritual words: "I, Philip, Duke of Edinburgh, do become Your Highness's man of life and limb, and of earthly worship; and faith and truth I will bear unto you, to live and die, against all manner of folks. So help me God."

The rain had intensified during the ceremony, and as the royal party left Westminster Abbey, great sheets of water poured down on them, soaking the guards standing sentry and the crowds that lined the route cheering as the queen's carriage made its way.

Back at the palace after the coronation, the queen took off her heavy crown with a sigh of relief and set it on the table. Prince Charles ran over, picked it up, and put it on his head, immediately toppling over amid gales of laughter. It was a rare moment of levity in what had been a grim march.

The young queen received universal praise, and her mother took some comfort in knowing that her magnificent coronation day was a result of the job Bertie and she had done to prepare their daughter for the throne. "Your father would be proud of you," she told Lilibet.

Among the accolades was an honor peculiar to the American media. The January 5, 1953, issue of *Time* magazine named "Queen Elizabeth II—Defender of the Faith" its "Man of the Year" for 1952—the second woman to receive that distinction. The first, ironically, was Wallis Simpson in 1936. *Time*'s cover featured a portrait of the queen's smiling face embedded in the crown of a giant red rose. The cover line read, "On a hardy stalk, a new bloom." The fatuous, clearly adoring image reflected the postwar romanticism of the American people. Like their British counterparts, they were willingly swept along on the tide of a fairy tale. People were hungry for a taste of magic, and the Royal Family obliged.

A STUNNING PORTRAIT OF THE YOUNG ELIZABETH BOWES-LYON.
(E. O. Hoppe/Mansell/Time-Life Pictures/Getty Images) ◆

THE DUKE AND DUCHESS OF WINDSOR (FORMERLY KING
EDWARD VIII AND WALLIS SIMPSON) ON THEIR
BITTERSWEET WEDDING DAY. (*Getty Images*) ◆

THE DUKE AND DUCHESS OF
WINDSOR MEET WITH HITLER IN
GERMANY, OCTOBER 22, 1937. IT
WAS WIDELY BELIEVED THAT
HITLER PLANNED TO OVERTHROW
KING GEORGE VI AND RETURN
EDWARD TO THE THRONE UNDER
GERMAN RULE. *(Keystone/Getty
Images)* ◆

KING GEORGE VI AND QUEEN
ELIZABETH SURVEY THE
DAMAGE AFTER THE BOMBING
OF BUCKINGHAM PALACE
DURING WORLD WAR II. THE
QUEEN EVEN MANAGES A SMILE.
THE COUPLE'S DIGNITY AND
OPTIMISM DURING THE WORST
OF TIMES WON THE HEARTS OF
THEIR PEOPLE. *(Fox Photos/Getty
Images)* ◆

IN A RARE BREAK FROM THE STRAINS OF WAR, KING
GEORGE VI AND QUEEN ELIZABETH RELAX WITH THEIR
DAUGHTERS, MARGARET ROSE AND ELIZABETH, AT THE
ROYAL LODGE, WINDSOR, APRIL 11, 1942. (*Lisa Sheridan/
Studio Lisa/Getty Images*) ◆

PRINCESS ELIZABETH
AND HER NEW HUSBAND,
PHILIP, WAVE TO
CROWDS FROM THE
BALCONY AT
BUCKINGHAM PALACE.
(*Central Press/Getty
Images*) ◆

PRINCESS MARGARET (*left*), PRINCESS ELIZABETH, AND GROUP
CAPTAIN PETER TOWNSEND IN THE ROYAL BOX AT ASCOT ON
JUNE 13, 1951. IN 1955 MARGARET'S HEART WOULD BE BROKEN
WHEN HER SISTER, NOW QUEEN, REFUSED HER PERMISSION
TO MARRY TOWNSEND. (*Keystone/Getty Images*) ◆

PRINCESS ANNE AND HER NEW HUSBAND, CAPTAIN MARK PHILLIPS, WAVE TO CROWDS FROM THE BALCONY OF BUCKINGHAM PALACE, NOVEMBER 14, 1973. (STF/AFP/Getty Images) ◆

Opposite: PRINCESS ELIZABETH AND PHILIP, DUKE OF EDINBURGH, ON THE GROUNDS OF CLARENCE HOUSE WITH CHARLES AND ANNE. EVEN AS AN INFANT, ANNE WAS TRYING TO CRAWL AWAY. (*Lisa Sheridan/Studio Lisa/Getty Images*) ◆

AT A PHOTO CALL AT BALMORAL BEFORE THE WEDDING, DIANA GAMELY DONS WELLINGTONS AND TROUSERS, POSING AS A SHY COUNTRY GIRL BESIDE HER PRINCE. THE APPEARANCE WAS DECEPTIVE. (*Tim Graham/Getty Images*) ◆

IN APRIL 1969, CHARLES AND ANNE TROT OUT THEIR SIBLING CHARMS AS PART OF THE PALACE PUBLIC RELATIONS CAMPAIGN—JUST AN AVERAGE FAMILY ON AN AFTERNOON RIDE AT WINDSOR CASTLE. (*Getty Images*) ◆

A RARE PHOTO OF LADY DIANA SPENCER AND CAMILLA PARKER BOWLES SHOWS BOTH LOOKING PENSIVE. (*Getty Images*) ◆

BY 1986 CHARLES AND DIANA WERE NOT EVEN TRYING TO HIDE THEIR MISERY AS
THEY WALK WITH THEIR BOYS, WILLIAM AND HARRY, AT HIGHGROVE, THE COUNTRY
HOME DIANA DESPISED. *(Tim Graham/Getty Images)* ◆

CHARLES STANDS APART AS DIANA, HARRY, AND WILLIAM SMILE FOR THE
CAMERAS. IT IS WILLIAM'S FIRST DAY AT ETON; WITH THEM IS THE
HOUSEMASTER DR. ANDREW GAILEY. *(Tim Graham/Getty Images)* ◈

THE QUEEN'S BELOVED WINDSOR PALACE IN FLAMES ON
NOVEMBER 30, 1992. IT WAS THE FINAL BLOW IN A
HORRIBLE YEAR. *(Johnson/Keystone/Getty Images)* ◆

PRINCESS MARGARET, SHOWING SIGNS OF WEAR IN HER LATER YEARS. *(Ken Goff/Time-Life Pictures/Getty Images)* ◆

MEMBERS OF THE ROYAL FAMILY GATHER OUTSIDE CLARENCE HOUSE IN CELEBRATION OF THE QUEEN MOTHER'S NINETIETH BIRTHDAY. *(Left to right)* PRINCE PHILIP, PETER PHILLIPS (SON OF PRINCESS ANNE), VISCOUNT DAVID LINLEY (SON OF PRINCESS MARGARET), PRINCESS ANNE, PRINCE EDWARD, QUEEN ELIZABETH, PRINCESS DIANA, PRINCE CHARLES, THE QUEEN MOTHER, AND PRINCESS MARGARET. *(Ken Goff/Time-Life Pictures/Getty Images)* ◆

THE QUEEN MOTHER, JOINED BY HER DAUGHTERS,
PRINCESS MARGARET AND QUEEN ELIZABETH, WAVES TO
ADMIRERS ON THE OCCASION OF HER ONE HUNDREDTH
BIRTHDAY, AUGUST 4, 2000. *(UK Press/Getty Images)* ◆

PRINCESS ANNE
WATCHES A FOOTBALL
MATCH WITH A GROUP
OF ORPHANS FROM
STAREHE BOYS'
CENTRE IN NAIROBI,
WHICH WAS BUILT IN
COOPERATION WITH
THE SAVE THE
CHILDREN FUND, OF
WHICH THE PRINCESS
IS PRESIDENT.
(Keystone/Getty Images) ◆

CHARLES AND CAMILLA, TOGETHER AT LAST. THEY WERE
MARRIED APRIL 9, 2005. *(Tim Graham/Getty Images)* ◆

SISTER DEAREST

You must either be mad or bad.

THE QUEEN'S PRIVATE SECRETARY,
SIR ALAN LASCELLES, TO PETER TOWNSEND

1953 ◆ LONDON

HE LOSS OF HER FATHER left Margaret curled alone inside the circle where her family used to be. Not only was it no longer "we four," it wasn't even "we three" or "we two." Her mother, struggling to rise out of her own grief, was busier than ever creating a new role for herself and preparing for the grand coronation festivities. Her sister barely had time for her own children, much less Margaret. And forget about her grandmother, who considered expressions of grief nothing more than sniveling. So there she was, twenty-three years old, ensconced in her suite of rooms at the palace, distanced from other family members, as she waited to move into Clarence House with her mother.

She didn't especially envy her sister her burdens, but she did envy her certitude. Margaret had never had a role in the grand scheme of things, and that hadn't bothered her as much when she could see her light reflected in her father's eyes. Grieving and lonely, Margaret sought solace from the one person at the palace she trusted most—her father's former equerry and newly appointed Deputy Master of the Queen's Household, Group Captain Peter Townsend.[1]

King George VI had appointed Peter as his equerry in 1944, an unusual gesture, since the prized position was usually reserved for members of the aristocracy and Peter was from the middle class. He was also a highly decorated fighter pilot who had performed heroically during the war, and the king had granted him the position as a way of honoring the brave men fighting for the future of England.

The king and Peter had hit it off immediately. They had much in common, including a lifelong battle with a stammer. As Peter later recalled of the king, "The humanity of the man and his striking simplicity came across warmly, unmistakably. . . . Sometimes he hesitated in his speech and then I felt drawn towards him, to help keep up the flow of words. I knew myself the agonies of a stammerer."[2]

The love between Margaret and Peter Townsend had been slowly simmering for years, since she was eighteen. That year she undertook her first royal mission, representing her father at the inauguration of Crown Princess Juliana as Queen of the Netherlands. In addition to various relatives and staff accompanying her to Amsterdam, her father had sent Peter Townsend. The thirty-four-year-old Townsend cut a dashing figure—tall and handsome, with a winning smile and a mop of wavy brown hair. Some said he resembled Gregory Peck. He was also married, with two children.

Inadvertently, the king and queen might have encouraged the relationship by drawing Peter into their circle. They were both quite fond of him and sometimes treated him as if he were a member of the family. The king once said wistfully, "I'd have liked a boy like Townsend."[3]

They thought little of their daughter's friendship with him. Margaret found him attractive and easy to talk to, and over the years they were often seen together, talking or out riding. Even the most alert gossipmongers never suspected anything untoward about their relationship, although Peter's marriage, a wartime union with Rosemary Pawle, had been rocky almost from the start and was heading toward divorce. Beautiful and ambitious, Rosemary did not relish the drab life of an equerry's spouse, and the two had little in common. While Townsend was away during the war, Rosemary had engaged in romances with other men, and her infidelity would eventually cause their breakup.

In Peter, Margaret found for the first time in her life a true friend—someone who was interested in her well-being, who cared for her not just because of her royal status. Margaret felt more herself with Peter than with any other man she knew. He had experienced things that young men in her set had not. He had struggled with the demands of working for the king and had been unhappily married—experiences that, in Margaret's eyes, gave him an aura of worldliness. His gift for words was extraordinary. He had a great capacity for understanding, and a talent for listening with warmth and discretion. For his part, Peter relished Margaret's unabashed joy in life and her ability to make him laugh. Laughter had been in short supply in his marriage.

Margaret had grown into a beautiful young woman, whose thousand-watt smile lit up rooms across London. She had always taken an interest in fashion—something her sister disdained—and the public voraciously studied her clothing and hairstyles and sought to emulate her. Like most men who earned Margaret's attention, Peter was enraptured by her beauty, but he saw something deeper in her luminous blue eyes. "Behind the dazzling façade, the apparent self-assurance, you could find, if you looked for it, a rare softness and sincerity," he wrote.[4] By the time of the king's death, Peter, newly divorced, was falling in love.

As Margaret's mother and sister had learned before her, if one is lucky enough to find one's true love and soul mate, even the greatest challenges of life become possible. Margaret was desperate for this all-consuming union that would give her life purpose, and quiet the ever-present pangs of loneliness. And now, at last, at age twenty-three, she had found it.

The young Queen Elizabeth had plenty on her plate the day her sister came to tell her the big news. The coronation was only weeks away, and the palace was still in mourning for Queen Mary. So when Margaret, glowing with happiness for the first time in months, told her that Peter had proposed and she'd accepted, the queen couldn't have been pleased with the timing. However, she initially responded with sisterly warmth. For a brief moment they were two girls together, marveling over the miracle of love. There was a spark of the old familiarity. Lilibet and Margaret had been each other's closest friends and confidantes— each the other's only friend, really—while they were growing up. Their unnatural upbringing cemented their dependence on each other. As a teenager in the throes of love, Lilibet had often whispered her feelings to her sister. She recalled now the intensity of falling in love and her own determination not to let anything stand in its way.

But then the queen grew serious. She asked Margaret if she was aware that as sovereign and as head of the Church of England, the queen must approve the marriage, and Townsend's divorce might be a problem. The queen's power was granted under the Royal Marriages Act of 1772, which decreed that the sovereign's consent was required for any royal marriage when the individual was under age twenty-five. At age twenty-five, the petitioner could announce his or her intention in writing to both Houses of Parliament; unless objections were raised within twelve months, the marriage could take place.

Margaret was shocked. She claimed to be completely unaware of this dusty old decree. What could some eighteenth-century edict have to do with *her*? This was the moment when Queen Elizabeth might have set her sister straight, for she must have known that she could not approve Margaret's marriage to a divorced man. Maybe she couldn't bear to dash her sister's hopes at that moment. Maybe she thought the whole mess would go away on its own. Maybe she even thought there was a way her sister could be granted her wish. After all, Elizabeth had herself flirted with bypassing the Royal Marriage Act when she accepted Philip's proposal before the king had given his permission for them to marry. Whatever her reasons, instead of laying the facts on the line, she demurred, and asked Margaret to wait for a year. To her great relief, her sister agreed.

What the queen did next doomed her sister's love for certain. Had there been even the smallest chance that the old rule could be bent, it was dashed when the queen chose to consult Lascelles, the rigid royalist, who could not tolerate the slightest detour from the rule. As if he were speaking to a foolish young girl and not his sovereign, he sternly told the queen that it was absolutely impossible for this profane marriage to take place. Furthermore, he strongly suggested that Peter Townsend be sent away at once to discourage any further potential for scandal. The queen initially rejected the idea of banishing Townsend, thinking it far too harsh. Her sister had agreed to wait a year; perhaps the situation would resolve itself by that time. But Lascelles was a skillful and powerful insider, and he could be quite persuasive. He told the queen that Townsend's continuing presence could only bring scandal to the throne.[5]

The queen was rattled by Lascelles's strong reaction. For the first time she realized that she would have to forbid the marriage. She should have immediately summoned Margaret and told her, but she chose once again to say nothing. She didn't yet have the words to deny Margaret the love she herself enjoyed.

When Lascelles informed Winston Churchill of the engagement, the prime minister's initial reaction was to be in favor of it. An old romantic, Churchill was sure something could be worked out. He'd had a similar reaction in 1936 to King Edward VIII's desire to marry Wallis Simpson. In Margaret's case he was soon set straight. Lascelles told him that short of renouncing her right to succession, Margaret could not marry a divorced man.

On June 30, 1953, Margaret and the Queen Mother set off on a fifteen-day tour of Rhodesia on behalf of the queen. While they were away, the palace struck, assigning Townsend to a new post as air attaché to Brussels. He was to leave before the princess returned to London. The British papers were silent, but headlines flashed in the American press: PRINCESS MEG'S BEAU BANISHED.

Separated and miserable, Margaret and Peter nonetheless waited out the year, as the queen had requested. Then Margaret eagerly approached her sister for a second time. She seemed to believe that the delay had something to do with protocol. Again, the queen didn't set her straight, instead asking her to wait one more year.

On the face of it, this request was just plain cruel. The queen was fully aware that her sister's marriage would not be allowed to go forward. Why not just settle the matter once and for all?

By now the British press had picked up on the romance. A reader survey conducted by the *Daily Mirror* during this period found that 67,907 out of approximately 70,000 respondents thought Princess Margaret should be allowed to marry Townsend. Alas, the monarchy was not a poll-driven institution.[6]

Whatever her private reasons, the Queen Mother failed her daughter as well, at first refusing to discuss the matter, although she thoroughly opposed the match. It wasn't just Peter's divorce that earned the Queen Mother's disapproval. It was also his station. What kind of precedent would it set if palace servants started marrying members of the Royal Family? Margaret bristled. Peter was *hardly* a servant. He had been like a son to the king. He was beloved by the family. The Queen Mother didn't budge. She finally appealed to Margaret by asking, "Would your father have approved?" In spite of the king's fondness for Peter, she assured Margaret that the answer was no. She reminded her daughter of all her father had sacrificed—indeed, his very life!—for duty. Could she not sacrifice this one thing?[7]

The fretting was vastly overblown, no doubt fueled by bitter memories of King Edward's abdication. But what did that have to do with Margaret? In reality, there was little if any chance that she would ever reign. Her sister was a young woman with two children whose place in the line of succession preceded Margaret's. It was likely that the queen would have more children.

It was becoming clear that if there was a will, there could be a way. Although the sovereign herself was bound by the Church of England, others were not. For many, it was much ado about nothing. If the monarchy was seriously concerned that Margaret might someday drag her tainted marriage to the throne, why not just ask her to renounce claims to the throne for herself and her progeny?[8] Apart from that, it didn't really matter. As the *Manchester Guardian* put it, "The mass of ordinary simple people would not care two hoots when she came to lay a foundation stone or open a town hall whether her husband had been married before or not."

Furthermore, during Margaret's waiting period Churchill had resigned due to ill health, and the new prime minister, Anthony Eden, was a divorced man. Margaret observed that the sky had not fallen when Eden took office.

None of this mattered to the tradition-bound royals. Even Philip, who despised the false pomp of the palace and might have been expected to sympathize, was opposed to the marriage. His early relationship with Margaret had been warm and playful—he like a big brother. But over the years Philip had grown to disapprove of Margaret's antics. He thought her spoiled and self-indulgent. Now he was intent on preventing any action that might rock his wife's boat.

Margaret was beginning to waver. The pressure was taking its toll. More than ever, she felt that her life did not matter, that the cold bureaucracy of the palace and the extreme scandal aversion of her family mattered more than her happiness. It drove her to despair.

Finally, she was told in no uncertain terms: *Give Peter up or you will lose your title, your privileges, and your income. You will be plain Mrs. Townsend; you will have to make ends meet on a small salary; Peter will lose his job; and neither of you will be invited to another royal occasion.* It was an impossible situation, and Margaret knew it. Her acquiescence was just one of the many sacrifices that she would make for her sister.

Her first action was to pay a visit to the archbishop. When she told him she had decided against marrying Peter Townsend, he beamed. "What a wonderful person the Holy Spirit is!" he declared.[9]

She and Peter met, and together they drafted a statement for the media. Peter would recall that after they had finished, "We looked at each other; there was a wonderful tenderness in her eyes which reflected, I suppose, the look in mine. We had reached the end of the road. Our feelings for one another were unchanged, but they had incurred for us a burden so great that we decided together to lay it down."[10]

Margaret, overcome with emotion, pledged undying love for Peter, and promised that since she couldn't have him, she would never marry.

Looking at her crumpled, heartbroken face, Peter felt his own sorrow well up. But he was older than Margaret, and more experienced in the ways of love and life. He told her that his only wish was for her happiness. He would go away, and if she fell in love again and married, he would be glad that she had found someone.[11] It was a noble response, but Margaret didn't really hear him.

Later that day Princess Margaret released this statement to the press:

> I would like it to be known that I have decided not to marry Group Captain Peter Townsend. I have been aware that, subject to my renouncing my rights of succession, it might have been possible for me to contract a civil marriage. But mindful of the Church's teachings that Christian marriage is indissoluble, and conscious of my duty to the Commonwealth, I have resolved to put these considerations before others. I have reached this decision entirely alone, and in doing so I have been strengthened by the support and devotion of Group Captain Townsend. I am deeply grateful for the concern of all those who have constantly prayed for my happiness.

It was a hollow victory for the palace. In a moment that might have transformed Margaret's life and demonstrated her sister's humanity, the queen failed. The incident was a crucible in Margaret's life. In many ways she would never fully regain her footing.

Most of the British press was firmly on Margaret's side. Referring to the fact that Prime Minister Anthony Eden was divorced, the *Manchester Guardian* decried the double standard, calling Margaret's decision "unnecessary and perhaps a great waste." Only the *Daily Mail* fawned, declaring in exaggerated prose, "One institution emerges calm, serene and unshaken . . . the British Monarchy."

American papers seized upon the incident as a sign of the British monarchy's false piety. An editorial in the *New York Post* asked: "What kind of conception of duty is it which demands that one should give up love and life, in the interest of some abstraction like the Monarchy or the Empire or the Church, all of which in the end draw their sustenance from love and life?"

Margaret kept Peter's letters, boxed up and labeled "my correspondence with Group Captain Peter Townsend," in the Royal Archives at Windsor Castle, with the instruction that they not be opened until the one hundredth anniversary of her birth.

Although abandoning Townsend was painful, Margaret believed that it would draw her closer to her sister. As she later told an interviewer, "In my own sort of humble way I have always tried to take some part of the burden off my sister. She can't do it all, you know."[12]

"She had a profound loyalty to her sister," Peter Townsend wrote later. "She was complex, very much herself—and it was quite a sorry little self that was. Inside herself was a mass of dynamite. But she kept a facade."[13]

Years later, Margaret would discover that Elizabeth had wanted the romance stopped from day one but had allowed her to fall even more deeply in love without warning her of the consequences. She said that if her sister and mother had ended the matter from the start, much of her suffering would have been avoided.

Margaret was twenty-seven, her love dashed, but she was not about to become an "old maid." She returned to her social life with full vigor, an eye out for marriage. In February 1958, at a dinner party hosted by her old friend and lady-in-waiting, Lady Elizabeth Cavendish, Margaret met a dashing freelance photographer named Antony Armstrong-Jones. Tony was handsome, independent, and unconventional. As a teenager he'd contracted polio, and one leg was an inch shorter than the other—a defect that enhanced his jaunty sex appeal.

Margaret was quite taken with Tony, but no sooner had they started a relationship than her old flame reappeared on the scene. In March 1958, while the queen and Philip were on a state visit to Holland, Peter visited London and headed straight to Clarence House for what was obviously an arranged meeting with Margaret. Somehow the press found out, because the front page of the *London News* boomed, THEY'RE TOGETHER AGAIN in bold type.

It was a deliciously romantic notion—the handsome captain, after nearly two years of self-imposed exile, striding onto the stage, crying, *The monarchy be damned. I will have the woman I love.* That wasn't Peter Townsend's style, but speculation raged. Had Margaret done an end run around her sister? It seemed impossible that the queen would allow such a meeting to occur while she was away. Amid the uproar, a palace spokesman told reporters that the queen had known in advance of the meeting. However, backstairs gossip and off-the-record statements presented a different story. The queen had not known, and when she heard the news in Holland, she was furious.[14]

The following day, Peter and Margaret had arranged to meet again at 4:00 P.M. But when he phoned shortly before the meeting, Margaret told him the visit was off. They should not be together while the queen was out of the country, she explained, in the perfect imitation of a medieval virgin.

Frustrated, Peter backed off, but four dozen red roses were delivered to Clarence House later that day.

Those close to Peter and Margaret believed that both still held out hope that one day a way would be found for them to marry. Even if that did not happen, Peter thought it was needlessly harsh to insist that they cut off all contact. In the queen's view, however, every press headline about her sister was like a knife to the heart of the monarchy. Margaret and Peter simply could not have a relationship of any sort. When she returned to England, the queen drove to Clarence House to meet with her sister. Later the palace made an unprecedented statement in response to the press frenzy, making it clear that rumors of a renewed romance were untrue and that "Her Royal Highness's statement of 1955 remains unaltered."[15]

Peter departed London, and Margaret and Tony began to be seen together often. If Margaret thought her dalliance with the middle-class man and his artsy friends was a small act of rebellion against her stodgy, protocol-saturated family, she was mistaken. Margaret's mother and sister fully embraced Tony, and even Philip encouraged the relationship. Whether the reaction was residual guilt or anxiety over Margaret's unsettled lifestyle, they seemed delighted with the match.

It's impossible to know whether Margaret was really in love with Tony, or whether she would have married him, if it were not for a letter she received from Peter in October 1959.

In the letter, Peter broke the news that he was planning to remarry. She was nineteen-year-old Marie-Luce Jamagne, a Belgian woman half his age. Margaret was crushed. When she'd pledged to Peter that she would never marry if she could not have him, she had assumed he felt the same way about her.

Her bruised feelings might have been the catalyst for a marriage that would prove disastrous. In December Margaret and Tony were privately engaged. A month later he formally asked the queen for Margaret's hand, and she gave her permission. However, since she was eight months pregnant at the time, she asked that they wait to announce the engagement until after the delivery.

The Queen's third child, Andrew, was born on February 19, 1960. On February 26 the palace released the announcement:

*Queen Elizabeth, the Queen Mother, announces the betrothal
of her beloved daughter, Margaret Rose*

Those who knew Tony couldn't imagine him marrying into this family with all of its restrictions. It seemed folly. Even his father bluntly predicted, "Without freedom and the ability to do what he wants when he wants, he won't survive."[16]

Nonetheless, the wedding was scheduled for May 6, 1960, and the glass coach was polished for use once more. Norman Hartnell designed the dress, and it was a glorious concoction. Margaret had never looked so ravishing.

More than 500,000 Londoners came out for the occasion. For the first and only time in her life, Margaret took center stage, with all the glory she had dreamed of. The girl who had always longed to be the star finally was—if only for one day.

ROYAL FAMILY VALUES

*Loneliness is something royal children
have always suffered and always will.
Not much you can do about it, really.*

LORD MOUNTBATTEN

1953 ◆ BUCKINGHAM PALACE

A DAY IN THE LIFE of the Queen of England was not that different from that of any working mum—if you believed the glowing early press. The life of the Royal Family was bustling with activity, and the queen cheerfully and efficiently juggled her many roles. One feature described an average day something like this:

8:00 A.M. ◆ The Queen and Philip begin their day, as they listen to a BBC broadcast of the news.

8:30 A.M. ◆ Over a breakfast of tea, toast and kippers, they peruse the morning papers. The Queen looks at *Sporting Life* first to check the horses, and if there's time she starts the *Daily Telegraph* crossword puzzle.

9:15 A.M. • The nanny, Helen Lightbody, brings in the children and the Queen's corgis, Susan and Sugar, for thirty minutes of play.

10:00 A.M. • The Queen begins her work day, reading documents, signing papers, giving audiences, making appearances.

5:00 P.M. • The Queen insists upon spending an hour with the children.

6:00 P.M. • Once a week the Queen meets with the Prime Minister. Evenings often involve official duties, but the royal couple prefers quiet evenings at home.[1]

Not exactly an average life, but the magazines pretended it was, and their female audiences thrilled to the idea of the queen sharing the busy complexity they were experiencing. It was a new era for women, and like it or not, Elizabeth II was the queen of "having it all"—an expression later coined by feminists in the 1960s and 1970s to denote empowerment. Women could raise families and save the world simultaneously. They could be loving wives and mothers at home and iron-willed leaders in the world.

Or, at least, that was the theory and the hope. The lovely young queen with her handsome husband and cherubic children appeared to be the perfect role model, the modern ideal who would launch a new Elizabethan era. Unfortunately, the queen's fixation was on the past, not the future. She relied to an obsessive degree on the old order and was more a female reincarnation of her father than the visionary embodiment of a fresh era. To put it mildly, Queen Elizabeth II wasn't one to mix it up with history.

As a woman she had none of her mother's gift for emotional expression or empathy, even with her own children. There were no lavish hugs and kisses either in public or in private.

"She is a stiffener of backs," her private secretary, Martin Charteris, once said. It's not really what one wants from Mummy. The queen's parents had been effusive in their love. Why could she not manage the same? For sensitive, high-strung Charles, the effects of his mother's remoteness were worsened by his father's harshness. Philip was intent on molding his son in his own image, turning the shy, sickly child with the awkward gait and big ears into a "man's man." Charles was terrified of his father, whose scathing rebukes often brought him to tears. Decades later, he remained emotionally bruised. "I can never remember my father ever telling me he loved me," he confided to a friend. "I can never remember him ever praising me for anything."[2]

In the end, the queen could not give Charles and Anne what she herself had had in abundance, while Philip could not give them what he had never had.

In the early years of her reign, the queen was equally unsuccessful in mollifying her husband. Perhaps a woman more experienced with men might have found a way to appease Philip. But young and inexperienced, with a chorus of advisors determined to keep Philip on the sidelines, she was helpless to make things right. She longed for the kind of partnership her parents had crafted from equal parts love and respect. But Philip was not a partner on the throne. He was not the male equivalent of the Queen Consort. There was no *King* Consort, because (as any card player knows) a king is always higher than a queen.

One hundred years earlier, Prince Albert, consort to Queen Victoria, had laid out the role in no uncertain terms, and it was clearly a bad fit for Philip. Prince Albert wrote:

> *The position of the Prince Consort requires that a husband should entirely sink his own individual existence in that of his wife; that he should aim at no power by himself or for himself; should shun all attention, assume no separate responsibility before the public, but make his position entirely part of hers, and fill every gap which as a woman she would naturally leave in the exercise of her regal functions.*[3]

Philip wasn't about to adopt such a simpering pose, and he dealt with his frustration by spending as much time as possible away from the palace, often in the company of Mike Parker. He was still tight with his Thursday Club clan, and he was frequently seen out on the town at times when a more devoted husband and father would be at home. Having grown up in the cozy nest of "we four," the queen suffered silently as her own foursome became increasingly fragmented.

Rumors of Philip's exploits abounded, and though infidelity was never proved, there was definitely a sense of "where there's smoke there's fire." At the very least, Philip enjoyed the company of beautiful women whose frank admiration and awe restored his trampled manhood.

The queen must have heard the rumors about her husband; his dalliances were an open secret. She coped by compartmentalizing. For her mother, love and duty had been woven together in a single sparkling strand. This was impossible for her daughter, who made it a point to separate her marriage and her work as much as possible.

In her memoirs, Eleanor Roosevelt recalls a telling conversation with a secretary while visiting the queen: "'It must be terribly hard,' I said to him, 'for anyone as young as the Queen to have so many official responsibilities and also carry on as a wife and mother.' He looked at me with what I thought was a surprised expression and said briskly: 'Oh, no. Not at all. The Queen is very well departmentalized.' How *does* one departmentalize one's heart, I thought!"[4]

Faced with excruciating public humiliation and personal pain, the queen reverted to her stony mask, never letting on that she was aware of the rumors swirling around her husband. For a time Lilibet and Philip each traveled alone, nursing their private wounds.

Philip's absences did not bring Lilibet closer to her children. Instead, she sought comfort from the only friends who would never let her down—her horses and her dogs. Her relationship with her corgis, whose love was unconditional, at times seemed deeper than her love for her children. In the evenings, after Charles and Anne had been brought to her sitting room to say their good nights, she turned happily to Susan and Sugar. A uniformed footman brought their dinner on a tray, and she lovingly dished out their meals of fresh meat and gravy and other delicacies, cooing and smooching all the while.[5]

The greatest test of their marriage came in 1956 when Philip was invited to open the Olympics in Melbourne. Rather than flying to Australia and making a week of it, he proposed making the Olympics the centerpiece of a five-month tour of the Commonwealth aboard the royal yacht *Britannia*.

Such a transparent plot to escape the palace noose and return to his days of freedom and fun at sea did not go unnoticed in the press, but Philip defended himself, even going so far as to characterize the journey as a hardship. "I believe there are some things for which it is worthwhile to make some personal sacrifices, and the British Commonwealth is one of those things," he said haughtily.[6]

Philip, Mike Parker, and a large crew set off on a blustery day in October, the queen sadly waving good-bye. Observers noted the tight set of her jaw as she watched her prince depart.

Toward the end of the tour, Mike Parker's wife, Eileen, stewing back home in London, filed for divorce. She accused Parker of being the ringleader in a series of sexual escapades, and said that the *Britannia* was nothing more than a party boat. Before the scandal could reach full steam and implicate Philip, Parker was given his walking papers. He left the tour before its end.

The lengthy tour and Mike Parker's abrupt dismissal gave rise to rumors in the American press that the royal marriage was in trouble. On the eve of Philip's return, an article in *Time* opined, "Last week the mongering winds were howling louder around Buckingham Palace than they had since the day of Wallis Warfield Simpson and Edward VIII."[7]

Philip was aghast at the rumors of his infidelities, insisting that he never had anything but the most honorable motivations for his actions. The stories would persist throughout his marriage. Philip would be linked with the stunning American film star Merle Oberon; Pat Kirkwood, the star whose legs were described by theater critic Kenneth Tynan as "the eighth wonder of the world"; and his childhood friend, nightclub owner Hélène Cordet. Cordet's two children, Louise and Max, were born out of wedlock, which was quite scandalous at the time. To this day there are those who believe Philip to be Max's father. Philip paid for the boy's education, and the two have remained close.

According to some biographers, Philip's most long-standing relationship was with the queen's cousin, Princess Alexandra of Kent, Marina's beautiful daughter. Even after Alexandra married Angus Ogilvy, a British aristocrat, the affair was so blatant that Mountbatten furiously wrote to Philip, "If news of this affair should enter the public domain you must realize the reflection this would have on the whole family and especially Lilibet."[8]

In spite of what seemed to be voluminous evidence, Philip always denied having any affairs. In 1992, decades into his marriage, he would respond to a British reporter's unprecedented question about infidelities explosively. "Have you ever stopped to think that for the last forty years I have never moved anywhere without a policeman accompanying me? So how the hell could I get away with anything like that?"[9]

Philip's response was inadvertently revealing for what he did *not* say—that he adored his wife, that he valued faithfulness, and that he was the luckiest man in the world with no inclination to stray.

The serene young woman whose path was unsullied by doubt for the first twenty-five years of her life would find nothing but confusion and dissent in the early years of her reign. Surrounded by an old guard whose influence seemed to outweigh her own, the queen struggled to assert authority in a role whose power was expressed in nuance and suggestion. She was accustomed to being told what to do, and she listened to the guidance of her advisors—particularly Lascelles—more closely than the modernists wished. She also depended heavily on her mother, just as Churchill had predicted. They spoke by phone every morning, and Lilibet frequently asked, "What would you do?" Sadly, Lilibet had never been taught to have a mind of her own. The weight of her role could paralyze her. "My father told me that I must always remember that whatever I said, or did, to anyone, they would remember it," she once said, and it's easy to imagine how unforgiving this must have seemed, how much it froze out spontaneity and inhibited change. Those who had longed to see the young queen craft a new era of openness were sadly disappointed. In a scathing editorial in the *Daily Mirror*, Cecil King criticized the stultifying palace atmosphere. "The circle around the throne is as aristocratic, as insular and—there is no more suitable word for it—as toffee-nosed as it has ever been," he wrote, in a striking digression from the usually sycophantic British press.

Lord Altrincham,[10] publisher of the *National and English Review*, devoted the August 1957 issue to articles about the monarchy. In a by-lined piece, Altrincham delivered a harsh critique of the queen and her outdated court, at times turning personal. Particularly deadly was his analysis of the queen's personality:

> *When she has lost the bloom of youth, the Queen's reputation will depend, far more than it does now, on her personality. It will not then be enough for her to go through the motions; she will have to say things which people can remember and do things on her own initiative that will make people sit up and take notice. As yet there is little sign that such a personality is emerging.*

In fairness to the queen, her role was less clear than it had been in the simple old days of the imperial monarchy. The Commonwealth was a murkier concept. This "family of nations" had no united purpose and little in common except for a history of British rule. Furthermore, the decade after World War II had brought repeated challenges to Britain's place in the world. While the war had served to elevate the United States in strength and position, it had diminished Britain. With Churchill's successor, Anthony Eden, an ineffectual leader whose disastrous confrontation with Egypt over the Suez Canal further marred Britain's reputation, everyone looked to the queen to provide a sense of purpose and moral direction. But the queen was increasingly isolated inside her palace.

The optimism and confidence she had experienced in the early days of her reign had been falsely fueled by the warm encouragement of Churchill. He always seemed a little bit in love with her; he was fond of making public declarations that elevated her in the eyes of the public.[11] When she ascended the throne, Churchill was there with a misty-eyed radio address: "I whose youth was passed in the august, unchallenged and tranquil glare of the Victorian era, may feel a thrill in invoking once again the prayer and anthem, 'God save the Queen!'"

With Churchill gone, there was no one to sing the queen's praises, no reminder of the greatness that lay ahead. She was utterly devoted to duty, but leadership is nine tenths public presence, and to her people she remained remote.

The ever-hovering Bobo MacDonald also played a role in keeping the queen entrenched in the past. Her childhood nanny had remained by Lilibet's side, her most trusted aide and confidante. She even shopped for the queen's clothes, which might explain the queen's prematurely matronly look. Philip barely tolerated Bobo, whom he considered a meddling old fogey.

The queen must have privately envied her mother her social skills and popularity. The Queen Mother, named "Woman of the Year" in 1954 by the *Daily Mirror,* was fully on the road again. That year she made a poignant solo trip to the United States. In 1952 a fund had been created in the king's name to give technical training to workers from the Commonwealth in the United States. The Queen Mother attended a lavish banquet at the Waldorf-Astoria in New York City to accept the fund, and she lunched with Eleanor Roosevelt at Hyde Park. Everywhere she went she was greeted by enthusiastic crowds. The old sparkle was returning to her eyes. She asked to be taken to F.A.O. Schwarz, and arrived at the Fifth Avenue toy store with a crowd of reporters in tow. "I'm interested in toys for a six-year-old boy and a four-year-old girl," the smiling young grandmother told the clerk, adding, "I'd like them to be *very* American." She left the store with a model steamshovel for Charles and a plastic tea set for Anne, her wide smile blazing for a dozen cameras.[12] At home and abroad, the Queen Mother garnered the affection of the people. They could relate to her, and easily adopted the title Queen Mum, which delighted her.

By the time Philip returned from his lengthy and controversial Commonwealth tour, the queen had made a decision: Her husband must be appeased. She began by granting him the title of prince. He was now Prince Philip, Duke of Edinburgh. Then in 1959 she made a gesture that must have thrilled Lord Mountbatten. In a remarkable concession, she quietly changed her name to Mountbatten-Windsor, and made the following declaration: "While I and my children will continue to be styled and known as the House and Family of Windsor, my descendents, other than descendents enjoying the style, title, or attributes of Royal Highnesses and the titular dignity of Prince or Princess and the female descendents who marry and their descendents shall bear the name Mountbatten-Windsor."[13]

A bit convoluted, perhaps, but the bottom line was that the name Mountbatten had finally insinuated itself into the royal lineage.

The following year the queen gave birth to Andrew, who was whispered to be a "reconciliation baby." Philip put a quick end to such talk with this cold remark: "People want their first child very much. They want the second child almost as much. If a third child comes along they accept it as natural, even if they have not gone out of their way for it."[14]

But the queen was delighted with her infant son. Overnight she discovered that strange and glorious state called mother love. It was as if she had saved up all of her hugs for this beautiful little boy. She spoiled Andrew rotten, and as a result the future Duke of York became a hell-raiser. Even as a child Andrew was openly arrogant—like his father but without the compensating charm or sense of duty. A naughty little boy, he pulled rank on the palace staff, threatening reprisals if they chastised him.

The couple's fourth and final child, Edward, was born in 1964, and he, too, basked in his mother's adoration. Charles and Anne were like "starter children," born before their mother learned how to nurture.

Mountbatten was keenly aware of Prince Charles's struggles. Ignored by his mother and belittled by his father, Charles was desperate for a father figure and advocate, and Mountbatten, now retired, insinuated himself easily into this role. Charles called him "my honorary grandfather."

According to Dame Barbara Cartland, a close friend of Lord Mountbatten's, "The fact that Prince Charles did not get on very well with his father made Dickie all the more important. There is no doubt that Dickie treated him like an adored son."[15]

This did not sit well with the Queen Mother, whose distaste for the meddling Mountbatten had grown with time. She was suspicious of his motivations and didn't much care for his philosophy of life. She also felt herself being replaced as Charles's caretaker and confidante. His parents' frequent absences had buttressed his grandmother's position as a surrogate mother to the boy. Mountbatten would have to be watched carefully.

Mountbatten and Philip were in agreement on one count: The young prince must be toughened up. To this end it was decided that he would be sent to Gordonstoun, the strict sink-or-swim environment of Philip's boyhood. In this oppressive, bullying setting Charles was expected to shed the tender skin of his youth and emerge ruddy and ready for bear. It had the opposite effect, shattering what little self-confidence Charles possessed. His time at Gordonstoun was a disaster. Charles was tormented unmercifully by his classmates, who mocked his sensitive nature, his outsized ears, and his station in life. He was so lonely and miserable that he cried bitterly when he had to return to school after holidays. Gordonstoun didn't make a man out of him, as Philip had predicted. It merely reinforced Charles's feelings of isolation and inadequacy.

R eady or not, the times they were a-changing. The 1960s were lived in Technicolor. The vivid entry on the scene of a dashing young American president and his glamorous wife emphasized the contrasting gray aura of the British monarchy. The Kennedys were both chic and casual. He was "Jack," not "Mr. President." She was "Jackie," not "ma'am." The First Couple possessed a flawless instinct for the cultural revolution emerging from the drab postwar era. In contrast, the Royal Family seemed old-fashioned and a bit frayed around the edges. The stiff palace protocol was a poor fit for the "hang loose" times.

Television brought a new irreverence into people's living rooms. Programs like David Frost's *That Was the Week That Was* dared to poke fun at the frumpy royals. Television also provided a wider platform for the monarchy's critics. "The English are getting bored with their monarchy," Malcolm Muggeridge smirked from the smoke-filled set of *The Jack Paar Program*.[16]

It was embarrassing, even intolerable, and by the late 1960s, many influential people were demanding that the palace pay attention. Chief among the modernists was Prince Philip. He had always despised the pompous phoniness of royal life, and for many years he had lobbied unsuccessfully for more fresh air in the dusty Buckingham Palace corridors. Now he said, "No one wants to end up like a brontosaurus, who couldn't adapt himself and ended up stuffed in a museum."[17]

For the myth of royal relevance to remain alive, it was essential that the people see its Royal Family as representative of their aspirations, a model of family the way it was supposed to be. This was a challenge for the rigid, secretive, dysfunctional Windsors, but in 1969 they rose to it by agreeing to open the palace gates to a television film crew. The documentary, produced by the BBC's Richard Cawston, would show the family at work and play, presenting its human side.

Royal Family first aired in July 1969 to rave reviews. More than twenty-three million Brits watched it the first time it aired, and viewers were charmed by the portrait of a loving, hardworking family. The biggest surprise was the queen, who appeared relaxed and smiling throughout—happily preparing food at a family barbecue, in trousers on the deck of the *Britannia,* dignified and industrious at her office desk. The verdict: Here was a family that worked hard on behalf of England and the Commonwealth, yet managed to be personally endearing and close.

The film's task of polishing the family's image worked up to a point, but one could hardly say that the Royal Family was normal. Prince Philip might stand at the grill during a family barbecue, but behind the scenes dozens of staff were busily at work. "It seems crazy in retrospect," Stephen P. Barry, former valet to Prince Charles, said, "but I can remember occasions at Balmoral, the Royal summer holiday home in Scotland, when there would be one hundred and twenty members of staff looking after only six of the family."[18]

10

BEING ANNE

*You start off in life very much
a tail-end Charlie, at the back of the line.*

ANNE, IN AN INTERVIEW, DESCRIBING
HER PLACE IN THE MONARCHY

1952 ◆ BUCKINGHAM PALACE

FROM BIRTH ANNE was a real pisser, an untidy amalgam of her heritage—boorish father, impish grandmother, stiff mother, haughty great-grandmother. These combined influences gelled to form a personality as bold as her older brother's was shy, as original as a new bloom.

The children's nannies, Helen Lightbody and Mabel Anderson, were well aware of their distinct personalities. Lightbody once remarked, "Anne will never walk if she can run, and when on horseback, even as a child, she would never trot when she could gallop."[1] Mabel Anderson put it this way: "He [Charles] was never as boisterous as Princess Anne. She had a much stronger, more extrovert personality.

She didn't exactly push him aside, but she was certainly a more force-ful child. . . . She was always the ringleader and up to every sort of prank you can think of. Charles just tagged along."[2]

A story is told of Anne when she was barely two. Her parents were in Malta, and their grandparents were caring for the children. Anne begged to be taken to church, and her grandmother agreed but solemnly told her she must behave very properly. During the service the congregation knelt to say a prayer for the Royal Family, asking God to bless and protect each member—the king, the queen, the Queen Mother, Princess Elizabeth, Princess Margaret, the Duke of Edinburgh. When Anne heard her father's title, she jumped up and yelled, "Duke of Cornflakes!" before collapsing into laughter.[3] That was Anne.

In childhood Anne grabbed a domineering role that she would never be allowed later. She was not soft or prettily feminine. In the nursery, she was the leader, Charles the follower. Her temper tantrums were legendary. One observer recalls: "If she wanted a toy, she would grab it from Charles. She also grabbed everything that Charles wanted—and everything he had she wanted." Her father's favorite, she could do no wrong in his eyes. Philip might actually have found a vengeful pleasure in seeing the scrawny little boy receive his comeup-pance from a girl.

As the children grew older and their proper roles began to take shape, Anne felt more like a misfit. She was a permanent lady-in-waiting who would never achieve authority. Even her younger brothers would leapfrog her to the throne. She resented being a girl in a boys' world. When Charles was sent off to boarding school, Anne felt lonely and iso-lated. Eventually, having observed their daughter kicking the corgis, the queen and Prince Philip both decided that it wasn't healthy for a young child to be living in such seclusion.

Two girls her own age were invited to join the young princess for schooling at Buckingham Palace. Having set up the school, however, neither parent appeared to pay any attention to her academic progress.

In fact, neither the queen nor Prince Philip ever visited her home classroom.

When Anne was thirteen, she was sent to Benenden, a private girls' boarding school in Kent, and she relished the opportunity to be in a normal environment and develop true relationships with her peers. On her first day, when her mother remarked worriedly, "The girls look so alike in their uniforms that I don't know whether I shall be able to pick out Princess Anne when I come next," Anne was pleased. That was exactly the point!

Anne was happy to be just one of the girls, and she was far more successful at it than her mother had been during her brief stint with the women's service during World War II. As one of Anne's housemates, Susan Forgan, said, "I never felt that I was talking to the daughter of the Queen. . . . She had a very good sense of humor." Anne made friends easily, and one in particular, Victoria Legge-Bourke, became a friend for life and Anne's lady-in-waiting. Later, her daughter would become Prince William and Harry's governess.

She wasn't an exceptional student; her favorite period was the ninety minutes each day she was allowed to ride her horse, High Jinks, who was stabled at Benenden.

From the moment Anne could sit in the saddle, riding was her passion, and also her greatest means of escape from the loneliness of her childhood. The one place where she felt totally self-confident was on horseback. Among the hay bales she could disappear into a private world, and she took riding seriously. After graduating from Benenden, she decided to take up the sport of eventing, and she trained rigorously—three hours early each morning before starting a day of royal engagements.

She found horses far more trustworthy than humans. They accepted her without question or criticism. They responded to her touch. She once put it this way: "When I'm approaching a water jump with dozens of photographers waiting for me to fall in, and hundreds of spectators wondering what was going to happen next, the horse is the only one who doesn't know I'm Royal."[4]

With her horse, Doublet, Anne rode her way into a coveted place at the 1971 Badminton Horse Trials, where she finished fifth out of a field of forty-seven. The winner that year was a handsome young riding instructor named Captain Mark Phillips.

Later that year Anne rode Doublet to win the individual European Three-Day Event at Burghley. Both of her parents were in attendance, which made the victory all the sweeter. She was enormously relieved that she hadn't let them down by losing. "To receive the prize from my mother and the medal from my father on a horse bred by my mother was very special," she said.

She was a natural, winning ribbons and medals at riding events across the country. After taking the Raleigh Trophy at the Individual Three-Day Event in Lincolnshire in 1971, she was voted BBC's Sports Personality of the Year.

It was Anne, not Margaret or even Diana, who broke the mold of royal women. She had no interest in putting on airs and did not even try to mask her feelings. It was a notable departure, as royal women for all time had been great maskers of feelings—her mother, grandmother, and great-grandmother being prime examples.

Anne came of age at a time when women were demanding equality and insisting on the right to their own identities. In this respect, she was very much a woman of her era. She did not flirt with the press, didn't know how to be coy and giggly. She refused to be their fairy-tale princess. Her determination to be true to herself—particularly when that "self" didn't fit any obvious mold—earned her unfair criticism from the press. They dogged her every move, delighting in her shows of impatience, capturing every downturn of her mouth, every extra pound gained. She was called "frumpy, dumpy and grumpy." The mean-spirited critiques must have hurt, but they never brought her to tears. "I'm me," she said defiantly. "I'm a person. I'm an individual, and I think it's better for everybody that I *am* me and shouldn't try to be anything I'm not."[5]

Anne always felt very awkward in the public light. She had strong reservations when the queen agreed to allow cameras into their home to film *Royal Family* in 1969. "I never liked the idea of the *Royal Family* film. I always thought it was a rotten idea. The attention that had been brought on one ever since one was a child, you just didn't want any more. The last thing you needed was greater access." At nineteen Anne was still awkward and pudgy. She hadn't grown into herself. Her embarrassment was plain to see in the film.

While her horsemanship was admired, Anne never had the love affair with the press other royal women had enjoyed at various times during their lives. She had neither her grandmother's charm nor her mother's graceful dignity under pressure. Reporters and photographers were astounded that Anne didn't even try to court them. They had the power to invent a person's public identity, and so they invented Anne as arrogant, unattractive, and ill-tempered.

Not only did the press seem to take pleasure in criticizing Anne, they also failed to give her proper credit for what she *did* do. Her calendar was always crowded with engagements, which she took on in addition to her riding schedule. She had an enthusiastic following among young girls who shared her love of horses and admired her as a role model.

Anne received frequent invitations to become a patron for charitable institutions—essentially serving as a figurehead for fund-raising purposes. When she was asked to become president of the Save the Children Fund at age twenty, it appeared the role would be mostly symbolic. However, something about this organization and its work with children in Third World nations touched an altruistic spark in Anne. She took on a real role, making her first trip to Kenya when she was twenty-one. In the coming years Anne would travel the world, raising money and publicizing the plight of children in India, Somalia, and Sudan. She insisted on seeing the children for herself so she could better understand their needs, and even went to Beirut at the height of the war in Lebanon. Those whose lives the princess touched often marveled at her complete lack of pretension and her genuine concern.[6]

Princess Anne always regarded herself as a "plain Jane." She had a protruding nose, eyes that were too close together, and a tendency to gain weight easily. The queen did little to ease Anne's anxiety, frequently telling her daughter to lose weight or take better care of her appearance. "Your hair makes you look like a sheepdog," she once remarked, asking Anne to please cover it with a hat.

As she grew older, though, the pudgy adolescent blossomed into an attractive young woman. She also discovered men and found that she had a lusty sexual appetite.[7] Among her many suitors was Andrew Parker Bowles, who would later marry Camilla Shand.

By the time she was in her early twenties, Anne was smitten with her fellow eventing competitor, Captain Mark Phillips, a riding instructor in the Queen's Dragoon Guards. It was not love at first sight for either of them, but it grew over the years as they competed together and attended the same events. They naturally began to see each other more often and soon found that in addition to a love of horses, they had a shared sense of humor and worldview. Once the press got wind of their relationship, they reported every public appearance of the couple, which naturally annoyed Anne. She refused to give the media even the slightest nibble.

An up-and-coming military man who was also a talented horseman, Mark Phillips came from a wealthy, though not aristocratic, family. He was well bred, handsome, and popular with women. He didn't give a hoot about Anne's royal position, and she glowed under the gaze of a man who seemed to love her just for herself.

The queen and Prince Philip were surprised by Anne's choice. They found Mark a bore, and Charles nicknamed him Fog, "because he's thick and wet"—whatever that meant. Mostly, the family was puzzled by Mark's plain disinterest in anything royal. When the queen offered him a title upon his marriage to Anne, he refused it, declaring that he and Anne would be Mr. and Mrs. Mark Phillips.

The palace announced the engagement in May 1973, and the wedding date was set for November 14, which was also Charles's twenty-fifth birthday.

The wedding at Westminster Abbey was a spectacular television event, with an estimated worldwide audience of five hundred million. Ironically, much of the commentary focused on how beautiful the bride looked, as if to say, Aha! At last the ugly duckling has emerged as a swan! It was an insult to Anne, who could only achieve public favor when she became a pretty face.

The newlyweds did not exactly ride off into the sunset together, although they would continue to compete. Once they were married, Mark was appointed Acting Captain Instructor at the Royal Military Academy at Sandhurst, and they moved into a house on the grounds. Mark's salary was £2,300; his wife would receive a £23,000 allowance from the Civil List—an increase of £8,000 over her single allowance.

On a cool evening in late March, five months into their marriage, Anne and Mark were returning to Buckingham Palace after a screening of *Riding Towards Freedom,* produced by the Riding for the Disabled Association, of which the princess was a patron. Anne's lady-in-Waiting, Rowena Brassey, sat with them in the back of the limousine. In front were the chauffeur, Alexander Callender, and a bodyguard, Inspector James Beaton. It was a normal moment that was about to become shockingly abnormal.

As their limo approached the Mall, a white Ford Escort suddenly appeared behind them. They didn't notice the car or the frantic demeanor of the man behind the wheel.

Twenty-six-year-old Ian Ball was in the final stage of a three-year plot to kidnap the princess. Delusional but organized, Ball had planned every detail. He had two Astra revolvers—a five-round .38 and an eleven-round .22—white cotton gloves, and four pairs of handcuffs. Months earlier, under the name Jason Van Der Sluis, he had rented a house in Sandhurst, which he'd stocked with food, toiletries, and bedding; this was where he planned to bring the princess.

In his pocket, Ball had a typed note, addressed to the queen and Prince Philip:

> *Your daughter has been kidnapped. The following are conditions to be fulfilled for her release. A ransom of £3,000,000 is to be paid in £5 notes. They are to be used, unmarked, not sprayed with any chemical substances, and not consecutively numbered.*

The ransom note also demanded:

A pardon in advance for the kidnapping, possession of firearms, and the murder of any police officers;

A stipulation that if his identity was revealed, a civil action against the police would be granted, for not less than £1 million;

A private plane to fly him and the Princess from Heathrow to Switzerland;

An audience with the Queen.

He promised to send Anne home from Switzerland when all conditions were met.

The occupants of the limousine were chatting gaily about the film and the dinner party they would attend that evening, when suddenly the white Escort accelerated and leapt out in front of the limo, cutting it off.

Callender roughly braked to a stop, and Beaton jumped out to see what was going on just as Ball came hurling toward him, firing a shot into the bodyguard's chest. Within seconds Ball had wrenched open the back door and was pulling on Anne's left arm, yelling that she must come with him. Mark grabbed her right arm and held on for dear life as a brief tug-of-war ensued. Mustering all of her strength, Anne pulled her arm out of Ball's grip and pushed the door shut.

The next moments were sheer chaos. Later, when she'd had a chance to digest the event, Anne would marvel at how long it took people in the crowded Mall area to realize that dangerous events were occurring, or to hear the *pop-pop* of Ball's pistol as he fired two more shots at Beaton and one at Callender. "It was very unreal," she said. "I was amazed that things were still going on outside as usual—cars and taxis passing us as though nothing was happening. I didn't have time to be frightened. I just got angry at them."

Police finally arrived to subdue Ball, but not before he had wounded a policeman and a journalist, in addition to Anne's driver and bodyguard.[8]

For the first time in memory, the media unanimously expressed real admiration for the princess, applauding her courage and calm. Her father was out of the country and crowed proudly when he heard about the incident. "God help that cretin," he said. "If he had succeeded in abducting Anne, she would have given him a hell of a time while in captivity."

Anne wasn't in any hurry to procreate. "Yes, in time, we will have children," she told the pestering media with a hint of exasperation. "Right now I've got this ambition to achieve." That ambition was to compete in the 1976 Montreal Olympics.

Anne's attitude about motherhood was revealing. "I know that some people think that you should have your children sooner rather than later, when you are closer to them in age, but I'm not so sure," she once said.

"My own family is a splendid example of inconsistency. There was one lot when my mother was very young and a second lot later on. But I don't think you are settled enough at the beginning of your marriage to have children."[9]

If one were searching for a subtext to these remarks, it might be that Anne, as one of the first "lot," had not fared as well as her younger brothers. However, unlike Charles, who was prone to whine that he'd been badly parented, Anne was fiercely loyal to her parents and took pains to praise them—especially her mother. As Anne grew older the two women had achieved a closeness that was cultivated and enhanced by their shared love of horses.

Anne and Mark were both intent on qualifying for the Olympics, but three months before the team was selected, Anne had a serious setback when she was thrown from her horse Goodwill at the Durweston Horse Trials in Dorset. She was knocked unconscious and suffered a hairline fracture of the vertebra. After the fall Anne said, "I have no idea what happened next, except that I eventually regained full consciousness nearly twenty-four hours later." With her usual toughness and will, Anne embarked upon an intense rehabilitation program and was one of the five selected for the Olympic team. Mark also qualified. The team did not bring home any medals, but it was a thrilling ride. After the Olympics, Anne decided to end her competitive career "because of pressure of time and the possibility of starting a family."

Meanwhile, Mark was having the problem typical of men who married into the Royal Family: *What about me?* He was in danger of becoming a mere extension of his wife's persona. With all of the restrictions inherent to his position, and the necessity of accompanying his wife on numerous engagements—a function he despised—Mark had slowly reached the conclusion that he would be unable to fully pursue his career or rise up in the ranks. What he wanted to do, he told Anne, was resign from the army and start a horse farm and riding academy. It was a romantic notion that they could ever be just a farming family, but Anne went along with the idea.

They found a property in the Cotswolds called Gatcombe Park, which included 730 acres of farmland and woodland, several out-buildings, a ten-bedroom house, and four cottages. The queen purchased it for them for five hundred thousand pounds, but it was in such a shambles that an additional infusion of money was needed to bring it up to spec. Embarrassed at having to accept more charity from his mother-in-law, Mark insisted on taking out a mortgage for £35,000 to pay for renovation. His remark to the press, "We're just a young couple with a mortgage," was widely ridiculed as an example of royal pretension.[10]

That year Anne gave birth to their first child, Peter. The press coverage of the baby's arrival was so positive, it led her to say, "Well, it's nice to think I've done something right for a change." She shouldn't have spoken so fast. When she was spotted leaving the hospital in the front seat of the car, holding her baby without benefit of a seat belt, there was a fresh storm of criticism.[11]

With offspring in the picture, the queen once again urged Mark to accept a title. It seemed unthinkable that Anne's children would re-main untitled. But Mark resisted once again. He thought the need for titles was just another example of the pretension he despised. He re-fused and Anne backed him up. The couple remained adamant that their children would not become hothouse flowers bred for life in the public eye. Anne's sole ambition for her children was that they be treated as individuals and allowed to pursue their own dreams.

In the beginning, Gatcombe was all Anne had dreamed of. In the ca-sual, country environment, she could be what she'd always wanted to be—herself. She spent long hours in the company of the horses, dressed in jeans and boots. The rambling main house was often full of guests, and it was a decidedly protocol-free zone.

Mark was content as well, no longer obliged to follow his wife to the deadly dull engagements that filled her calendar. He had a gift for business, and his breeding-and-training operation was going strong. However, within five years, there were signs that the marriage was in trouble. Anne had longed for a normal marriage but now seemed to be losing the battle. The fractured nature of family life at Gatcombe was impossible to ignore. Anne and Mark were circling in separate orbits.

There are many explanations for what happened to the Phillipses' marriage, but one is Anne's maturing process. She had grown out of the awkwardness and insecurity that dogged her younger years and had become a woman of substance, strength, and even allure. Indeed, she had changed far more than her husband, who was happiest mucking around on the farm, and who stayed away from royal circles as much as possible.

Anne had come to terms with her royal role and even embraced it, as she saw the opportunity to do real good in the world. But she missed the passion that had died in her marriage.

In 1979, when Anne was twenty-nine, Sergeant Peter Cross was assigned to her protection detail. Cross, thirty-two, was big, blond, and ruggedly handsome, and he and Anne hit it off immediately. Although Cross was also married and the father of two, he could not resist Anne.

It was the perfect setup for an affair. Mark was often away, having taken his riding school on the road, and as Anne's protector, Cross had reason to be constantly at her side. They were extremely discreet, and if anyone noticed heated glances passing between them, they never spoke of it.

The affair continued until at least late 1980, when Anne discovered that she was pregnant. It isn't known whether she feared she might be carrying Cross's baby, but in any case, the affair had to end to avoid any suggestions to that effect.[12]

Cross didn't fare too well in the breakup. He was transferred out of the Royal Protection Department and placed on regular uniformed patrol; soon he left the department altogether.

Royal paramours are the most disposable of creatures, and Anne probably didn't lose much sleep over the fact that her lover was essentially exiled from a promising career. She settled in at Gatcombe to await the arrival of her second child. In May 1981 she gave birth to a daughter. Always one to buck the trend, she called the girl Zara, a name of Arabic origin meaning "dawn."

The whispers that Zara was really Peter Cross's child never quite died down. When she was four, Cross sold a series of articles to *News of the World*, offering a sanitized version of his relationship with Princess Anne. He made a point of noting that within minutes of giving birth to Zara, Anne phoned him with the news that she had a beautiful daughter.[13] The questions about Zara's paternity would continue throughout her young life, in part because she was such a standout on the family tree. With dazzling blond looks and an electric personality, Zara brought a welcome charge of energy to the Royal Family. Her arrival also seemed to transform and soften her mother. Anne and Zara were extremely close, bonding along the horse trails of Gatcombe.

CHAPTER

11

ALWAYS A ROSEBUD,
NEVER A ROSE

*In human terms, it is possible
to feel sympathy for Princess Margaret—
but humanity is not what monarchy is all about.*

NEW STATESMAN, REGARDING MARGARET'S MARITAL WOES

Summer 1960 ◆ KENSINGTON PALACE, LONDON

WHEN FOUR-YEAR-OLD LILIBET had learned of the birth of her sister, Margaret, she'd raced to spread the news. Coming upon Lady Cynthia Asquith, she exclaimed, "I've got a baby sister, Margaret Rose. I'm going to call her Bud." Amused, Lady Asquith asked, "Why Bud?" "Well," replied the precocious child, "she's not a real rose yet, is she? She's only a bud."[1] It was an unwitting prediction of Margaret's life.

With marriage to Tony, it was hoped that Margaret would blossom, but she never became quite settled or fully formed. Even during happy times, Margaret seemed doomed to poor press. Her marriage set off a new spate of discussions about royal expenditures. The queen gave

Margaret and Tony the use of the *Britannia* for their Caribbean honeymoon, at an estimated cost to the realm of ten thousand pounds a day. Margaret and Tony's friends Colin and Anne Tennant had made them a wedding gift of a plot of land on a tiny, remote Caribbean island named Mustique, and they visited the island on their honeymoon trip. Margaret excitedly made plans for the glorious retreat she would create there.[2]

Then there was the refurbishment of a large apartment at Kensington Palace for the couple, at a cost to taxpayers of £56,000. From the start Margaret and Tony were spending up a storm.

After the wedding, it was assumed the couple would settle into a pseudo-royal life, in the model of Margaret's parents before her father became king. But Margaret and Tony were not your average couple, and in the early period of their marriage they showed very little inclination to settle down. They kept an active nightlife and continued to bandy about with their favorite group of bohemians and intellectuals. Margaret was always in demand for the social cachet she lent, but those who knew her well understood that she was not an easy guest—or an easy friend, for that matter. She was emotionally stunted—on one hand, arrogant, on the other, needy. She craved attention, which she got plenty of, but more than that, she craved respect, which was in short supply. Her mercurial personality could bring people up short. One moment she could dazzle with the warmth of her smile, only to become still as stone and glacial in the next.

The irony of Margaret's manner was that while she longed to be free, she was deeply attached to her station in life and would sometimes put even her closest friends in their places. She could become petulant and icy at the drop of a hat if she thought her company was forgetting she was a princess and sister of the queen.[3] If only she could have sustained the chill, she might have lived happily ever after. But Margaret's desperate need for approval always got her into trouble.

Tony did not provide a steady counterbalance. He was certainly no Peter Townsend. He got along well with his in-laws, but he soon became bored and restless following Margaret around on her endless engagements. Initially, he thought he might retire from photography when he married Margaret, because he did not want to be accused of impropriety or unfair access. But he soon realized that this would doom him to a suffocating life, not to mention a dependent one, and that was intolerable. Instead, he plunged into his photography career with new intensity, and was often away from home. Margaret easily found fill-ins to escort her on her evenings out, but she was devastated by her husband's increasingly long absences.[4]

In some respects, her marital circumstances were not that different from her sister's. Lilibet's husband also traveled obsessively. Rarely a month went by when Philip wasn't going on, returning from, or planning an extended trip. While Lilibet might have suffered from his absences in the early years, time and distance seemed to have a mellowing effect on her marriage. The old adage "Absence makes the heart grow fonder" rang true in Lilibet's life. Not so for Margaret.

Nor could motherhood settle Margaret down. Maternal instincts did not come naturally to her. In fact, before their marriage, Tony and Margaret had agreed that neither wanted children. That made some sense, as both were intensely needy—perennial children themselves. They changed their minds, but David's birth in 1961 barely registered a blip on the radar. When he was only two months old Margaret and Tony departed on a Caribbean vacation, ignoring the raised eyebrows and murmurs of disapproval. Who would leave a new infant to take a vacation? Margaret said she needed a rest, as if she had just completed a particularly arduous job, and could now hand over to staff responsibility for the gritty details of mopping up.

Their second child, Sarah, was born in 1964, the year the queen gave birth to her youngest, Edward. Her arrival was also followed by a vacation for her weary parents. Childbearing could be so exhausting.

Margaret loved her children, but she was ill equipped to be their emotional anchor, and neither she nor Tony seemed to think that parenthood required any fundamental change in lifestyle. The children were raised mostly by their nanny, Miss Verona Sumner. Sumner was very haughty, treating the children like precious artifacts that should not be exposed to anything or anybody crude.[5]

The press was on full alert for any signs of trouble in the marriage, figuring that with two such volatile people it was inevitable. Within five years, the signs were glaring. While Tony was often away "on assignment," Margaret was regularly seen at Soho clubs with a virtual army of escorts. There were whispers of affairs on both sides. Margaret was linked with, among others, the actor Peter Sellers and Robin Douglas-Home, nephew of the famed political operative Sir Alec Douglas-Home.[6]

The queen and the Queen Mother heard the rumors, of course. They were most alarmed by Margaret's appearance. She didn't look well. She was dieting herself to pencil thinness, drinking too much, and chain-smoking Gitanes. But they chose not to interfere.

By its tenth anniversary, the Snowdon marriage existed in name only. Margaret wanted and expected to be the center of Tony's universe, but he craved independence. While some couples, trapped in a poor match, try to make the best of it, such concessions were not in either Margaret or Tony's nature, and their vitriol was often on public display. Where they had always been popular at dinner parties, they were now viewed as the eggshell couple, constantly in danger of breaking into nasty exchanges. The violent rows brought out the worst in both parties, especially near the end, when Tony would leave nasty notes for his wife to find, such as, "You look like a Jewish manicurist and I hate you!"[7]

The queen, who despised controversy and hated to meddle in personal matters, pulled herself together to have stern talks with Margaret and Tony, urging them to do something to salvage their crumbling marriage. But Elizabeth wasn't much of a marriage counselor, and while Margaret loved and respected her sister, she felt that she was mostly interested in putting a stop to the public displays. Margaret was also well aware of her sister's own marital struggles and didn't think she had much standing to give advice on the matter.

In 1972 Tony became involved with Lucy Lindsay-Hogg, a beautiful divorcée, and in 1974 Margaret, then forty-two, began an open affair with twenty-four-year-old Roddy Llewellyn.

Llewellyn was the son of Harry Llewellyn, the dashing avant-garde businessman who had first distinguished himself as a horseman, winning a Gold Medal at the 1952 Helsinki Olympics. Harry had two sons—Dai, who followed his father into business, and Roddy, who never quite settled down. Roddy hung out with a lowbrow artsy set, which included a group of aging hippies who organized a commune.

Discretion was never Margaret's strong suit, and her affair with Roddy soon became a public secret. When she invited him along on a vacation trip to Mustique, the paparazzi followed en masse, and photos of the cavorting duo hit tabloids worldwide.

The palace fumed. Once again Margaret was proving an embarrassment to the queen, who privately complained that she couldn't do a thing with her sister. For the most part she and Philip viewed Margaret's behavior through a selfish lens: How did it affect the queen? How could she do this to her sister?

After the Mustique incident, the queen called a meeting of the Privy Council to discuss the possibility of a formal separation for Margaret and Tony. On March 19, 1976, the announcement came from Kensington Palace:

> *Her Royal Highness the Princess Margaret, Countess of Snowdon, and the Earl of Snowdon have agreed mutually to live apart. The Princess will carry out her public functions unaccompanied by Lord Snowdon. There are no plans for a divorce.*

After the official separation, things went on much the same as before. Tony continued to see Lucy Lindsay-Hogg, albeit with some discretion, while Margaret flaunted her affair with Roddy. There was no salvaging this marriage, and Margaret and Tony finally did divorce in

1978, when Margaret was forty-eight. Shortly after the divorce was final, Tony married Lindsay-Hogg. Margaret continued to see Roddy, who was now taking a turn as an aspiring pop star with his own publicity agent. "Of course I took advantage of the publicity that surrounds my friendship with Princess Margaret," he said, without the slightest hint of embarrassment.[8]

As Margaret approached the half-century mark, her beauty eroding, having never found the importance or respect she craved, she chased youth and hung on to what dim spotlight she could find.

She had metamorphosed over the years from England's beloved princess to the most unpopular member of the Royal Family. A 1978 poll conducted by the Opinion Research Center found that 73 percent of the people disapproved of her relationship with Roddy, and many thought her a useless bit of fluff with none of the dignity or devotion to duty of her mother or sister. Although she lived like a princess at Kensington Palace, the public felt she did relatively little to advance the monarchy and was mostly in the news because of her behavior with Roddy Llewellyn and others.

In *Sunday People,* under the heading "Readers Vote NO for Margaret," it was revealed that, according to its mail, three out of four readers said the princess failed to justify her £55,000 Civil List allowance.

Margaret had been a focus of royal critics for some time, not for the unseemliness of her exploits but because of their expense. Willie Hamilton, perhaps the most outspoken member of the Labour Party, loudly decried Margaret's "expensive, extravagant irrelevance." Hamilton huffed, "If she thumbs her nose at taxpayers by flying off to Mustique to see this pop singer chap, she shouldn't expect the workers to pay for it."[9]

Criticism that Margaret was a drain on the public purse wasn't entirely fair. She presided over some eighty organizations, including the Royal Ballet Company. However, for some years, the people's government had been looking at palace finances with a keener eye, and Margaret seemed a fitting poster girl for royal extravagance.

B y the end of the 1960s, with England battling economic blight, the royal purse strings were being pulled on a regular basis. A newly emboldened press was openly expressing what many of the citizenry wondered: Why are we paying so much for the upkeep of this family?

Matters were made worse by the family's own myopic view of its wealth and its constant campaign for more money from the Treasury. In a 1969 interview on *Meet the Press,* Prince Philip set tongues wagging when he said, without a hint of irony, "We go into the red next year . . . inevitably, if nothing happens we shall either have to—I don't know, we may have to move to smaller quarters."

Smaller quarters? It was an outrageous claim. The very idea of the Royal Family being "in the red" was ludicrous, considering its palatial estates, its buckets of jewelry, and its wall-to-wall priceless paintings— not to mention the private jets and yachts.

The Royal Family derived its income from three sources. The Civil List, paid for by the government, covered all costs of the queen, her family, and their staff related to official duties. The Privy Purse, also paid for by the government, covered the family's personal expenditures in the line of duty, although the distinction between private and public was often murky. Personal income from the family's estates and investments was not taxed and was rumored to be in the hundreds of million of pounds.

As the 1970s advanced, a period of inflation triggered by rising oil prices threatened the nation. Over one million people were out of work, yet what they saw from the palace was shameless opulence. For example, the royal yacht *Britannia* cost more than three million pounds a year to operate. A virtual floating palace, it had a crew of nearly two hundred at all times, even when it was inactive. If the Royal Family was on board, one hundred additional crew were added. The *Britannia* was used not just for official trips. It was the Royal Family's favorite honeymoon and vacation cruiser. Both Margaret and Anne had used it for their honeymoons, and the Queen Mother used it for three weeks each sum-mer to take her to the Castle Mey in Scotland, which she had purchased after her husband's death.

Not incidentally, the Queen Mother was a big spender. She lived lavishly at Clarence House, with six cars, three chauffeurs, five chefs, two pages, three footmen, two dressers, and thirty more assorted sec-retaries, maids, treasurers, and housekeepers. As a hobby she bred racehorses, and she was known to spend vast sums on her favorite pas-time, racing. Dubbed "the First Lady of Chasing" by jockeys, she was especially fond of Dick Francis, who later became a bestselling novel-ist whose thrillers centered on the racing world.

It was a paradox of both the queen and the Queen Mother that while duty-bound and service-oriented, they both held such a strong sense of entitlement. The most persistent question was why the queen didn't pay taxes on her private income, especially income produced by her estates, the Duchy of Cornwall and the Duchy of Lancaster. The palace argued that she did pay taxes on the Duchy of Cornwall, but this wasn't entirely true, as they were only local taxes as opposed to federal income taxes on their revenues. Prince Charles had a similar deal for the Duchy of Lancaster, which he'd inherited at age twenty-one.

In spite of all its wealth, the Royal Family continued to petition Par-liament for Civil List increases to keep pace with inflation, and these sailed right by with only perfunctory efforts to trim the outlandish bud-get. Publicity about the palace's "hard times" reached a peak when the queen visited a local nursery school and was approached by a four-year-old girl. Pressing ten pence into the startled queen's hand, the girl said, "Here you are, Queen. I want to help you with your palace."[10]

12

CRASH OF SYMBOLS

I'm against compassion. It's so patronizing.
MARGARET THATCHER

July 1982 ◆ BUCKINGHAM PALACE

THE ALARM BELLS were ringing all over Buckingham Palace, but the queen was alone in her bedroom with a deranged man. She had been awakened shortly after 7:00 A.M. by the sound of footsteps, and as she sat up, the curtain surrounding her bed was pulled aside and a stranger plopped down on top of the coverlet and gazed at her morosely. "I'm not here to harm you," he assured the alarmed queen. "I think you are a really nice woman. I love you."

The queen's uninvited early-morning guest was a thirty-one-year-old schizophrenic named Michael Fagan, who told her he just wanted to talk to her about his marital problems.[1]

Without hesitation, the queen pressed an alarm button by her bed and sternly ordered the man, "Get out." But Fagan stayed put.

Remarkably, the alarm failed to bring a response. The queen's

footman, Paul Whybrew, was out walking the corgis, and the night policeman had gone off-duty at 6:00 A.M. So the queen took matters into
her own hands, calmly getting out of bed and leading Fagan to the door.
He asked for a cigarette, and she took him into a nearby pantry on the
pretense of looking for one. Fagan would later say with admiration that
the queen did not appear to be the least bit afraid of him.

Not until Whybrew returned with the corgis was any action taken.
The police were finally summoned, and they dragged Fagan away.

When an account of the break-in was leaked to the press, there was
an uproar. Was palace security really so inadequate that intruders could
wander willy-nilly through its hallways and into the queen's bedchamber? It turned out that this wasn't even Fagan's first visit; on a prior occasion he had climbed through a window and stolen a bottle of wine.

While press attention focused on the disgraceful lack of security,
some people were asking, *Where was Prince Philip?* Obviously not in
bed with the queen. Accounts varied: He'd left the palace early for an
engagement; he'd slept through the commotion in his own rooms
down the corridor; he'd slept overnight at his club.

The queen was furious that the incident had given the press yet another opportunity to speculate on the state of her marriage. The implication was that her husband should have been beside her in bed to
face down the intruder, but, once again Philip had been missing in
action.[2]

Coverage of the break-in was huge, and although the queen got
high marks for her courage, the prevailing image was that the palace,
and perhaps the marriage, was in tatters.

The Royal Family needed all the good press it could get. The past
twelve years had been turbulent for the image of the monarchy, and
Philip continued to be the wild card. He often seemed irritated, and
he had an extremely thin hide when it came to criticism of any sort.
When as head of the World Wildlife Fund he was blasted for continuing
to hunt, he spat out, "Everything which is pleasant must of necessity
be sinful. The bloody moralistic Brits!"[3]

Margaret Thatcher could sometimes seem more regal than the queen, especially when she used the royal "we," which she liked to do. "We are a grandmother," she announced when her son and his wife had a baby. Moments like this caused heartburn at the palace. When Thatcher became the first female prime minister in 1979, her forceful personality and imposing demeanor pushed her to the head of the class, leaving the increasingly Old World queen in the dust. At fifty-four, Thatcher was six months older than the queen, and her rise to power meant that the queen was no longer the central female face of the monarchy. It would be a twelve-year crash of symbols—jarring and out of sync.

It wasn't that Margaret Thatcher tried to present herself as a modern alternative to the queen. In fact, she was a fiercely loyal monarchist, of whom it was remarked, "Nobody would curtsy lower." That being said, she was a dominating figure who seized power with relish, a lifelong political operative who was highly opinionated.

It was no secret that the two women did not get along.[4] The queen resented Thatcher's imperious air during their weekly meetings and complained that the prime minister didn't come to discuss matters and seek advice but to lecture her, often stridently, on policy. It must have felt a bit intimidating for a woman whose formal education had consisted largely of lessons by aging courtiers on her family's lineage and royal protocol, and erratic home schooling by Crawfie. The queen had often expressed regret that she and her sister had not had more in the way of formal education. She'd once told Margaret that she didn't think either of them could have passed a university entrance exam. Margaret Thatcher had studied at Oxford and had trained in the law. She had been education minister. Her conversations—or lectures—to the queen on policy could leave the queen feeling like a schoolgirl.

There is a somewhat bitchy story about the time the two women arrived at a function wearing the same dress. Thatcher was appalled, and she told the queen, "Next time we attend a function together, we must speak to each other to see what we are going to wear so we won't wear similar dresses." The queen gave Thatcher the tiniest, implacable smile, and replied, "Her Majesty never notices what another person is wearing."[5] Touché!

The real problem between Thatcher and the queen, however, was not on matters of style but on critical issues of substance. The queen carried the banner for the status quo. Her prime minister was a revolutionary. Thatcher, the only woman to this day to lead a major Western democracy, came to power during a time of global conflict. She was stalwartly against concessions to IRA demands, skeptical about the viability of a European Community, and unyielding on the global stage. The Soviets dubbed her "the Iron Lady." She was a leader in the style of Churchill, and although the nation was not at war, Thatcher made it clear that they were fighting what amounted to a war to restore Britain to global greatness.

Thatcher was also the first true neoconservative leader, and her attitudes about domestic programs didn't sit well with the queen. In spite of their opulent lifestyle, the Windsors were great believers in social responsibility and compassion for those less fortunate. It was a key myth, essential to the survival of the matriarchal monarchy, that the queen's subjects lived in the shelter of her protective cloak. It was beside the point that the maternal posture did not always translate into real help. It was a position the queen promoted. (She was quite embarrassed when Prince Philip joked, at the height of the recession in 1981, "Everybody was saying we must have more leisure. Now they are complaining they are unemployed."[6]) Thatcher, on the other hand, believed that people were better off when they were made to stand on their own two feet. She opposed many social programs, saying, "I'm against compassion. It's so patronizing!"[7]

Thatcher's model of world and domestic policy was similar to the one adopted by the new president of the United States, Ronald Reagan, who was elected the year after Thatcher became prime minister. The two were like a power couple on the world stage.

The queen liked Reagan. For one thing, they shared a love of horses. But she didn't care for Nancy Reagan, whom she saw as something of a behind-the-scenes schemer, and who treated the queen and Philip as if they were just another glamorous Hollywood-style celebrity couple. The Reagans had absolutely no use for protocol, and they didn't even try to hide it. In 1982, when they visited England and stayed at Windsor Castle, President Reagan used a morning ride with the queen as an opportunity to stage an impromptu press conference. The queen sat by and quietly fumed, feeling used for political purposes.

In every encounter with royalty, the Reagans stumbled on matters of propriety. Michael Deaver, Reagan's deputy chief of staff, has told the story of the queen's visit to California in 1983.[8] After a cruise to Mexico on the *Britannia,* the queen and Prince Philip had arrived in San Diego, where they were entertaining guests aboard the royal yacht. Deaver, who had flown to California from Washington to join the party, was feeling jet-lagged, and by midnight he was seriously flagging.

"I realized how tired I was," he recalled, "and I just slipped off down to my little room. I had a valet assigned to me who had laid everything out, and I had just gotten into bed and turned the lights off when there was a knock on the door. It was the queen's private secretary. And he said, 'Michael, are you in there?' And I said, 'Yes.' And he said, 'Well, one shouldn't retire before the Queen.' And I said, 'I'm terribly sorry—it's three A.M. my time, and I know we have a full day tomorrow, and I didn't think I would be missed.' And he said, 'Well, you ought to remember that.' And I said, 'I certainly will.'"

In truth, the queen was the odd woman out in the blooming relationship between Thatcher and Reagan, and it didn't help that she and Thatcher were at odds on most major issues. Unlike Thatcher, the queen could not make her political views public. She could not make speeches about domestic policy, or put forward her opposition to apartheid in South Africa when Thatcher was promoting a hands-off policy. It was a frustrating period for the queen.[9]

The press, with little actual information to go on, played a key role in fanning the flames of controversy, essentially inventing a picture of the two as engaged in frequent catfights, which wasn't even close to true.

Thatcher's removal from power in 1990 was brutal and abrupt—what some say amounted to a coup d'état. Ironically, the harbinger of her downfall was her success in pushing through Parliament a substantial increase in the Civil List payment to the Royal Family, from £3.9 million to £7.9 million.[10]

The queen's family was adding to her heartburn. As she gloomily observed her eldest son, the heir apparent, flitting from one nubile beauty to the next, she was at a loss to understand, much less justify, his behavior. Charles was self-indulgent in the extreme, doing precisely what he liked without fear of consequences. As he turned thirty, he seemed no closer to finding a life partner than he had ever been.

Shy as a child, pushed around by his father, Prince Charles was a late bloomer when it came to the opposite sex. He was uptight, unable to put himself or others at ease. He had been created Prince of Wales when he turned twenty-one[11] and seemed far too young for the title to have any meaning. Even a stint in the Royal Navy didn't mature him; he came out in 1976 with little more sophistication than he'd entered with. It didn't help that he was unattractive, with big ears and a pouting mouth that made his smiles look like he had a bad case of indigestion. However, at some point he'd discovered that women would excuse his personal flaws for a grab at the gold ring—a chance to bed and perhaps to wed the future King of England. He was flattered by the attention and took full advantage of it.

His mentor, Lord Mountbatten, was always at hand with advice. He told Charles, "I believe, in a case like yours, that a young man should sow his wild oats before settling down. But for a wife he should choose a suitable and sweet-charactered girl before she meets anyone else she might fall for." Charles took the sowing-wild-oats part of the advice to heart. As for settling down, he wasn't terribly interested. His social life was so promiscuous that Mountbatten warned him in 1978 that he should cool his jets lest he begin "on the downward slope that wrecked your Uncle David's life and led to his disgraceful abdication and futile life ever after."[12]

Charles was a case of arrested development, rebelling at twenty-five the way most young men did at sixteen. He definitely liked the perks of his position—including a £250,000 income from the Duchy of Cornwall—but he bristled at palace control, insisting that he be allowed to "find" himself. For a time that took the form of a spiritual journey, seeking out gurus and even experimenting with Buddhism—not exactly fitting for the future head of the Church of England.

There is no question that Charles was vastly limited by his lack of purpose in life. King-in-waiting is hardly a suitable career, especially when one's mum is in the bloom of health. The queen, as hardy as one of her prized horses, was not about to die early or step down from the throne. As noted historian David Cannadine wrote, "Monarchy is a very brutal institution. The heir to the throne has no job until either his mother or his father dies. It's an institutionalization of an oedipal trauma."

The meddling hand of Lord Mountbatten was once again at work, trying to match Charles with one of his own, and the Queen Mother was not at all pleased. She had always been watchful of Mountbatten's influence over her impressionable grandson, which she blamed on Philip's inability or unwillingness to be a proper father figure. She herself had remained close to Charles, but for all her hovering she could not fill the role of a male advisor.

The Queen Mother believed, with good reason, that Mountbatten had but one lifelong ambition—to turn the House of Windsor into the House of Mountbatten, in spirit if not in name.

Charles had known Mountbatten's granddaughter Amanda Knatch-bull since childhood, and he found her attractive and amusing. Suddenly, in the late 1970s, the two were frequently seen together, and rumors, no doubt planted, that Amanda might be the girl to land the Prince of Wales were appearing in the press.

Mountbatten was furiously at work behind the scenes, reshaping Amanda into a proper royal-to-be. He spent large sums to send her to Paris for a wardrobe makeover, and the formerly low-key girl began wearing the finest couture.

The Queen Mother was adamantly opposed to the match, although Prince Philip welcomed the idea, saying, "Good. It beats having strangers come into the family."[13]

Then, on August 29, 1979, while Mountbatten was sailing with family members near his Irish holiday home of Classiebawn Castle, his boat was blown out of the water, allegedly by IRA terrorists.[14] Mountbatten, his fourteen-year-old grandson Nicholas, and the Irish boatboy were killed instantly. His daughter Patricia Brabourne, his son-in-law John, and Nicholas's twin, Timothy, survived. John's mother, the eighty-two-year-old Lady Brabourne, died the next morning. Patricia Brabourne, memorializing her father, said dreamily, "He went out like a shooting star."

Had Lord Mountbatten not been blown to the kingdom beyond, the next Princess of Wales in the earthly kingdom might have been Amanda Knatchbull, not Diana Spencer.

13

TO DI FOR

I am very happy that the girl
he has found to marry is a long-legged,
good-looking blonde. I feared he
might decide on someone awful.

QUEEN ELIZABETH, ON THE ENGAGEMENT
OF PRINCE CHARLES AND DIANA SPENCER

Summer 1980 ◆ ALTHORP

HE PRINCE OF WALES and (God willing)
future King of England was sitting on a hay bale
on a mild summer day, looking into the warm, sympathetic blue eyes of a young woman he had known for years
but was only now truly seeing for the first time. He found himself
opening up to Lady Diana Spencer, sharing his grief over the violent
death of Lord Mountbatten. Miracle of miracles, she seemed to understand.

He'd felt adrift in the months since Mountbatten's death. He had
lost the man whose advice he had always trusted most, and these days

he often felt he had nowhere to turn. He certainly couldn't share his aspirations and doubts with his father. No one understood the depth of his grief in this "buck up" environment. He hadn't expected it from a girl not yet out of her teens.

At nineteen, Diana was very different from her older sister, Sarah, whom Charles had dated briefly several years earlier. She was unspoiled yet brilliantly perceptive. "You looked so sad when you walked up the aisle at the funeral," she said, her eyes filling. "It was the most tragic thing I've ever seen. My heart bled for you when I watched it. I thought, it's wrong, you are lonely, you should be with somebody to look after you."

Charles was deeply moved by Diana's genuine sympathy.[1] She had struck exactly the right note—placing all of the focus on him, nurturing his tendency toward self-pity, striking a vulnerable spot.

After that night, he began to call on the young kindergarten teacher at the West London flat she shared with three girlfriends. By the fall the ever-hovering gossips were buzzing about the prince and Diana Spencer. Could she be the one? Charles found Diana appealing, but the growing pressure to find a suitable bride dictated the intensity of his pursuit. He wasn't smitten, but Diana looked very good on paper. She met the criteria—including her virginal status. (Ironically, all of the women who went to bed with the prince were instantly disqualified on this account.)

The Spencers were an aristocratic family with long-standing connections to the palace. Diana's great-grandfather had been a courtier to both Edward VII and George V. Her paternal grandmother, Lady Cynthia Spencer, and her great-aunt, Lady Delia Peel, had been ladies of the bedchamber to the Queen Mother. Her maternal grandmother, Lady Fermoy, was currently lady-in-waiting to the Queen Mother. Her father, Johnny Spencer, formerly the Viscount Althorp and now Earl Spencer, had served as equerry to the queen's father and to the queen.

Diana's family had also had its share of scandal and crisis. Her mother, Frances, was beautiful, vivacious, and strong-willed. She bore three daughters in a row (Diana, the third, was supposed to be a boy[2]) and finally a son, Charles. When Diana was six, Frances Althorp fell in love with an older, married man. She left the family and later married him. The divorce was bitter, and Frances lost custody of her children. They were raised by Johnny Spencer, and the girls in particular were fiercely protective of him. When he announced his intention to marry Raine Dartmouth in 1976, they felt betrayed. (Diana once said she smacked her father across the face when he told her.)[3] The children despised Raine, whom they dubbed "Acid Raine."

By all appearances Diana seemed to have come through her rocky childhood with poise and good spirits, but Charles was beset by doubts. Did he want to marry this girl? Did she fit the bill? He began his familiar and maddening mating dance—approach, delay; approach, delay. Did he love Diana? One thing was certain: He loved his freedom. Had Charles not been heir apparent, he might have spent his entire life in happy bachelorhood. He wanted to come and go as he pleased. He told a friend, "It's just a matter of taking an unusual plunge into some rather unknown circumstances that inevitably disturbs me, but I expect it will be the right thing in the end."[4] His words sounded like a male version of "Close your eyes and think of England."

His family watched with worry while Charles went about his ambivalent courtship. The queen was determined not to interfere, but she feared Diana would bolt, as others had, in the face of Charles's chronic dillydallying. She needn't have worried. Diana wasn't going anywhere.

Diana Spencer during those years is often portrayed as naïve and romantic, a young woman madly in love with a prince who was only marrying her as a brood mare. The truth is more complex. Diana might not have been an intellectual or a sophisticate, but she was shrewd. Far from being the insecure, blushing girl her pose would suggest, she had a strong sense of personal destiny and entitlement. The public viewed her as the lucky commoner who snagged a prince, but Diana quickly came to believe that *he* was the lucky one, thank you very much, and he'd better learn to show it.

The Queen Mother strongly supported the match, but Lady Fermoy warned against it. In her opinion, Charles and Diana were ill suited. "The marriage will end in tears," she predicted.[5] No one else saw what she did. No doubt they were blinded by relief that Charles might finally be willing to tie the knot and get on with the business of producing an heir.

The queen was quite pleased. She confided to a friend, "I am very happy that the girl he has found to marry is a long-legged, good-looking blonde. I feared he might decide on someone awful."[6] But it wasn't just Diana's looks that pleased the queen. She also believed Diana's youth— she was almost fifteen years Charles's junior—and her submissive air would perfectly suit her son. But Charles continued to waffle. Few knew that the true source of his agony was a woman named Camilla.

When Charles met Camilla Shand in 1971, she was unmarried but involved in an on-and-off relationship with Andrew Parker Bowles, a man who had once dated Charles's sister, Anne.

Charles found her unlike the other girls he had known. Saucy and irreverent, she was undaunted by his status. Her first words to him were instantly captivating. "My great-grandmother was your great-great-grandfather's mistress," she informed him with a wicked smile. "How about it?"[7]

Camilla had the irresistible appeal of a girl who was not beautiful but oozed confidence and a sexual charge. She was extremely bright, a great wit, and she didn't care what anyone thought of her. For the first time in his life, Charles was fully and truly in love.

They began a passionate affair, and Andrew Parker Bowles faded into the background. Had Charles popped the question, Camilla would have accepted instantly. Instead, he wallowed in uncertainty. He could have any woman he wanted. He was only twenty-five. Should he wait?

The obstacle of her lost virginity aside, Camilla would probably have been an ideal partner for Charles, an equal who could have given him what he needed most, boosted his self-esteem, and brought the moody prince a semblance of happiness. However, Camilla had an important critic in Lord Mountbatten, who was eager to press his granddaughter for the job. "Have fun with her by all means," he counseled Charles, "but for God's sake don't get involved. She's far too common. You could never marry her. The country wouldn't have it."[8]

Charles continued to delay, but a woman like Camilla wasn't about to sit still and wait indefinitely. If Charles didn't love her enough to be sure that she was the one, others did. While Charles was at sea on naval duty, Andrew Parker Bowles reentered the picture. He was a great catch and the object of many women's longings. Tall, handsome, charming, and reasonably well off, Andrew was bred to be a good husband and father. Most important, he absolutely adored Camilla. When he proposed, she accepted, and they were married.

Spurned but undaunted, Charles leapt back into the fray, dating one gorgeous girl after another, many of them one-night stands. Although women were drawn to the *idea* of Charles, the reality was less satisfying. His narcissistic personality made him a terrible suitor. He was spoiled and self-involved. He didn't seem to realize that a relationship was a two-way street—that merely being in his presence was not enough to sustain a girl's interest. He didn't try to understand what women needed; he only wanted to see his own image reflected in their adoring eyes.

Over the years he remained close to Camilla. She was the one he trusted, and he often visited her, regaling her with stories of his exploits and seeking her opinion of one woman after another. In 1980 he bought Highgrove, a property near the Parker Bowles estate, Bolehyde Manor. By the time he became involved with Diana, he and Camilla had resumed an intense sexual relationship.[9]

The Queen Mother, whose relationship with Charles was very close, was more aware than any other member of the Royal Family that Charles had been carrying on a long affair with Mrs. Parker Bowles. While he was single, she didn't view the liaison as worrisome. Indeed, she and Charles would spend hours discussing the object of his secret affections. But even the Queen Mother believed it was time for him to find an appropriate wife.[10]

Prince Philip offered some manly advice to his wavering son. Try the marriage, he said, and if after five years it wasn't working out, he could return to the bachelor life.[11]

At last persuaded, Charles proposed to Diana in February 1981. She accepted, breaking into a fit of giggles. A relieved palace promptly announced the engagement, and the wedding was scheduled for July 29. Now that they were engaged, the prince gave Diana permission to call him Charles rather than "sir."

Once the deed was done, Charles reverted to his old ways, as if the proposal alone were enough to hold things in place. He had, in effect, put a down payment on marriage, and there was little more for him to do. He didn't recognize that Diana's view of love came from a regular diet of Barbara Cartland romances. (Incidentally, Cartland was the stepgrandmother of Diana's stepmother, Raine.) To her, if you were in love, engaged to be married, you wanted to be with your loved one every minute. Instead, Charles essentially left her in the hands of his family and palace courtiers, whose job it was to teach her the ways of the Windsors. She found them dull and rigid. Her fiancé's lack of ardor was a constant snag in her romantic bubble.

Diana also detested the outdoorsy, tromping-through-woods activities that Charles relished. Because Charles had been so mired in his own thoughts, he had failed to notice how little he and Diana had in common. Early on, she'd tried to impress him by implying a love of the outdoors. Her healthy countenance seemed to bear that out, but it wasn't so.

In a television interview, when asked if they were in love, Diana blushed prettily and responded, "Of course." Charles mumbled, "Whatever in love means." Seated beside him, her hand linked in his, Diana seemed momentarily stunned by his reply. Later she would admit to having been "devastated."[12]

She was equally horrified by the way she thought she looked in the television camera's unblinking eye—pudgy and matronly. She began a rigorous diet, which soon led to an eating disorder. Diana's battle with bulimia began here.

No one, least of all Charles, noticed that Diana was dropping weight at an alarming rate. Charles was off to Australia, leaving his bride-to-be a virtual prisoner in the palace. In fairness, the queen made a valiant effort to draw Diana in, but the girl was unhappy and impossible. She seemed to hate everything about the royal life. She sobbed, brooded, refused to join the family for meals, and created end-less little dramas. With Charles absent much of the time, Diana wan-dered the corridors, bored and restless. She took to wearing headphones and losing herself in music, shutting out the world around her. As the wedding gained its own unstoppable momentum, even Charles was beginning to see his intended in a new light—and the picture was not flattering. Where was that sympathetic, sweet, adoring girl whose shy smile glowed from the pages of every magazine and newspaper in the world? Diana in the flesh was moody, spoiled, immature, and explosive.

One note that sounded an alarm to Diana's highly sensitive radar was Camilla Parker Bowles. Camilla was always around, and Diana wasn't blind. She'd heard the rumors, and she could see with her own eyes that Charles catered to Camilla in an unnatural way. When she confronted him, Charles brushed her off as ridiculous, but Diana knew that Camilla was a third party in their relationship. One incident proved particularly humiliating for Diana. The *Sunday Mirror* printed a front-page story stating that a blond woman was seen sneaking onto the prince's train one night when the prince was traveling. The woman remained for several hours before sneaking back off. The press picked up the story, suggesting that the blonde could be none other than Di-ana. Diana was horrified, and she vigorously defended her honor and her intact virginity, saying that she was never there. Even the palace defended her. The story went away, but surely Diana realized that if the blonde on the train wasn't her, it must have been Camilla.

Ordinarily, it would have been intolerable, but Diana's ambition was great enough to convince her to stay the course. She was heartbroken, however, when, days before the wedding she opened a package addressed to Charles, thinking it was a wedding gift, and discovered a bracelet engraved with the letters F and G entwined. (The letters stood for Charles and Camilla's pet names for each other, Fred and Gladys.) Furious and distraught, Diana confronted Charles, demanding an explanation. He coolly told her that the bracelet was a farewell gift to Camilla. Diana later said that she gave serious thought to canceling the wedding, but the forces that were already in motion were overwhelming. Her friends and family told her, "Your face is on the tea towels." It's unlikely that Diana ever really considered backing out. More likely, she thought of Charles's interest in Camilla as a challenge that she, with youth and beauty on her side, could overcome.

The day before the wedding, Charles told his bride-to-be that he didn't love her, and, according to some accounts, he spent that night with his mistress.[13] The next day, as the world watched its fairy-tale couple, few observers guessed that Charles was quietly sulking and Diana was already regretting her decision.

The Wedding of the Century took place on July 29, 1981, at St. Paul's Cathedral, with the entire world in attendance. An estimated 750 million viewers watched the dazzling procession on television. For that single day, it really did look as if Charles and Diana were stepping out of the pages of a fairy tale. The queen beamed with happiness, and even Charles gazed on his bride with delight and awe.

The wedding left no rosy afterglow, and the honeymoon was an unmitigated disaster. Charles was distant, and his lack of interest set

Diana off on a bulimic binge.[14] Back in London, as the newlyweds prepared to move into their renovated apartment at Kensington Palace, it was already dawning on some palace insiders that the marriage was a terrible mistake.

The public image was much different. The world fell hard for Diana. She possessed a natural charm and charisma that most people found thrilling. Beautiful, fashionable, dripping empathy from every pore, she walked among them like a storybook princess.

No one could have predicted the extent of Diana's popularity. Di madness took hold of the country and the world and never abated. The shy Di who coyly batted her eyelashes at the prince seemed transformed overnight into a dazzling star, whose warmth and common touch rivaled the Queen Mother's. Initially pleased by her popularity, the royals watched with increasing alarm as Diana was anointed "the People's Princess." Far from walking a step behind her husband, she was front and center, in all her glory.

Diana used her power to make demands on the palace. The Royal Family was accustomed to having others bend to its will, but Diana was a walking temper tantrum, insisting that they bend to hers. She believed she could get away with it, because regardless of what the stodgy royals thought, she was a star on the larger screen of international life. Diana's arrival marked a convergence of tabloid journalism with a charismatic personality who sparkled and glowed in the light of the camera. Those who met her—from commoners to world leaders— literally fawned and stammered in her presence. She could make grown men blush.

Americans worshipped Diana. She was Jackie Kennedy squared, a refreshing splash of glamour. They adopted her as their own, and every magazine editor knew that the simple route to high sales was a picture of Princess Di on the cover.

Charles responded to his wife's popularity first with pride, then with envy, often sulking in the background as she waded into the crowds.

Diana might have expected Charles to be more attentive when she became pregnant. Instead, he grew more distant, fleeing the presence of his overly emotional wife. On one occasion, when Diana was three months pregnant, they were having an argument. As she cried and threatened suicide, Charles walked away without a word. Diana responded by throwing herself down a flight of stairs. The Queen Mother heard the noise and hurried out to find Diana collapsed in a heap on the floor. The eighty-two-year-old woman was so distraught that she nearly fainted, and when moments later the queen arrived on the scene, she went immediately to console her mother, not Diana.[15]

Was Diana truly trying to kill herself? To lose the baby? To get attention? Even she professed not to know. To ascribe a motivation is to suggest it was a rational decision, as opposed to a wildly irrational leap of despair.

For one thing, Diana was convinced that Charles was still having an affair with Camilla. This was probably not technically true at that point, although he continued to see her. Charles and Camilla went hunting together and engaged in other countrified pursuits that Diana abhorred. Diana thought that her husband was flaunting the relationship; it's more likely that he was just boorishly insensitive.

There had been frequent warning signs of Charles's true nature from the outset. At first Diana made excuses for his stiff demeanor, his reluctance to kiss or cuddle or even to take her hand in public. She invented an image of him as a poor boy who only needed an infusion of love to become a gallant Prince Charming. But in truth, Charles despised the courting rituals, and he had little use for cuddling, either before or after marriage. He once said, tellingly, before he met Diana, "I don't know how the idea got about that I am amazingly successful with women—my constant battle is to escape."[16] And escape he did, from the suffocating embrace of his wife.

Charles, who had adjusted to the chilly temperature of his family, found Diana too hot to handle. She raged, she sobbed, she demanded, she accused. His only recourse, as he saw it, was to withdraw so he wouldn't be burned by her fiery temperament.

He didn't hesitate to criticize Diana and put her down. "My husband made me feel so inadequate in every possible way," she said. "Every time I tried to come up for air, he pushed me back down again."[17]

In the beginning, the queen was sympathetic to Diana. She understood that any outsider, especially a young girl, could be expected to have problems adjusting to royal life. But flinging oneself down staircases while pregnant with a future heir to the throne of England went well beyond an adjustment problem. Was Diana mad? When Charles reluctantly told his mother about Diana's bulimia, she was shocked.

Charles had first learned of Diana's eating disorder on their honeymoon. He didn't really understand it, but few did at that time. In the early 1980s, bulimia had not yet made its way into public light. Even when it did, most people had difficulty grasping that the obsessive cycle of binge eating followed by purging involved a complex pathology.

Experts emphasize that bulimia is not about food, per se; rather, food is the vehicle used to express intense inner feelings of inadequacy and neediness. In the bingeing phase, the bulimic loses control, eating large amounts of food in an effort to compensate for feelings of loneliness or depression. The act of purging is essentially an act of regaining control, and it is followed by a brief period of calm before the next episode begins. In severe cases, the cycle of bingeing and purging may repeat itself several times in the course of a day.

Diana's bulimia followed a standard pattern, and it provided her with fleeting moments of comfort. "It always felt better after I'd been sick to get rid of the anger," she said, "and I'd be very passive afterwards. Very quiet."[18]

No one around her grasped the severity of Diana's condition. In a family where problems were addressed with the admonition to buck up, to grin and bear it, or just to bear it, Diana's bulimia was seen as defiance.

Desperate for a solution, the queen called in the pros. A slew of psychiatrists descended on Kensington Palace,[19] but they made little impact.

If Diana felt at a loss to control her environment, she insisted on having control of her children. From the moment of William's birth, June 22, 1982, she rejected the royal model of motherhood, which was distant and overly reliant on surrogates. "There is no substitute for a mother's arms," she said pointedly. Nannies were employed, but they would not take her place. Diana left no confusion about who was mum.

When William was nine months old, she insisted on bringing him along on a tour of Australia and New Zealand—something that would have been unthinkable in earlier times. She was a full-fledged member of the "baby on board" generation, not about to let others raise her children.

By the time Harry came along in 1984, the family seemed to have settled down. Charles clearly loved being a father, Diana was warm and doting, and the two little boys were adorable. But the picture of contentment was just a façade. Diana was desperately unhappy, and she and Charles argued constantly about their very different ideas of parenting.[20] Diana didn't want her children to be warped as her husband had been by his peculiar upbringing. When Charles suggested hiring his beloved old nanny, Mabel Anderson, Diana flatly refused. She insisted the boys be schooled outside the stuffy hothouse of Kensington Palace, beginning with Miss Mynor's Nursery School in Notting Hill, when they were mere tots.

Her parenting philosophy was simple: "I hug them to death," a contrast with her husband's mother, who made do with a handshake. But the hugs could be suffocating, and Diana's mothering could be wildly inconsistent, depending on her moods—hugs one moment, a smack on the bottom the next, followed by more hugs and tears.

Unlike their mother, William and Harry loved Highgrove, and this was Charles's domain. The boys felt relaxed in the country, where they could put on old clothes and race through the fields playing soldier, as boys do. Charles had turned Highgrove into a virtual farming estate, with vegetable and flower gardens, egg-laying hens, rabbits, and dogs. It was a comfort zone for father and sons.

As a father Charles was as engaged as his personality allowed. Clearly his sons were the best thing that had ever happened to him. They grounded him and gave him an appreciation of life outside his abstract interests.

Diana was jealous of the boys' time with their father, and she criticized Charles constantly, reminding him that *she* was the mother and the primary figure in their children's lives. Diana's obsessive mothering was undoubtedly influenced by the absence of a nurturing mother in her own childhood, and by the stiff propriety of the world she now inhabited. As she smothered her sons with kisses, she was really longing to be smothered herself.

From a distance, Anne watched the fanfare surrounding her sister-in-law with some distaste. She thought Diana silly with her closets of designer clothes and constant star turns before the media. For her part, Diana thought Anne was remote—weren't they all?—and stuck-up. She recalled Anne once saying to her, "It's difficult for Charles with a wife like you."[21]

Diana cattily figured that Anne, whose relationship with the press had never been friendly, was jealous of her looks and charm. The women traded small snubs—minor jabs in the scheme of things, but meaningful nonetheless. For example, when Prince Philip suggested Anne as a godmother to Harry, Charles thought it a splendid idea, but Diana refused to consider it. Anne said nothing, but she made a point of having a prior engagement on the day of Harry's christening.

They might have disliked each other, but Diana inadvertently did one big favor for her sister-in-law. In the mid-1980s, when rumors began making the rounds that Mark Phillips had fathered a love child with a young riding student, they were swallowed up by the mountain of press focused on the marriage of Charles and Diana. And when Anne's former lover, Peter Cross, sold a series of articles about his affair with Anne,[22] people barely noticed. In placing herself at center stage, Diana took the heat off Anne.

By 1985, Anne and Mark were married in name only, their union taking years to disassemble. Anne, thirty-five, was far too vibrant to be put out to pasture, but she didn't look for a way to dissolve her marriage until she had good reason. That reason appeared in 1986 in the form of Commander Timothy Laurence, the queen's equerry. Laurence, thirty-one, was tall, dark, and handsome. He was also single. As their attraction grew, they began an affair.

Tim Laurence was more than just a fling. He was the real thing. Although he was a commoner, he and Anne were equals intellectually, and their attachment was passionate. As their relationship matured, Anne began to talk seriously with her mother about arranging a formal separation from Mark. Then, in 1989, four personal letters from Laurence were stolen from Anne's briefcase and given to *The Sun*. The letters were never printed by the paper, but Buckingham Palace was forced to acknowledge that they were from Laurence.

The queen liked Laurence very much, and with her daughter a safe distance from the throne in the line of succession, she granted permission for the Phillipses to separate and, eventually, to divorce. Mark would continue to run the farm at Gatcombe and would receive a settlement of £750,000. Anne would be granted custody of the children, with generous visitation rights for Mark.

14

THE PRINCESS OF WAILS

*If only they had spent as much time
checking out her mental health
as they did her virginity!*

THE QUEEN MOTHER OF PRINCESS DIANA

June 1992 ◆ LONDON

HEN THE SERIALIZATION OF Andrew Morton's book *Diana: Her True Story* first appeared in *The Sunday Times* on June 7, 1992,[1] it was instantly dismissed by the palace as pure gossip and fabrication. But slowly it began to dawn on the Royal Family that Morton's account had a distinctly inside-the-palace flavor. Nobody wanted to believe that Diana was personally involved; surely even *she* would know better than that. But Charles insisted to his mother that he could *hear* her voice in the text.

The revelations were so detailed and so intimate as to cause speculation that Diana had an indirect hand in the book, most likely using friends as surrogates to supply information to Morton. Not until years after her death would the world learn the truth: that Morton's information came directly from the princess in the form of taped conversations with her friend Dr. James Colthurst. It had all been secretly arranged in advance with Morton, who wrote down questions and gave them to Colthurst, who then visited the princess at Kensington Palace, taped her replies, and passed the tape to Morton.[2] It worked like a charm, and the resulting book was a riveting tale of a suffering princess trapped inside the tower of her marriage, scorned by her husband, abused by the palace, and helpless to defend herself against the dreadful power of the throne.

Andrew Morton's book was like the first loose stone of an avalanche. Once it was serialized, other journalists scrambled for a piece of the action. This was the biggest celebrity story of the era, and for once the palace was unable to staunch the flow.

If the portrait Diana painted of the Royal Family made it seem Machiavellian, she revealed herself to be equally tarnished. Diana was adept at playing the victim, but the blame for her behavior could not be pinned solely on "them." Her flaws were deep-rooted, their seeds planted long before she became Charles's bride, although the couple shared one quality—narcissism. Two individuals whose constant chorus was "me, me, me," could have no hope of becoming "we." Diana was greedy for love and attention. Even her very real contributions to important causes—raising awareness and support for AIDS and the victims of land mines—were propelled by her own sense of victimization. "I know what it is to suffer," she said over and over again.[3]

Her personal life was a shambles, composed of equal parts self-destruction and thirst for revenge. Her willingness to stray from her marriage, which her defenders mildly refer to as a "search for love," revealed a mushy inner core.

There is no question that she was doing what she could to knock Charles off his pedestal, the monarchy be damned. Judging by the mountain of tapes and personal accounts that spilled out in the years to come, the princess was indiscriminately telling her side of the story to anyone who would listen.

The palace fought back. After Morton's book, the word was *Diana is unstable. Pass it on.* Diana told friends they were trying to make her out to be crazy. She feared they would have her put away. Her friends cautioned her not to behave as if she *were* crazy—to tone it down a notch. It was advice she seemed incapable of taking.[4]

In hindsight, it is difficult to imagine how things were allowed to go this far. The crisis in Charles and Diana's marriage had been building for at least seven years by the time Morton's book was published, and it was unimaginable that it would resolve itself on its own. By 1985, Diana was desperately seeking male comfort. The first object of her obsession was Sergeant Barry Mannakee, one of her protection officers. She anointed Mannakee her primary confidant, and whether he liked it or not, he was a sitting duck for her outpourings. Mannakee was kind and understanding, and because he took her side, Diana adored him. "I fell deeply in love," she later admitted,[5] although she never acknowledged an outright affair. It hardly mattered, because when Charles caught wind of the relationship, he had Mannakee sacked. Soon afterward, Mannakee was killed in a traffic accident, and in spite of strong evidence to the contrary, Diana told her confidantes he had been murdered by her husband's goons.[6]

Disgusted by his wife's ceaseless wailing, Charles simply gave up trying. As far as he was concerned, there was no longer a marital bed or a marriage to be nurtured. "I feel like I'm in a kind of a cage, pacing up and down in it and longing to be free," Charles wrote.[7] He had completely abandoned his oft-stated philosophy of marriage, so easily adopted in the abstract. "Marriage is something you ought to work at," he'd primly asserted before he was married. "I intend to work at it when I get married." His idea of working at it was a mystery, most of all to his wife. In truth, he couldn't bear to work at it, and he despised conflict. When the going got tough, Charles got going—as far away from Diana as possible. Lost in self-pity, he complained, "Nobody but me can understand how absolutely bloody it is to be the Prince of

Wales."[8] Diana was equally disillusioned, and for the first time the rift between them was apparent in their public appearances.

Enter Major James Hewitt, a cavalry officer with the Life Guard Household Division, which protected the sovereign. Diana met the handsome redhead at a cocktail party in 1986. When she learned that Hewitt was an expert horseman, she confided to him that she'd been terrified of horses since she fell off her pony as a child. Hewitt offered to help her overcome her fear, and she began riding lessons. Hanging around the stables, all doe-eyed and flirtatious, Diana reined Hewitt in. They began an affair that would last five years.

Adding fuel to the fire, Sarah Ferguson strode into the royal midst in 1985. Prince Andrew, whose wild philandering had earned him the nickname "Randy Andy," and who was linked with, among others, the soft-porn actress Koo Stark, was finally settling down. The bride he chose was a bit untamed, and she was certainly not a virgin, but she was from a proper family and Andrew loved her. That seemed enough.

The palace can almost be forgiven for ignoring the signs that Fergie was unsuited for the royal life. For one thing, the couple was genuinely, goofily besotted, and that was a huge relief after Charles and Diana's tortured engagement and marriage. Also, Fergie was intensely likeable; people were drawn to her natural smile and her lack of pretension. She was energetic and outdoorsy. Unlike Diana, she was not obsessed with being the national fashion plate. When a reporter asked what changes she'd be making once she married the prince, Fergie saucily replied, "I'll just be myself."

Andrew and Fergie's wedding, on July 23, 1986, briefly diverted public attention from the gloomy innards of Charles and Diana's marriage. It was a lavish, romantic occasion, and the newlyweds' first public kiss as husband and wife, on the balcony of Buckingham Palace, was so hot it drew blushes.

Despite their different personalities, Diana and Fergie had always enjoyed each other's company, and they became closer after Fergie's marriage. As members of the small society of the royal sisterhood, the two outsiders were frequently together, whispering confidences and giggling like schoolgirls.

Andrew, unfortunately, was like his brother in one respect. Once he had his girl, he felt the marriage would take care of itself. He'd do as he liked, and he expected Fergie to happily go along. His naval duties kept him at sea for long stretches, and when he came home Fergie's plans for hot romance were foiled by his desire to zone out in front of the TV. When he took up golf, she thought she'd lose her mind.

Fergie wasn't like Diana; she didn't look for power in her marriage by whining and wailing. But Andrew was so dense, so insensitive to her needs, so, let's face it, *dull,* that it drove her to despair. It wasn't that Andrew didn't love her. He was madly in love with her. He just wasn't willing to translate his love into the kind of practical action that keeps a marriage afloat. Fergie felt her lifelong sense of fun, her optimistic spirit, draining out of her. By the birth of their first child, Beatrice, in 1988, the marriage was strained.

Into this volatile setting walked Steve Wyatt, whose mother was a Saks heiress and a friend of Princess Margaret. Steve's stepfather, an oilman, was one of the richest men in Texas. Wyatt lived in London, but he was visiting family in Texas when the duchess arrived for a tribute to three hundred years of British opera at the Houston Grand Opera. Fergie and Steve became friends, and then more. She might have been a duchess, but her life was dreary as all get-out compared to Wyatt's Texas-sized jet-set existence.

By 1990, the year Eugenie was born, Fergie wasn't even trying to hide the fact that she was disillusioned with her marriage. Six weeks after delivering Eugenie, she left the infant in her father's care and took off with Beatrice to a luxurious resort on the coast of Morocco. Her host was Steve Wyatt.[9]

Diana and Fergie used each other as sounding boards, and they agreed that their royal marriages were a perverse tangle. The two made a pact: They would walk away together, united.[10] But it never happened. In the end, it was Fergie who became the sacrificial lamb, although some would argue that she did herself in. In January 1992, compromising photos of Sarah and Wyatt taken in the South of France were discovered by cleaners at Wyatt's London apartment. Their publication forced Andrew out of his passive state of denial, and soon after the couple agreed to separate. Fergie might still have salvaged her marriage had she cared to, and had she been discreet. Instead, she became even bolder. On August 20, 1992, the *Daily Mirror* published photos of Fergie cavorting in St.-Tropez with her financial advisor, John Bryan. She was topless. He was sucking her big toe. The marriage was over. By some reports Fergie was deliberately vilified to set an example for Diana.[11] *This is what we can do to you.* The attacks were brutal: Fergie was frivolous, she was fat, she blew through the taxpayers' money with shocking abandon, she was indiscreet, she was a freeloader, she was stupid, she was promiscuous, she was an embarrassment. Fergie could not withstand the onslaught. She literally crawled away from her marriage with her tail tucked between her legs. It would take her many years to regain her self-esteem.

The showdown between Diana and her nemesis, Camilla Parker Bowles, occurred in the late winter of 1989 at a party to celebrate the fortieth birthday of Camilla's sister, Annabel Elliot. Diana watched numbly as her husband catered to his mistress, flinching when they exchanged private smiles and intimate looks. At one point she noticed that the two had disappeared, and she wandered the house looking for them. She found them in the basement, happily chatting with one of the guests. Taking a deep breath, Diana marched up to the group and asked to have a private word with Camilla. Charles and the other guest left the two women alone. "Camilla," Diana said, "I would just like you to know that I know exactly what is going on between you and Charles. I wasn't born yesterday. I'm sorry I'm in the way. I obviously am in the way and it must be hell for both of you, but I do know what's going on. Don't treat me like an idiot." It was a brave speech, but it had absolutely no effect, except to make Charles angry.[12]

The constant theme of their marriage was Camilla. The other woman tortured Diana. She believed that during her husband's long absences from Kensington Palace he was in Camilla's arms. Their arguments were loud and full of spite. According to Diana, Charles once told her, "I refuse to be the only Prince of Wales who never had a mistress."[13] Frankly, it doesn't sound like a statement the prince, who had always denied the affair, would make. It didn't matter. Even if he didn't say it, Diana believed he felt entitled to cheat on her if he so desired. It was the male prerogative.

Behind closed doors, the queen and Prince Philip were steaming with anger. Now that Andrew Morton's book had created a blast of unfavorable publicity, they felt it was time, at long last, to intervene in Charles and Diana's marriage. They suspected that Diana herself was at least indirectly the source for Morton's most shocking revelations, although she denied it, but they were most disappointed in their son. Yes, Diana's behavior was intolerable, but Charles was older, more mature, and accustomed to a lifetime of royal service. He should have tried harder to be a friend to Diana, instead of shutting her out.

It was time to call this wayward couple on the carpet. Charles and Diana were ordered to a meeting at the palace, where the queen and Philip scolded them as if they were naughty children. Charles glowered as Diana cried that she had done everything humanly possible to save her marriage, but Charles refused to meet her even partway. He had made it impossible for her, she insisted, by bringing another woman into their marriage. She told them she knew of the affair with Camilla Parker Bowles, that she had seen the letters Camilla had written, calling Charles "my most precious darling" and saying, "My heart and body ache for you."[14] These were not the words of a platonic friend and shooting buddy.

The queen and Philip took turns sternly admonishing the couple that they must try harder to work out their difficulties—a marriage took time and work, but if a couple truly cared for each other, they could make these adjustments. They had good reason to believe it. In the fortieth year of their marriage, the queen and Philip had come through their own troubles and were bound by tremendous love and respect. Philip could still make the queen blush with a compliment, and he was extremely protective of her. Speaking from the experience of someone who believed in marital redemption, the queen urged Charles and Diana to go back and give it another try.

After the meeting, Philip began to write Diana a series of letters. His intention was to be a fatherly advisor, but Diana found the letters disturbing. They seemed to imply that she was the problem, not Charles, and she deeply resented that. "Can you honestly look into your heart," Philip wrote, "and say that Charles' relationship with Camilla had nothing to do with your behavior toward him in your marriage?"[15] Diana read a not-so-subtle threat into his words: *Don't mess with the family. We know about you.*

What was wrong with the younger generation? It was a question being raised in millions of households, but most families struggled privately with their errant offspring. The queen didn't have that luxury. It distressed her that marriage vows, taken with such fervor and hope, could simply be tossed aside for reasons of incompatibility, that extramarital affairs would be broadcast to the world without a hint of discretion. Both the queen and the Queen Mother had wedded their lives to a code of faithfulness, not just to the monarchy but to their marriages as well. If a marital vow could so easily be broken, who was to say that an oath to the throne of England would not also be treated casually?

The relationship between the queen and Diana was never bitter; in fact, the queen always made an effort to support Diana and to be kind to her—an exhausting task by any measure. Countless times Diana had pounded on her office door, needing to talk.[16] The queen always listened quietly as Diana unloaded a litany of complaints. Inevitably she'd turn on the spigot, sobbing and begging the queen to do something about her son. The queen expressed her sympathy and tried to advise Diana, but she let her know there wasn't much she could do about Charles. "He's impossible," she agreed with a helpless shrug.[17]

The simple fact was that the two women just didn't understand each other. Diana thought the queen was trapped in her gilded cage— almost a machine in her lack of spontaneity. The queen thought Diana was a puddle of emotion, unwilling to cope with the simplest realities of royal life. If a personality could be brewed up in a laboratory, composed of equal parts the queen and Diana, the result would be the ideal balance.

The other Windsor women didn't share the queen's sympathy for Diana. The Queen Mother was firmly in Charles's camp and spoke with him every day. She was his primary advisor in matters relating to Diana, and her advice was rarely critical of her beloved grandson. Diana feared and abhorred the Queen Mother for what she suspected was her complicity in Charles's affair with Camilla.[18] The Queen Mother froze Diana out as only she could do, leaving the princess to speculate that this must have been the way Wallis Simpson felt.

Anne made an effort to include Diana and her children in gatherings at Gatcombe, but Diana despised the muddied country style of Anne's home. When they visited, Diana's boys were usually too nicely dressed for romping. They, however, loved Gatcombe, and especially worshipped their older cousin Peter, who graciously took them under his wing.

Diana's closest relationship was with Princess Margaret, her neighbor at Kensington Palace. Margaret knew better than anyone how difficult it was for a romantic young woman to find the balance between happiness and duty in royal life, and she was initially sympathetic to Diana's difficulties. But Diana never had a true ally in Margaret, whose first loyalty, as always, was to her sister. After the publication of Andrew Morton's book, Margaret grew noticeably cooler, and she eventually stopped speaking to Diana altogether.

Someone at the palace decided that Diana needed a comeuppance. Unbeknownst to the princess, a cellular-telephone conversation she'd had three years earlier with a sports-car dealer named James Gilbey had been picked up by the security detail. In August 1992 a tape and transcript of the conversation found its way to the media and became public. On the tape, Gilbey was heard professing his love for Diana and calling her "Squidgy," and the ensuing scandal was dubbed "Squidgygate."

Diana was humiliated. She insisted that Gilbey had just been a good friend. There had been no affair. Nothing improper. Lucky for her the media withheld an extremely graphic portion of the tape, in which Gilbey and the princess were obviously engaging in steamy phone sex.[19]

15

THE QUEEN'S
HORRIBLE YEAR

*It is not a year I shall look back on
with undiluted pleasure.*

QUEEN ELIZABETH, SPEAKING ON
THE FORTIETH ANNIVERSARY OF HER ASCENSION

November 20, 1992 ✦ LONDON

*I*T WAS THE QUEEN AND Philip's forty-fifth
wedding anniversary, but there was no celebration
to speak of. Philip was away in Argentina, so the queen
followed her regular schedule of working, feeding the corgis,
and watching television before retiring.

While she slept, catastrophe struck. Thirty miles away at Windsor
Castle, which was undergoing restoration, a flame from a neglected
restorer's lamp in St. George's Hall caught the edge of a curtain, then
streaked rapidly along walls and corridors to Brunswick Tower and the
surrounding apartments. As smoke and flame billowed into the night
sky, Prince Andrew, who was staying at the castle, awoke and quickly

organized a fire brigade. Thanks to his swift action, nearly all of the priceless artifacts were rescued, but in the sopping aftermath a large portion of the castle that had stood for centuries was a charred ruin. Finally, Andrew picked up the phone and called his mother.

In the early light of morning, the queen appeared, a small figure in a head scarf, her mouth set in a tight line to hold emotions in check. She looked frail and sad as she picked among the sooty remains of the place that held so much personal and national history. Her shoulders slumped with the weight of one more burden in what had been a ghastly year. Sir Edward Ford, an old courtier, said to her later that day, "You deserve *annus miribilis,* but get instead *annus horribilis.*"[1]

The queen agreed that 1992 had, indeed, been horrible. Four days later, looking unusually vulnerable, she made a speech at a Guildhall luncheon to mark her fortieth year on the throne, and she picked up on the theme. "It is not a year I shall look back on with undiluted plea- sure," she said, sounding a little shaky. "It has turned out to be an *an- nus horribilis.*"

As she spoke, it almost seemed as if she were trying to work things out in her own mind. "I am quite sure that most people try to do their jobs as best they can," she told the hushed gathering, "even if the re- sult is not always entirely successful." She added, brows knit, "There can be no doubt that criticism is good for people and institutions that are part of public life. . . . But we are all part of the same fabric of our national society and that scrutiny . . . can be just as effective if it is made with a touch of gentleness, good humor and understanding."[2]

It was as close as she had ever come to begging for a letup in the re- lentlessly negative coverage of her family. A woman so intensely pri- vate that she had never given a personal media interview, the queen was suffering from the steady onslaught of bad press. In a lifetime spent trying to do the right thing, she felt very alone and helpless to control the scandalous behavior of the younger generation.

It had all come to a bitter fruition in this, her fortieth year on the throne: the Andrew Morton book, the Squidgy tapes, Andrew and Fergie's separation, Anne's divorce, and the fire. The weeks ahead promised more discomfort. On December 9 the palace would announce formally that Charles and Diana were separating. On December 12 Anne would be married to Tim Laurence in the Church of Scotland, which allowed remarriage for the divorced.

In the wake of the fire at Windsor Castle, the public was willing to spare the queen a bit of sympathy. She *had* had a bad year. The fire was an awful blow. Poor lady. But the sympathy almost instantly turned to outrage when the palace handed the taxpayers a bill for the restoration of the castle, estimated at sixty million pounds.

The initial reaction was shock. Wait a minute, wasn't Windsor Castle *insured*? "Why should we pay for a palace that we're not allowed to visit, that we pay to maintain?" asked journalist Anthony Holden. "She [the queen] didn't take out fire insurance? If my house burns down and I haven't taken out fire insurance is the Queen going to pay for it? No way."[3]

The outcry over the bill for restoration of Windsor Castle brought the whole royal money mess back into the spotlight. The Windsors were finally shamed into agreeing to pay taxes on their private estates, and after much discussion it was announced that the renovation money would not come out of the taxpayers' pockets but would be raised in other ways.

The money question just wouldn't die, however. The image of the Royal Family living off the fat of the land was too firmly entrenched, especially as an indulged younger generation flaunted its wealth on the party circuit. A 1993 Gallup Poll found that 80 percent of respondents agreed that "too many members of the family lead an idle, jet-set kind of existence."

The Civil List increases that were Margaret Thatcher's parting gift to the queen underscored how much money was flowing from the public pot into the coffers of family members. Everyone got big raises in January 1991, including the Queen Mother (from £334,400 to £643,000); Prince Philip (from £186,500 to £359,000), and Princess Margaret (from £107,100 to £213,000).

True to form, Prince Philip highlighted the family's insensitivity with another gaffe. During a 1993 visit to grieving residents of Lockerbie, Scotland, after a plane exploded and crashed into the town, killing everyone on board and several people on the ground, he crassly compared the tragedy to the fire at Windsor Castle, remarking, "People usually say that after a fire it's the water damage that's the worst. We're *still* trying to dry out Windsor Castle."

When the announcement came, very few people greeted it with shock. The signs had been there for a long time. The statement, dated December 9, 1992, read:

> It is announced from Buckingham Palace that, with regret, the Prince and Princess of Wales have decided to separate. The Royal Highnesses have no plans to divorce and their constitutional positions are unaffected.[4]

It went on to say how awfully sad the queen and Prince Philip were, but what can you do, these things happen. However, it was the line about unchanged constitutional positions that raised eyebrows. Exactly how was *that* going to work? If Charles became king, did anyone truly believe that Diana would be crowned Queen Consort? The unavoidable image of the two staring daggers at each other from vying thrones sent a shudder through the population.

The Archbishop of Canterbury, in an attempt to clear up the confusion, stated that a separation should have no real effect on the couple's status, *as long as there were no extramarital affairs*.[5] It wasn't easy to stuff *that* cat back into the bag. In fact, no sooner had the archbishop spoken than the dirty linen hit the fan with the airing of a taped conversation between Charles and Camilla picked up by a ham-radio operator and sold to the media. Not only was it sexually explicit, it was also crass and distastefully juvenile. Of the six minutes, one passage drew the most reaction:

CAMILLA: *Mmmm . . . I need you all the week, all the time.*

CHARLES: *Oh God. I'll just have to live inside your trousers or something. It would be much easier!*

CAMILLA: (Laughs) *What are you going to turn into? A pair of knickers?* (Both laugh)

CHARLES: *Or, God forbid, a Tampax, just my luck!* (Laughs)

CAMILLA: *You are a complete idiot.* (Laughs) *Oh, what a wonderful idea!*

CHARLES: *My luck to be chucked down the lavatory and go on forever swirling round on top, never going down!*

Another passage exposed Charles's enormous ego. At one point, when Camilla demurred that she'd never achieved anything, Charles replied, "Your greatest achievement is to love me."[6]

When the queen's private secretary informed her about the tape, she shook her head in despair. "Just when we thought things couldn't get any worse," she said with a long sigh. Diana, however, felt vindicated. She wanted to scream so the whole world could hear: *You see . . . you see! This is what I've had to deal with!*

With the separation, Charles hired his own nanny to watch the children when they were in his care. Alexandra (Tiggy) Legge-Bourke, the daughter of Princess Anne's close friend and lady-in-waiting, was sweet-tempered, high-spirited, loving, and lots of fun. The boys took to her immediately. Tiggy's worshipful attitude toward Charles, reported in the media, drove Diana crazy, but worse was Tiggy's remark that she felt like a mother to William and Harry.

Diana was furious and refused to speak to Tiggy when she called about the boys. She became suspicious that Tiggy was having an affair with Charles (she wasn't). After learning that Tiggy had been hospitalized briefly for gynecological problems, Diana approached her at a party and said how sorry she was to hear she'd lost her baby. The implication was that Tiggy had had an abortion. Tiggy was outraged and threatened to sue, but she dropped the idea.[7]

That year William asked Tiggy to come to Eton's Founder's Day in place of his mother. He wanted to avoid the embarrassment of the press hounds who turned every Diana sighting into a free-for-all. When he told Diana, however, she promptly burst into tears. In her mind it was a betrayal. She couldn't see it objectively as the action of a boy who was desperate to stay out of the limelight. Boys of William's age would just as soon not have their mothers around at all. William's need to blend into the woodwork was the most natural thing in the world.

Diana might have adored her sons, but her fierce neediness placed a heavy burden on them. In particular, she treated William like a friend and sounding board, sharing far too many intimate details of her struggles.

The year of her separation was exhausting. Diana was sick of being poked, prodded, and watched by hordes of reporters. At the end of 1993, she announced that she was taking a break from public life. Her "retirement" lasted less than six months. Diana fed off the media; she couldn't exist without its chattering chorus.

In June 1994 Charles launched a counteroffensive to Diana's media monopoly, agreeing to be interviewed on British TV. He chose a sympathetic journalist, Jonathan Dimbleby, who was in the process of writing a flattering book about Charles. In the interview Dimbleby cast the prince as long-suffering but only human. He'd lob a softball—"Did you try to be faithful?"—and Charles, looking oh so serious and full of regret, replied that he had, until it became clear that the marriage had "irretrievably broken down." Not his doing, of course. It was a shamefully self-serving production, but it earned Charles more support than ridicule.

In November Dimbleby followed up with *The Prince of Wales: A*

Biography, a 620-page ode to the prince, written with his full cooperation. In careful, lovingly written prose, Charles was presented as a
deep thinker, an activist, a responsible leader, and a wonderful father.
The text skirted past salacious details and absolved the hardworking,
sensitive, and dedicated prince of all blame for the crisis in his marriage. Instead, the blame was directed at the architects of his twisted
childhood—his cold mother and bullying father.[8]

While it might be true that the queen and Prince Philip were not
up for any awards as Parents of the Year when Charles was a child, the
prince was now forty-six years old and long past the age when it was
appropriate to blame his parents for anything. Charles had been a full-
fledged, sentient adult for twenty-five years at this point, and he'd had
every opportunity to set his life on a different course. Yet he had not,
and now he was refusing all responsibility by casting the blame in his
parents' direction. He seemed totally unaware of the pain and embarrassment his marital and extramarital activities had caused his mother.
His self-satisfied excuse that his mum didn't hug him enough as a
child was cowardly and hurtful.

Charles and Diana moved in separate, well-armed camps, each
striving to deliver a knockout blow to the other side. They had coteries
of friends and supporters working behind the scenes. But too often
friends were hard-pressed to get the positive view across because the
gutter reality was so much more interesting. In 1994 James Hewitt
published a book detailing his five-year affair with the princess, a betrayal she found devastating.[9] Then in August a peculiar story about
the princess hit the airwaves. It seemed that a prominent art dealer
named Oliver Hoare had befriended Diana, and the two met often.
Hoare claimed he was just lending support; others suggested they
were having an affair. Whatever the truth, Hoare broke off the relationship in an effort to save his flagging marriage. There followed an
eighteen-month barrage of hundreds of hang-up calls to Hoare's home
phone. Terrified, Hoare and his wife went to the police, and the calls
were easily traced to Princess Diana's cell phone and her personal line

at Kensington Palace.[10] There was no way to wiggle around the facts of the matter. Diana was responsible for the calls.

Diana ducked the bad publicity by immersing herself in charity work. In spite of the revelations about her affairs and her peculiar behavior, she was still winning the publicity war. On November 20, 1995 (the forty-eighth wedding anniversary of the queen and Prince Philip), Diana appeared on the BBC program *Panorama*.[11] The interview with journalist Martin Bashir had been taped in secret without the knowledge of anyone at the palace or even many close to the princess. It was shown worldwide.

Diana sat across from Bashir, dressed in black, her eyes heavily made up in the tragic countenance of a woman who spends her days crying. She answered every question he put to her, beginning with one about her alleged affair with James Hewitt.

"Did your relationship go beyond a close friendship?" Bashir asked.

"Yes, it did, yes," Diana answered.

"Were you unfaithful?"

"Yes, I adored him," Diana said. "Yes, I was in love with him. But I was very let down [when he published his book]. It was very distressing for me that a friend of mine, who I had trusted, made money out of me. I really minded about that. And he'd rung me up ten days before it arrived in the bookshops to tell me that there was nothing to worry about, and I believed him, stupidly. And then when it did arrive, the first thing I did was rush down to talk to my children. And William produced a box of chocolates and said, 'Mummy, I think you've been hurt. These are to make you smile again.'"

Diana told Bashir that the Royal Family had always resented her because she attracted so much attention, and their resentment had turned to fear. "They see me as a threat of some kind," she said, with a long-suffering sigh. "I think every strong woman in history has had to walk down a similar path, and I think it's the strength that causes the confusion and the fear. Why is she strong? Where does she get it from? Where is she taking it? Where is she going to use it? Why do the public still support her?"

Diana expertly brushed aside her own scandals as palace attempts to discredit her. She saved her most ruthless verdict for Charles, wondering aloud if he was really fit to be king, and suggesting he wasn't up to the job.

Bashir asked the princess why she was giving this interview. Diana drew herself up and gazed directly into his eyes, speaking with the sincerity of a political pro in an election speech. "Because we will have been separated three years this December, and the perception that has been given of me for the last three years has been very confusing, turbulent, and in some areas I'm sure many, many people doubt me. And I want to reassure all those people who have loved me and supported me throughout the last fifteen years that I'd never let them down."

Diana was triumphant in the days following the interview. Public support had never been so high. She took tremendous comfort in the knowledge that the people were on her side. She had been noble and righteous. She had put the palace on notice. They could not afford to treat her with disrespect. The public wouldn't have it.

Her self-delusion was complete in that moment. For while the public might have chosen Diana in a popularity contest, graver matters regarding the future of the monarchy were beyond public control. It was the queen's duty to protect the throne, and she regarded Diana's interview as a fatal strike. By impugning Charles and questioning his fitness to be king, Diana was attempting to undermine her husband, saying in effect, *I don't care about being queen. I will be the mother of the king.*

The sham had gone on long enough. On December 18, handwritten letters were delivered to Charles and Diana from the queen, stating plainly that they must begin divorce proceedings without delay.[12]

Diana was stunned. This was not the result she had expected. Indeed, even after all that had transpired, she was still holding out hope that her marriage could be salvaged. In her letter, the queen wrote that she had already set the wheels in motion for a divorce by discussing the matter with the prime minister, the Archbishop of Canterbury, and others. Diana was deeply offended. "It's *my* marriage!" she cried. "It's nobody else's business."[13] But even she had to know that was not true. Her marriage did not belong to her. Her sons did not even belong to her. Under law the queen had full dominion over Diana's children. She could take them away if she wished.

Days earlier Diana had felt she held all the cards. Now she saw she held none. She began to sob.

16

PALACE COUP

I'd like to be queen of people's hearts,
in people's hearts, but I don't see
myself being queen of this country.

PRINCESS DIANA IN AN INTERVIEW
WITH MARTIN BASHIR, NOVEMBER 20, 1995

March 1996 ◆ BUCKINGHAM PALACE

THEY WERE THREE little letters that meant
so much, and the last time the Queen Mother had
had a heated debate about them was almost sixty
years earlier to the day. Wallis Simpson had been desper-
ate for the title HRH, and Bertie might have given it to her, too, if only
to stop the incessant phone calls from his brother. The Queen Mother
had stood firm then and she was standing firm now. Princess Diana
was not going to walk away from her marriage as Her Royal Highness.

The title had important implications, both real and symbolic. The
difference between being Her Royal Highness Princess Diana and Diana, Princess of Wales, was the difference between being royal and not

being royal. Without the title Diana would have to give up her palace associations, including her patronage of more than one hundred charities. She would have no standing in the Royal Family. She would curtsy to her own sons. The tagline "Princess of Wales" would not signify that she was *the* Princess of Wales; indeed, if Charles ever remarried, his second wife could be made Princess of Wales. It was confusing only to those outside the rarified world where titles had meaning in the first place. Insiders knew that being stripped of HRH was as good as banishment.

When divorce negotiations had first begun following the queen's letter, Diana, in an emotional moment, had recklessly said she cared nothing about the title and would gladly give it up. The queen took her at her word, and when the two met privately in February, the queen said she thought that an appropriate title was Diana, Princess of Wales. By then Diana had spoken to her advisors, and they'd said she was nuts to give up HRH. Now she pleaded with the queen. "I have worked hard for sixteen years, and do not want to see my life taken away from me," she said. "I want to protect my position in public life."[1]

The queen did not immediately reply. It would do no good to remind Diana that it was her very public antagonism toward the Royal Family that had brought her to this point. She could not now expect to continue as a representative of the palace she disdained. Finally, the queen put off the decision, saying it was a matter she would discuss with her son.

Diana, however, took it as a no and leaked to the press that the queen was stripping her of her title. She expected the sympathy ploy to be effective, but it backfired. The palace issued an extremely chilly correction: It was Diana's choice, not the queen's.[2] This was technically true.

The Queen Mother was perfectly clear where she stood on the question: Diana did not deserve a royal title. The queen was less sure. Foremost in her mind was Diana's inviolable status as the mother of the heir. If William (or, for that matter, Harry) ascended the throne, should not his mother be royal? In the end, she deferred to her mother, and Diana was told that after the divorce she would be Lady Diana, Princess of Wales.

Typically, Diana responded to the news with a fresh bout of sobbing. William tried to comfort his mother, promising, "Don't worry,
Mummy, I will give it back to you one day when I am King."[3]

Negotiations over money took months, with Diana's lawyers initially
suggesting a payout of £62 million. They eventually settled for a £17
million lump sum and the apartments at Kensington Palace, which
would assure Diana a life of luxury, no matter where her future led.

The divorce became official on August 28, 1996. The stark legal
language of a divorce decree is always sad, reminding the parties of
necessity that they were once full of hope. In the Waleses' case, it was
a grave constitutional moment as well. Two generations of the Royal
Family had been virtually tied up in knots over the question of divorce—first over the abdication of Edward VIII when he planned to
marry a divorced woman, then over Princess Margaret's thwarted desire to marry a divorced man. Now the heir apparent was divorced,
and it didn't seem the least bit *apparent* that he could inherit the
throne and the standing as the head of the Church of England and
Defender of the Faith.

And what of Camilla? She was now divorced as well, her marriage
having been permanently smashed by "Camillagate." These questions
had the public buzzing and the palace brooding, but for the time being
it was decided that the best action was no action. Charles and Camilla
continued their relationship but took pains to keep a very low profile.

Following her divorce, Diana began a furious program to reinvent
herself, a process made difficult by the vying compulsions that
pulled her in opposite directions. The first was to be strong, independent, self-assured, and complete in herself. She longed to embody the
serenity of women like Mother Teresa who needed no reassurance to
be secure in their paths. She envisioned herself as a warrior princess,
selfless and good, an advocate for the poor and helpless.

But the opposite compulsion was stronger, its pull darker and more
tenacious. Diana was a woman who needed the approval of a man to

make her feel worthwhile. She was easily dazzled by lavish displays of affection.

The first beau of her postdivorce period, a prominent heart surgeon named Dr. Hasnet Khan, loved his work more than he loved her, and the relationship ended. The second was Dodi Fayed, who wooed her with a zeal that took her breath away.

Dodi was the forty-one-year-old son of Mohamed Al Fayed, the Egyptian-born owner of Harrods Department Store. Fayed was worldly and charming, and he showered Diana with gifts. She felt safe and happy in his controlling arms; he touched a deep need in her. Diana had once joked to her friend Ingrid Seward, "I need someone like Aristotle Onassis."[4] Dodi was her Onassis.

As pictures of Diana and Dodi flooded the newspapers during the summer of 1997, the queen expressed some concern about the relationship. Diana had let it be known that, at summer's end, she would make an important announcement.[5] What was she up to? Fear of an engagement between the mother of a future king and an Arab with family ties to a violent underworld was enough to ruin the queen's summer break at Balmoral. Following numerous conversations with the Queen Mother and Margaret, in which she sought advice on how to handle the situation, the queen summoned her daughter, Anne, to her summer home. She believed the family had to be prepared for the worst.

The Royal Family was in the final stretch of its holiday at Balmoral, enjoying the waning days of summer. On August 31, 1997, at 2:00 A.M., Prince Charles was roused from his bed with the news that Diana had been in an automobile accident in Paris. He was initially told that her companion, Dodi Fayed, was seriously injured, but that Diana was believed to be fine. Even so, Charles climbed out of bed and asked that the queen be informed. He instructed that his sons be left sleeping.

A little over an hour later, the phone rang with the news that Diana had been pronounced dead at the Pitie-Salpetriere hospital at 4:00

A.M. Paris time (3:00 A.M. in London). It had been almost a year to the day since the divorce.

At Balmoral, as the horrible reality sank in, the family began an unusually emotional wake. Charles, in particular, was in shock, pacing the room, tearful and trembling. As he struggled to comprehend the news, he could not bear the idea of telling his sons, still slumbering blissfully in their quarters. Where would he find the strength for such an odious task?

The queen, also shaken, gently suggested they let the boys sleep until they had all the information. Charles nodded slowly, his thoughts on Diana, whose broken body was lying in a distant hospital morgue. He announced that he would fly to Paris to bring her body home. The remaining night hours passed with phone calls to Diana's family and friends and discussions of the arrangements. Diana's sisters, Lady Sarah McCorquodale and Lady Jane Fellowes, shocked by the news, demanded to accompany Charles to Paris.

Finally, as the sky turned light, Charles sighed deeply and headed toward his sons' rooms. It was time to tell them that their mother was dead.

The queen had never led with her heart, but she felt Diana's death deeply. It was impossible to avoid thoughts of what might have been had her son been a different man and Diana a different woman. But these, she knew, were foolish thoughts. Her concern now must be for her grandchildren. Her inclination, supported by Philip and the Queen Mother, was to hold a small family funeral. She wanted to do the right thing, but as Diana was no longer royal, it was a sensitive matter. The queen didn't want to go overboard. Unfortunately, overboard was what the public wanted.

It quickly became apparent that, once again, the Royal Family had underestimated Diana's place in the hearts of the people. As the dawn broke in London with the news of her death, crowds began to gather outside Buckingham Palace. Soon the outcry grew loud: Where was the queen? Why wasn't the flag at half-mast over Buckingham Palace? The London papers took up the cry: "Has the House of Windsor a heart?" asked the *Daily Mail*. *The Sun's* headline demanded, WHERE IS OUR QUEEN? WHERE IS HER FLAG?

In Scotland, the queen was initially puzzled. The Royal Standard—the Windsor family flag—was never lowered to half-mast, even for the death of the sovereign.[6] And what was the queen expected to do? To her credit, she realized rather quickly—though not quickly enough for the critics—that the people expected her to lead the nation in mourning. This was no time for protocol. She hurriedly arranged to return to London, where she mingled with the crowds outside the palace and lowered the Royal Standard for a brief time. That evening, dressed in black, the queen gave a television address to the nation.

"What I have to say to you now, as your queen and as a grandmother, I say from the heart," she said. She went on to pay tribute to Diana as "an exceptional and gifted human being," adding, "I admired and respected her—for her energy and commitment to others and especially for her devotion to her boys."

The rancor directed at the queen was not earned. She alone had always tried to treat Diana fairly and with respect. She alone had risen above the petty bickering and resentment. Despite what anyone thought, she'd had affection for the girl who had so foolishly wed her impossible son. Now, trying desperately to stay in tune with the public mood, she was willing to put on a massive funeral for the mother of her grandchildren.

As the media circus gathered momentum in London and the world press turned its spotlight on Diana, thousands of miles away a tiny woman whose life was sanctified by service to the poor slipped away, barely noticed. Mother Teresa was eighty-seven.[7]

On the morning of September 6, more than a million people lined the streets of London, and some two and a half billion more watched on television, as Diana's coffin was borne on a gun carriage for the four-mile journey from Kensington Palace to Westminster Abbey. The coffin was draped with the Royal Standard—and covered with white lilies and a floral arrangement. On top of the coffin was a card addressed to

"Mummy" from Harry. Princes William and Harry walked the last mile behind their mother's coffin, flanked by Diana's brother, Earl Spencer, Prince Charles, and Prince Philip.

The service was broadcast over a public-address system linked throughout the city. Tens of thousands of people gathered in Hyde Park to watch the service on huge television screens as Elton John played and sang a tribute rendition of his popular song "Candle in the Wind," with lyrics dedicated to Diana. It had originally been written— irony of ironies—about Marilyn Monroe.

Charles Spencer, the brother who had never been particularly close to Diana, the very one who had refused to give her shelter at his estate after her divorce when she was desperate to escape London,[8] gave the eulogy. Standing at the lectern, in a perfect simulation of a lone defender, Spencer's false indignation struck the sole sour note of the day. Casting his sister as a victim of the Royal Family, Spencer proclaimed in a ringing voice, "She would want us today to pledge ourselves to protecting her beloved boys, William and Harry, from a similar fate and I do this here. Diana, on your behalf we will not allow them to suffer the anguish that used regularly to drive you to tearful despair."

Of all the gall!

William and Harry stared ahead, expressionless, as did the rest of their family. They were all well practiced in masking their disdain. Still, it was an inescapable reality that in death Diana held the Royal Family and the world in her hands, with a power she was never able to achieve in life. She had orchestrated the perfect palace coup.

The conspiracy theories about Diana's death would not end; they only seemed to gain momentum with the passage of years. Although the French investigation concluded that the driver, Henri Paul, was three times over the drunk-driving limit and breaking the speed limit—most likely to escape paparazzi chasing them—many people believed the explanation was simply too pat and refused to credit the official report.

It might have been expected. When you elevate an individual to such mythic status as the world elevated Diana, it becomes impossible to accept that she was felled by ordinary events—because people were drinking too much or driving too fast, because careless actions beget fatal consequences, because the paparazzi are a bloodthirsty throng, because accidents do happen.

For those who idolized Diana, it was simply intolerable that her light could be so casually extinguished. It was much more plausible and, ultimately, more satisfying to spin a web of murderous intrigue. The first Diana conspiracy site popped up on the Internet in Australia only hours after her death was announced. "The whole thing seems too pat and too convenient," it said, putting blame for the crash on Western governments, arms manufacturers, and the Royal Family. Eventually, there would be around forty thousand sites devoted to conspiracy theories. Some of these theorized that, like Elvis and JFK, Diana was actually alive and in hiding—immortal, frozen in time. The World Wide Web was awash with crackpots. However, other conspiracy theories thrived because they contained fragments of truth. The most tenacious of these involved a Royal Family and/or Secret Service plot to prevent Diana's marriage to Dodi Fayed—or worse still, to prevent her from bearing his child, who would then become a stepbrother to the future King of England.

Chief among the conspiracy theorists were members of Dodi's family, who revealed that Dodi had given Diana a $205,000 diamond ring the night they died, and that Diana had recently given Dodi her late father's cuff links and gold cigar clipper.[9] Rumors of conspiracy had special traction in Cairo, where Western and "Jewish" plots were a stock in trade. In the daily *Al-Ahram*, Anis Mansour, a former advisor to Anwar Sadat, said Diana was "killed by British Intelligence to save the monarchy."

Mohamed Al Fayed told newspapers that Diana had been threatened by Prince Philip weeks before the crash. Fayed said: "Diana told me personally during a holiday in the South of France, 'If anything happens to me, make sure those people are exposed. The person who is spearheading these threats is Prince Philip.'"[10]

Fayed's accusation picked up steam after Diana's butler, Paul Burrell, publicized a letter in which Diana predicted her own death in an arranged "car accident." Burrell also revealed that Diana kept a packet of letters from Prince Philip in a red mahogany box, and said that the letters were more than harsh.[11]

In January 2001, Burrell found himself in the bull's-eye of the intrigue when a team from Scotland Yard descended on his home one daybreak. The stunned former butler watched in horror as they collected some 310 items that had been the personal property of Princess Diana. As Burrell protested that some of the items were gifts and others had been placed in his care for safekeeping, he was arrested for theft. Among the items were the Spencer-family photo album, a white envelope marked "Oprah Winfrey," containing a strip of negatives, a rug in a Versace carrier bag, nineteen CDs signed by Diana, a computer disc marked "Princess Private," several designer handbags, several pairs of shoes, an orange-and-black marble Cartier clock, and a framed picture of William with the model Naomi Campbell.

Burrell consistently claimed he had no intention of using the items for his own personal profit—he was merely keeping them in trust for William and Harry. His version was summarily dismissed, even when he informed the police that he had told the queen that he'd kept some items belonging to Diana for safekeeping. Instead, he was prosecuted and scheduled for trial. He was also tried in the media, where he was ridiculed as the lowest of the low—a man who would take advantage of his close relationship with Diana to steal from her.

The mournful toll of Great Tom, the state bell at St. Paul's Cathedral, cut through the early-morning sounds of London on February 9, 2002. On the street, people spontaneously glanced skyward as if to see the clouds part, for they knew Great Tom had but one purpose—to signal the death of a member of the Royal Family. Their first thoughts might have turned to the Queen Mother, now a century plus one year, but the bell pealed not for mother but for daughter. Margaret Rose was dead at age seventy-one.

The queen had been woken shortly after 6:30 A.M. with the news. She struggled out of bed, composing herself for the call to her mother, who was staying at Sandringham House in Norfolk, but her voice cracked when she spoke the words, "Mummy, Margaret is dead."

The Queen Mother was inconsolable. Frail and battling the flu, she collapsed into her grief and spent the remainder of the day crying in her room. At Buckingham Palace, Lilibet was equally inconsolable. She, too, took to her room, so choked with anguish that she was unable to speak for an entire day.

Margaret's death could not have come as a great shock to her mother and sister. She had been desperately ill for years, and had suffered three strokes since 1998. But the finality of death, the way it created a freeze-frame around Margaret's damaged soul, meant that the Queen Mother and the queen would never find redemption from their guilt. They would not receive absolution for their complicity in keeping the terrible secret they had shared and held close since 1955.

It would all come out in the years after Margaret's death, when state papers released under the fifty-year rule revealed that Margaret might have married Peter Townsend, after all. In 1955, shortly before Margaret decided that she had no choice but to bow to the command of duty and give up the love of her life, the palace, in full consultation with the queen and Queen Mother, had worked out a deal with the government that would have allowed her to marry. The deal called for Margaret to renounce her rights to succession, at which time prime minister, Anthony Eden, would have sent the following letter to Commonwealth ministers:

> United Kingdom ministers understand that it is Princess Margaret's wish that, despite her renunciation of her right to the succession, she should continue to live in the UK and to carry out her duties as a member of the royal family.

> *The UK government are, however, advised that neither her pro-*
> *posed marriage nor her renunciation of her rights to the succession*
> *need in themselves affect either her style and title as Her Royal*
> *Highness Princess Margaret or the provision made for her under*
> *the civil list. The Civil List Act 1952 provided that she should re-*
> *ceive, on her marriage, a further sum of £9,000 a year in addition*
> *to the £6,000 a year which she has already.*

It never happened because the queen and the Queen Mother never told Margaret it *could* happen. She was led to believe right up until the end that marriage to Peter Townsend would mean the loss of all royal rights and privileges.[12] So, while they undoubtedly believed it was the right thing to do at the time, there could be no question that her mother and sister betrayed Margaret. The consequences of their betrayal papered the walls of Margaret's life. As they watched Margaret in her last years being overwhelmed by her demons, they must have been sickened by their knowledge. Although she had given up her sixty-a-day cigarette habit after a serious lung infection several years before her death, she continued to drink Famous Grouse whiskey, often starting before noon. She suffered her first stroke in 1998 while vacationing in Mustique, followed by two more in 2001. They left her half blind and with damaged movement on the left side, and she became increasingly reclusive, holed up in her Kensington Palace apartment in the grip of a deep, numbing depression. A source close to the princess said a few months before her death, "She really has lost the will to live."

Margaret made her last public appearance in August 2001, when she joined her mother at a performance of the Royal Ballet on the occasion of the Queen Mother's 101st birthday. Slightly slumped in a wheelchair, wearing large, dark sunglasses to protect her eyes, Margaret looked diminished in the company of the beaming, rouge-cheeked Queen Mum.

Her only comfort in the final years was her children. Against all odds, David and Sarah had grown into responsible, well-balanced

adults, with fulfilling lives beyond the spotlight. They had both inherited their parents' creative streaks. David, Viscount Linley, was a
renowned cabinetmaker, and Sarah (Chatto) a professional painter.
Both had stable marriages with two children apiece. (David's younger
daughter, Margarita, was born several months after Margaret's death.)

Remarkably, Margaret's children had made peace with their parents' wandering ways. There were no embittered guilt trips, à la
Charles. In the end Margaret might have taken comfort in the thought
that perhaps she was not such a bad parent after all. David and Sarah
were at her bedside, holding her hand and stroking her brow, as she
slipped away.

It had been Margaret's express desire to be cremated, and she had
instructed that no ceremony be performed at the crematorium, and no
family or friends be present. So late on the day after her death, the
queen stood with David and Sarah, tearfully watching as her sister's coffin was loaded into a hearse at Windsor Castle, from where it would be
escorted by two kilted bagpipers to the Slough Crematorium, eight
miles away. Her mother was too ill to attend. Margaret's ashes, in a cas-
ket, would later be placed in the Royal Vault in St. George's Chapel.

In honor of Margaret's life and death, Britain's Poet Laureate, Andrew Motion, penned a poignant tribute. Titled "The Younger Sister,
14" his poem captured the drama of Margaret's life, and the simple
truth of her human struggle, concluding:

> A daughter gone before her mother goes;
> A younger sister heading on before;
> A woman in possession of the fact
> That love and duty speak two languages.

ROYAL IS AS ROYAL DOES

. . . love and duty speak two languages
POET LAUREATE ANDREW·MOTION

March 31, 2002 ◆ LONDON

IN THE YEARS SINCE the century's turn, the queen felt a growing sense that she was witnessing a climactic denouement in a powerful drama involving her family, and especially its women. As she rode horseback in the chilly morning sun through Windsor Great Park on Easter Saturday, her thoughts drifted to Margaret, then to her mother, lying ill nearby at the Royal Lodge. Suddenly she saw a Range Rover barreling across the field toward her, and she cantered to a stop knowing at once why her equerry had tracked her down. She dismounted, and listened in silence as the aide breathlessly told her the doctor said to come quickly. Leaving the equerry to return her horse to the stable, she slipped behind the wheel of the Range Rover and drove herself across the park to the Royal Lodge.[1]

The queen entered her mother's room and found her barely

conscious. She quietly asked that Canon John Ovenden, the Queen Mother's personal chaplain, be summoned, and that her faithful household servants be assembled to make their farewells. They entered silently, forming a wide circle around the bed as the canon leaned in close and haltingly led the elderly woman in her final prayers. Tears fell down their cheeks in silent tribute. The Queen Mother died peacefully at 3:15 P.M.

The queen then asked to be left alone with her mother, and she sat by her bedside for an hour, memorizing the peaceful features, saying good-bye with a heavy heart. When she emerged, she found her husband waiting and they embraced.

Even in death, royal protocol had to be observed. As heir to the throne, the Prince of Wales was to be told first, and the queen knew that Charles would be sick with grief. He had visited his grandmother two days earlier before leaving on a vacation with his sons to Klosters, Switzerland, and the queen knew he would berate himself for not being there in the final moments.

She reached Charles in his hotel suite at 4:30 P.M., and he broke into tears as soon as he heard her voice. After the call, he put his head in his hands and sobbed.

In London, Great Tom began to peal at St. Paul's Cathedral, spreading the sad news. Anne arrived from Gatcombe Park as crowds began to gather outside Buckingham Palace, the Royal Lodge, and Clarence House, laying bouquets of flowers next to the gates.

There was no doubt about the details of the state funeral. The Queen Mother was to be laid to rest with a display of high ceremony not seen since the death of her husband, King George VI, a half century before. And that was exactly how she wanted it. Her funeral was not an event she had trusted anyone else to design to her satisfaction. She had laid out her instructions back in 1979 during a meeting with the Lord Chamberlain. So determined was she that it should go without a hitch that she had her funeral, code-named Tay Bridge, rehearsed many times and had the rehearsals videotaped. After viewing the results, she would make constant improvements.[2] Her intention was to provide a moment in history that the world would never forget. It would be regal, dignified, and flawless.

Late the next day, as gray clouds gathered overhead, the Queen Mother made the first leg of her final journey the few hundred yards from the Royal Lodge to the Royal Chapel of All Saints in Windsor Great Park. With her family gathered around her, the queen watched with overwhelming sadness as six pallbearers bore the coffin, draped with the Queen Mother's Royal Standard, to its temporary resting place. A small wreath of pink camellias picked from the Royal Lodge garden had been placed on top. One of her most faithful servants clutched a potted jasmine, an Easter present from Prince Charles, which had been by her bedside when she died.

For the queen, trained from an early age to repress her feelings, keeping her composure was an ordeal. Her eyes were puffy from crying, and at one point she felt her legs give way under her. Philip held her tight.

As they left the chapel, the public lined the narrow streets of the ancient town. The sense of grief in the air was palpable as townspeople and tourists paid homage to the best-loved royal. Across the road from the castle, in the Castle Hotel, a lone harpist played the Queen Mum's favorite Scottish music. Around the castle's entrance the crowds were ten to twelve deep. They had come from all over the country, many of them seniors who recalled her inspiration during the dark years of World War II.

After the service, Anne stayed by her mother's side, and the queen was grateful for her daughter's company. Late into the evening they reminisced about the gracious grandmother who had been the matriarch of the House of Windsor. During the last few days of her life the ailing old lady had become increasingly unwilling to see people other than her own close family. Since Margaret's death, she had wanted to talk about her younger daughter. In their last meeting, she had surprised Lilibet by asking her to leave her alone for a few moments.

When the queen returned, she found her mother dressed immaculately from head to toe and wearing pearls and her favorite earrings.

Mother and daughter smiled as they recalled the Queen Mother's passion for horse racing and how she became utterly obsessed with the sport after Lord Mildmay persuaded her to buy a steeplechaser. Within a year of acquiring the animal, she had confided to her daughter: "I am completely hooked."

Apart from their loving reminiscing, the queen and Anne had serious matters to discuss. In recent years the queen had come to rely heavily on her sensible, loyal daughter, whose advice she trusted. Now the two turned to the delicate subject of whether Camilla Parker Bowles should attend the funeral. In the nearly five years since Diana's death, Camilla had remained at Charles's side, but their situation had yet to be resolved. They agreed that Camilla was worthy of admiration for the quiet, dignified way she had conducted herself since Diana's death. It had been rough going for a while; a great deal of spite was expressed toward Camilla, and there were even death threats, as if she were personally responsible for Diana's tragedy. But Camilla's gracious good spirit had cooled most of the anger. More to the point, in this great hour of Charles's grief, it would be cruel to deny him the comfort of Camilla's presence. They decided that Camilla should attend.

Anne had a request of her own—to walk behind her grandmother's coffin, alongside her brothers. The queen smiled at her daughter, who rarely asked for anything but always gave so generously. The rite was, like so many others, reserved for males, but it seemed most appropriate that Anne should share this honor. She immediately approved her daughter's request. As Anne prepared to leave for home at 9:30 P.M., the queen's eyes welled up. "I shall miss her terribly," she said with a trembling voice. "What shall I do?" Anne felt enormous compassion for her mother, who had relied on *her* mother for so much. She was at a loss for words.

Left alone for the first time that day, the queen sat quietly, ignoring the tray of sandwiches that her concerned maid placed by her side.

She was a woman of enormous power and privilege, yet none of it mattered in the face of mortality. She was thankful, though, for the strength and good sense her mother had bequeathed her. She hoped it would sustain her throughout the remainder of her reign.

The Queen Mother's coffin remained in the Queen's Chapel at St. James's Palace for four days until Westminster Hall was prepared to receive it the following Friday. Crowds gathered to watch as the bier was carried through London to Westminster Hall for the formal lying-in-state. It was followed by a procession headed by the Prince of Wales, Prince Philip, and William and Harry, along with other male members of the Royal Family. By her brothers' side was Princess Anne, dressed in naval uniform.

The night before the funeral, the queen gave a televised address, which Anne had helped her write, to the nation. With unusual emotion, she shared what was in her heart.

At the ceremony tomorrow, I hope that sadness will blend with a wider sense of thanksgiving, not just for her life, but for the times in which she lived a century for the country and the Commonwealth not without its trials and sorrows, but also one of extraordinary progress, full of examples of courage and service as well as fun and laughter. This is what my mother would have understood, because it was the warmth and affection of people everywhere, which inspired her resolve, dedication, and enthusiasm for life.

As the cameras turned off at Buckingham Palace, the queen, who had rehearsed her speech several times in front of Anne, was relieved that she had managed to get through it without breaking down.

More than a million people lined the street the following day to say good-bye to the woman who had been their national mum for as long as they could remember. During the hourlong service at Westminster

Abbey there were words of grace, music of poignant beauty, deep and heartfelt prayers, and a memorable sermon from the Archbishop of Canterbury, Dr. George Carey. But no moment was as moving for the queen as the reading of this anonymous poem, which was a tribute to the Queen Mother's spirit. The poem began with these words:

> *You can shed tears that she is gone*
> *or you can smile because she has lived.*
> *You can close your eyes and pray that she'll come back*
> *or you can open your eyes and see all she's left.*

Then it was time for Lilibet to walk one last time behind her mother. She approached the coffin with Philip at her side, aware that this was truly the end of an era, in the nation's life and in her own.

Prince Charles accompanied the Queen Mother's hearse back to St. George's Chapel for the burial as the queen returned to Buckingham Palace, where she shut her door and could be heard weeping uncontrollably until the early hours. She allowed no one, not even her husband, to enter.

In the weeks following the funeral, the queen found herself spending more and more time with Anne. Charles had gone off to Scotland to try to come to terms with his grief, and the two women now found themselves alone at the helm, bound by the sense of duty that was imbedded in the women of the family, if not the men. Life simply had to go on, even in a period of mourning.

The queen was more dependent on Anne than ever. The death of the Queen Mother marked a turning point for the House of Windsor. She had set the standard for a whole generation and in her daughter had given the British a monarch devoted to duty and public service, a woman who could be counted on to act circumspectly until her last breath. The queen looked down her family's line and saw only that the next generations were seething with rebellion.

When her mother spoke, the family had listened and obeyed. She wasn't so sure that any of the younger royals would heed even her instructions, and she worried that Charles, as king, would have no clout at all. Maybe Anne, so strong and self-assured, so regal in the true sense of the word, could exert meaningful authority.

The queen was weary. Although she adopted a business-as-usual demeanor, everyone around her sensed her lingering sadness. She couldn't bring herself to get back on the horse she'd been riding when she received the news of the Queen Mother's decline.

Through all the dramas of the years, the specter of Diana had never been far from people's minds. Nearly two years after Paul Burrell's arrest for pilfering personal items of Diana's, and one week before he was scheduled to testify in his own defense, police received a call from Queen Elizabeth. She had just "recalled" that Burrell had told her he was holding some of Diana's property in safekeeping for her children. He wasn't a thief. The trial ended abruptly.

Burrell was giddy with relief. "The Queen has come through for me, the lady has come through for me!" he cried. Others suspected that the queen's sudden intervention was motivated by a desire to protect her family and not because she had a real interest in Burrell. Burrell's testimony threatened to expose disturbing facts about the Royal Family, including revelations of the alleged homosexual rape of a former male servant by a senior aide to Prince Charles. Burrell was prepared to testify that Diana had made a tape recording of the alleged rape victim's story and had placed it in her red mahogany box, which had disappeared.[3]

Once released from the grip of the law, Burrell went on to publish his account in a book titled *A Royal Duty,* and to appear on television internationally, heating the embers of conspiracy theories surrounding Diana's death. Diana knew their secrets, Burrell said. She was a danger. Perhaps they decided she had to be stopped.

To believe that, one would also have to believe that the final months of Diana's life were spent in a search for truth and justice, not in the heady flight of a bird set free. With seventeen million pounds in her bank account, her global popularity undiminished, and the attentions of a man with eyes for her alone, Diana was not looking back into the gloomy underworld of the palace. She was the victor, and she was too intent on reaping the spoils. The women of Windsor could have their flawed prince and their suffocating dungeon. They had chosen duty and would bear its burdens. She had chosen freedom and would do as she pleased.

KINGDOM COME

*One of the strongest natural proofs
of the folly of hereditary right in Kings,
is that nature disapproves it, otherwise
she would not so frequently turn it into ridicule,
by giving mankind an Ass for a Lion.*

THOMAS PAINE, WRITING IN *COMMON SENSE*, 1776

January 2005 ◆ LONDON·

WHERE ON EARTH was Prince Charles? His younger son was embroiled in an international scandal that the monarchy could ill afford, but there was no sign of a strong father to rein him in. On vacation in Scotland with Camilla Parker Bowles, Daddy wasn't inclined to intervene.

Trouble had followed twenty-year-old Prince Harry (who, don't forget, is third in line to the throne) through bouts of binge drinking, drug abuse, and brawls, but it was his appearance at a post–New Year's Eve costume party that might have done irreparable harm to the dignity of the throne. A photograph of a maniacally grinning Harry, hoisting a drink and a cigarette while dressed as a member of the Nazi Afrika Korps, complete with red swastika armband, made the front pages of newspapers around the world. The uniform was purchased with the aid of Harry's older-but-not-wiser brother, Prince William, second in line to the throne.

The sickening display set old wounds smarting on the eve of the sixtieth anniversary of the liberation of Auschwitz. Harry's pro forma written apology—"I am very sorry if I caused any offense or embarrassment to anyone. It was a poor choice of costume and I apologize"—only made things worse. He clearly didn't understand. Aging soldiers and Holocaust survivors shed bitter tears to think that the monarchy would one day be in the hands of those who cared so little for their sacrifices or the horrors they had suffered. And leave it to Fergie to pierce the open wounds further by racing to Harry's defense. "I am behind him one hundred percent," she told reporters, inexplicably adding, "His mother would be proud of him."

Prince Charles spoke to his sons by phone from his vacation house, and one expects that he expressed strong disapproval. However, a nobler man, a wiser man, a man worthy of the throne, would have swept onto the scene with blazing scepter and riot act in tow. The people longed to hear Charles's outrage, but alas, there was only silence.

Perhaps he was distracted by his wedding plans, for he had finally asked Camilla Parker Bowles to be his wife. The announcement was somewhat anticlimactic, as the couple had been living together for many years. By and large the public professed not to care—perhaps because it no longer believed that the personal lives of the Royal Family were worth caring about. In the eyes of many, the escapades of the Windsors were little more than a soap opera that had lingered on the telly a season too long. What did their marriages, divorces, trysts, and traumas have to do with the real lives of the people?

The media attempted a desultory show of tut-tutting as the nuptials approached. Much was made of the palace's announcement that the queen would not attend the civil ceremony. And the monarchial purists, whose numbers shrink with each passing year, expressed shock that the Archbishop of Canterbury gave his blessing to the marriage, since the Royal Marriage Act expressly forbids royals—especially one who is next in line for the throne and might someday bear the title Supreme Governor of the Church of England—to marry in civil ceremonies. On the whole, however, nobody much cared, as long as the taxpayers didn't have to foot the bill for the reception.

King George V once referred to the Royal Family as "the Firm," and there are certain immutable truths about every great firm, be it the Windsors or IBM. Every firm has a unique culture—the defining moves and unspoken rules that, taken together, form the secret recipe for its success. As a family firm, the House of Windsor in the past century has had a culture that is matriarchal—the doting mother who always knows best. At least that is the ideal. The extent to which the Royal Family has measured up to this ideal is offset by another reality of family firms—the tendency to prop up its heirs, even when they lack the wisdom and devotion of the founders.

A great firm demands loyalty from its members, and the belief in a purpose larger than personal need. The Windsor Firm does not live or die by the actions of individuals, no matter how craven or foolish. Dianaphiles and antimonarchists like to say that the Princess of Wales drove a stake through the heart of the monarchy, wounding it fatally. It's hardly plausible that a single woman could accomplish what twelve hundred years of wars, schisms, abdications, and infidelities could not. Still, successful firms ride the waves of crisis; they adapt to new realities, and here the Royal Family is vulnerable. The British monarchy is like an old cloak—stained, frayed at the edges, ripped in some places, and desperately in need of mending. It is fair to ask: What function does it perform, and is it essential? Is the Firm worth saving? Are its best days behind it?

The answer is in doubt. The British people are almost evenly divided about whether the monarchy should continue. A 2004 poll conducted by MORI found that only 47 percent wanted to keep the monarchy in its current form when the queen retires or dies. Advocates for a republic are louder than ever in their call for Britain to join the twenty-first century and freely elect a president. It is absurd, they claim, for members of the House of Commons to swear an oath of allegiance to a sovereign whose position is hereditary and whose influence over the bread-and-butter issues of government is only vaguely advisory.

Far from uniting its subjects under a common banner, the monarchy embodies class, racial, and religious divisions. Writing in *The Guardian*, columnist Jonathan Freedland points out that "the crown symbolizes the very essence of our political culture—declaring loud and clear that power in Britain flows from the top down, with the throne at the summit of the pyramid. So long as the head of state belongs, automatically and irrevocably, to a single pampered family, we can but be subjects of their kingdom, not citizens of our own land."

The high price of supporting the Windsors in their many castles and palaces (to the tune of roughly sixty-five million pounds a year) is both real and symbolic. The argument put forth by the monarchy's supporters—that the money generated by tourism far outweighs the cost to taxpayers—sounds like an accountant's sleight of hand. Even if it were true, one has to ask whether it is enough for the Royal Family to serve as the proprietor of a great theme park, displaying relics of past glories to gawking tourists.

The republican movement in Britain is gaining momentum for one reason: The queen is seventy-nine as of this writing, and even if she achieves a longevity close to her mother's, she cannot rule forever. As the royal subjects stare gloomily down the line of succession, there is little cause for cheer in the graying indifference of Charles or the Gen X creeds of his heirs. The laws of succession have come under fresh scrutiny in an era when women have achieved equality in virtually every other realm but the narrowly constructed monarchy. This hereditary roll of the dice occasionally produces straight flushes but more often has maddening results. Queen Elizabeth, the Queen Mother, who cherished her role, was forced into retirement by the death of her husband, King George VI, just as she was hitting her stride. One day she was the queen, the next day she was curtsying to her daughter. While the present queen, Elizabeth II, has grown into the role she has inhabited since 1952, the prospect of her retirement or death has set off the panic buttons.

Recently, the queen gave her approval for Parliament to consider a law that would give royal daughters the right to inherit the throne before their younger brothers. Under current law, Prince Andrew, Prince Edward, and their children (male and female) rank ahead of Princess Anne in the line of succession. She ranks number nine; even Andrew and Fergie's daughters and Prince Edward's infant daughter, Louise, precede her. If the law changes, Anne will be fourth in line, after Prince Harry. Anne's position in the future monarchy may be unprecedented in any event. If Charles becomes king, it has been announced that Camilla will be not queen but Princess Consort. In that case, it is possible that Princess Anne, an increasingly popular and stable influence, might perform many of the queen's duties.

Anne might be the last woman of Windsor. Technically, there are others coming up, but it's hard to imagine the bungee-jumping, studded-tongued Americanized royal offspring walking the path of duty or adhering to codes that once inspired an empire. If the monarchy must end, let it end before the cretins take over, while the strong, dutiful women of Windsor are still alive to lead it gently to its rest.

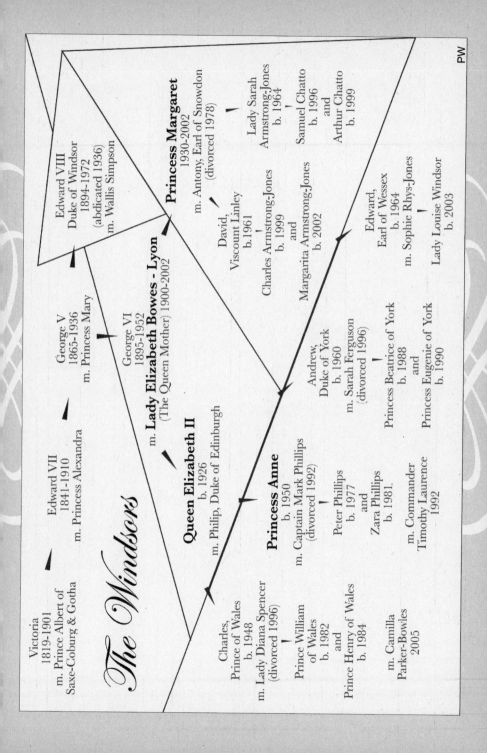

The Windsors

Victoria
1819-1901
m. Prince Albert of
Saxe-Coburg & Gotha

Edward VII
1841-1910
m. Princess Alexandra

George V
1865-1936
m. Princess Mary

Edward VIII
Duke of Windsor
1894-1972
(abdicated 1936)
m. Wallis Simpson

George VI
1895-1952
m. **Lady Elizabeth Bowes - Lyon**
(The Queen Mother) 1900-2002

Princess Margaret
1930-2002
m. Antony, Earl of Snowdon
(divorced 1978)

Queen Elizabeth II
b. 1926
m. Philip, Duke of Edinburgh

David,
Viscount Linley
b.1961
Charles Armstrong-Jones
b. 1999
and
Margarita Armstrong-Jones
b. 2002

Lady Sarah
Armstrong-Jones
b. 1964
Samuel Chatto
b. 1996
and
Arthur Chatto
b. 1999

Charles,
Prince of Wales
b. 1948
m. Lady Diana Spencer
(divorced 1996)

Prince William
of Wales
b. 1982
and
Prince Henry of Wales
b. 1984

m. Camilla
Parker-Bowles
2005

Princess Anne
b. 1950
m. Captain Mark Phillips
(divorced 1992)

Peter Phillips
b. 1977
and
Zara Phillips
b. 1981.

m. Commander
Timothy Laurence
1992

Andrew,
Duke of York
b. 1960
m. Sarah Ferguson
(divorced 1996)

Princess Beatrice of York
b. 1988
and
Princess Eugenie of York
b. 1990

Edward,
Earl of Wessex
b. 1964
m. Sophie Rhys-Jones

Lady Louise Windsor
b. 2003

PW

THE WINDSOR LINE
OF SUCCESSION

1. PRINCE CHARLES

2. PRINCE WILLIAM

3. PRINCE HARRY

4. PRINCE ANDREW

5. PRINCESS BEATRICE

6. PRINCESS EUGENIE

7. PRINCE EDWARD

8. LADY LOUISE WINDSOR

9. PRINCESS ANNE

10. PETER PHILLIPS

11. ZARA PHILLIPS

NOTES

Research for *The Women of Windsor* involved hundreds of sources, including more than forty books, archived and current magazine articles and newspaper reports, national archives in Great Britain and the United States, and a number of royal websites. In addition to more than 250 individual source notes below, the following sources were used:

PERIODICALS

The BBC, The Guardian, Daily Mirror, International Herald Tribune, The Sun, The Daily Express, the *London Times, Vanity Fair, Time,* the *New York Times,* the *Washington Post, Newsweek, Life, People,* the *Daily Telegraph,* the *Evening Standard, Ladies' Home Journal, Good Housekeeping,* and *Talk* magazine.

WEBSITES

www.royal.gov.uk (official site); www.royalarchives.com; www.royaltymagazine .com; www.nationalarchives.gov.uk; Royal Insight; www.alt.talk.royalty; www.royalty.nu; Monarchy Out, Throne Out; www.royalstart4all.com; and www.etoile.co.uk.

PROLOGUE: DRAMA QUEEN

1. Diana, Princess of Wales, interview by Peter Settelen. Videotape aired by NBC News, December 2004.

2. These tapes were made in 1991 by Dr. James Colthurst, a friend of the princess, and passed on to Andrew Morton; they form the basis for Morton's 1992 book, *Diana: Her True Story.*

3. The letter was produced by Paul Burrell.

4. The memorandum, written in response to an employee's question about promotion prospects, was leaked by a private secretary in Prince Charles's household. The secretary has made an accusation of sexual harassment against a senior member of the household.

CHAPTER 1: MERRY MISCHIEF

1. There are many sources detailing the courtship attempts of Bertie. Suite101.com, a historical website, gives this particularly charming dialogue in "20th Century Queen: The Life of the Queen Mother," August 1, 2000.

2. Longford, *Queen Mother.* The comment was made by Lord Gorell (John Gorell Barnes), author and editor.

3. Letter from the queen to Neville Chamberlain upon the occasion of her mother's death in 1938. Recorded by Bradford in *Elizabeth,* p. 77.

4. The Boer Wars were the South African Wars of 1880–1881 and 1899–1902, fought between the British and the descendants of the Dutch settlers (Boers) in Africa. They ended with the signing of the Treaty of Vereeniging in May 1902. The peace settlement brought to an end the Transvaal and the Orange Free State as Boer republics. However, the British granted the Boers three million pounds for restocking and repairing farmlands and promised eventual self-government, which was granted in 1907.

5. Forbes, *Elizabeth,* p. 18.

6. Ibid., p. 36.

7. Ibid., p. 26.

8. Ellis, ed., *Thatched with Gold,* p. 126.

9. *The Lost Prince,* screenplay by Stephen Poliakoff, 2004.

10. Brendon and Whitehead, *The Windsors: A Dynasty Revealed,* p. 29.

11. Forbes, *Elizabeth,* p. 34.

12. Several sources detail the relationship between Kaiser Wilhelm and George V and Queen Mary, including: Picknett, *War of the Windsors,* p. 17; Pope-Hennessy, *Queen Mary,* pp. 288–89; and Bradford, *Reluctant King,* pp. 63–64.

13. Women had only partially won the right to vote. Until 1928 the vote was granted solely to women householders, householders' wives, and women university graduates age thirty and older.

14. Ellis, ed., *Thatched with Gold,* pp. 195–96.

15. Picknett, et al., *War of the Windsors,* p. 49.

16. Forbes, *Elizabeth,* p. 47.
17. Ellis, ed., *Thatched with Gold,* pp. 195–96.
18. Cozens-Hardy, *Glorious Years.*

CHAPTER 2: WE FOUR

1. A number of sources provide details about the early married life of Bertie and Elizabeth, including Duff, *Elizabeth of Glamis;* Forbes, *Elizabeth;* Lacey, *Queen Mother's Century;* Morrow, *Queen Mother;* Bradford, *Reluctant King;* and Pope-Hennessy, *Queen Mary.*
2. Duke of Windsor, *King's Story,* p. 187.
3. Ibid., p. 182.
4. Ibid., p. 258.
5. The Duchy of Cornwall and the Duchy of Lancaster are private estates established in the Middle Ages, separate from the Crown, for the personal ownership of the Royal Family.
6. Ellis, ed., *Thatched with Gold,* p. 176.
7. Bradford, *Reluctant King,* p. 116.
8. Ibid., pp. 122–23.
9. Duff, *Elizabeth of Glamis,* p. 109.
10. Ibid., p. 122.
11. Bradford, *Elizabeth,* p. 29.
12. Crawford, *Little Princesses,* p. 70.
13. Kelley, *The Royals,* p. 50.
14. Bradford, *Elizabeth,* p. 41.
15. Warwick, *Princess Margaret,* p. 49.
16. Brendan and Whitehead, *The Windsors,* p. 59.

CHAPTER 3: CLASH OF THE TITANESSES

1. Duke of Windsor, *King's Story,* pp. 256–57.
2. According to Bradford, the king's private secretary, Clive Wigram, recounted the incident. *Reluctant King,* p. 141.
3. Kenneth Rose.
4. There are various sources for the analysis of Edward's skewed relationship with women and his sexual difficulties, most notably Thornton, *Royal Feud;* Ziegler, *King Edward VIII;* and Fox, "Oddest Couple."
5. Godfrey, *Letters from a Prince: Edward Prince of Wales to Mrs. Freda Dudley Ward, March 1918–January 1921.*
6. Picknett, et al., *War of the Windsors,* p. 76.

7. Ibid., p. 81.
8. Ibid., p. 97.
9. The one-year delay allowed for a proper period of mourning, but the person next in line for the throne automatically ascended with the death of the sovereign.
10. Duke of Windsor, *King's Story.*
11. Bradford, *Reluctant King,* p. 172.
12. Ziegler, *King Edward VIII;* Pope-Hennessy, *Queen Mary;* and Picknett, *War of the Windsors.*
13. Duke of Windsor, *King's Story,* p. 334.
14. Pope-Hennessy, *Queen Mary,* p. 575.
15. A morganatic marriage is contracted in certain countries, usually between persons of unequal social rank, and prevents the passage of the husband's titles and privileges to the wife and any children of the marriage. One such example involves Queen Mary's paternal grandmother, Claudine Rhedey, who married Prince Alexander of Württemberg.
16. Brody, *Gone with the Windsors.*
17. Edwards, *Royal Sisters,* p. 63.
18. Crawford, *Little Princesses,* p. 39.
19. Duke of Windsor, *King's Story.*
20. Ellis, ed., *Thatched with Gold,* pp. 195–96.
21. Crawford, *Little Princesses,* p. 64.
22. Bradford, *Elizabeth,* p. 66.

CHAPTER 4: THE MOST DANGEROUS WOMAN IN EUROPE

1. Pritchard, ed. *Poetry of Niagara.*
2. Bradford, *Reluctant King,* p. 283.
3. Ibid., pp. 277–79.
4. Ibid. pp. 242–43.
5. From recently declassified correspondence between Rudolf Hess and Adolf Hitler.
6. Ibid
7. Bradford, *Reluctant King.*
8. The National Archive, handwritten letter from King George VI to Chamberlain, Ref. PREM 1/467.
9. Ziegler, *King Edward VIII,* p. 361.
10. From the transcript of King George VI's handwritten notes for a memorandum on his conversations with President Roosevelt. The Franklin D. Roosevelt Presidential Library archives. The notes, dated 10 and 11 June 1939, read in part, "Debts. Better not reopen the question. Congress wants repayment in full, which is impossible, & a small bit is of no use, as they will want more later."

11. Douglas-Home and Kelly, *Dignified & Efficient,* p. 141.

12. On Constitutional Mall and fronting the Lagoon of Nations, the British Pavilion consisted of two buildings connected at the first-floor level and divided into several sections. A replica of the crown jewels was displayed in the Royal Room. The Silver Room contained many coins and medals struck by the Royal Mint. The Court of Honor contained an elaborate display of heraldry and a collection of antique silver-gilt plate. Other exhibits and displays were devoted to public works and industry. Historical documents linking the English-speaking world were viewed in the Magna Charta Hall. The pavilion also housed an art gallery, cinema, restaurant, and a section devoted to official publications.

13. Roosevelt, *On My Own.*

14. The period between the declaration of war and the first bombs was called "the phony war."

15. Lacey, *Queen Mother's Century,* p. 79.

16. Crawford, *Little Princesses,* p. 103.

17. Pope-Hennessy, *Queen Mary,* p. 609.

18. Bradford, *Elizabeth,* p. 93.

19. Ibid.

20. Bradford, *Reluctant King,* p. 324.

21. Radio broadcast, September 27, 1940.

22. Bradford, *Reluctant King,* p. 350.

23. Franklin D. Roosevelt Presidential Library archives.

24. From the transcript of King George VI's handwritten notes for a memorandum on his conversations with President Roosevelt. The Franklin D. Roosevelt Presidential Library archives. The notes, dated June 10 and 11, 1939, include this one: "If London was bombed USA would come in. Offensive air warfare was better than defensive & he hoped we should do the same on Berlin." The United States was not completely out of the war. The Lend-Lease Act, passed by Congress in 1941, gave the president power to sell, transfer, lend, or lease war matériels. The president was to set the terms for aid; repayment was to be "in kind or property, or any other direct or indirect benefit which the President deems satisfactory."

25. Roosevelt, *On My Own,* p. 31.

26. Ibid., p. 36.

CHAPTER 5: HEIR PRESUMPTIVE

1. A male heir is heir *apparent,* as in "It is apparent that he is next in line for the throne." A female is heir *presumptive,* as in "Presuming no male children are born, she is next in line for the throne."

2. The Girl Guides were the British version of Girl Scouts. During the war, Crawfie's

group kept vegetable gardens, cooked soups and cakes for the soldiers stationed at Windsor Castle, and had campouts.

3. Crawford, *Little Princesses*, pp. 137–42.
4. Ibid., p. 101.
5. Vickers, *Alice*, p. 201.
6. Ellis, ed., *Thatched with Gold*, p. 226.
7. Parker, *Prince Philip*, p. 80.
8. Crawford, *Little Princesses*, p. 52.
9. Ibid.
10. Bradford, *Reluctant King*, p. 399.
11. Franklin D. Roosevelt Presidential Library archives.
12. Bradford, *Reluctant King*, pp. 358–59.
13. Margaret's recollection, for a BBC commemoration of the fiftieth anniversary of the end of World War II, May 8, 1995.6

CHAPTER 6: LILIBET'S PRINCE CHARMING

1. Picknett, et al., *War of the Windsors*, pp. 86–87.
2. The king wrote to his mother about this overture, expressing his and the queen's feelings on the matter: "We both think she is far too young for that now. She has never met any young men of her own age. . . . We are going to tell George that P. had better not think any more about it at present."
3. Parker, *Prince Philip*, p. 91.
4. Crawford, *Little Princesses*, p. 178.
5. Bradford, *Elizabeth*, p. 185.
6. Ellis, ed., *Thatched with Gold*, p. 226.
7. Duff, *Elizabeth of Glamis*. p. 274.
8. Erickson, *Lilibet*, p. 101.
9. Bradford, *Elizabeth*, p.135.
10. Crawford, *Little Princesses*, p. 201.
11. Edwards, *Royal Sisters*, p. 178.
12. Bradford, *Elizabeth*, p. 124.
13. Kelley, *The Royals*, p. 96.
14. Vickers, *Alice*.
15. There are several sources for details about the Thursday Club, including Parker, *Prince Philip*; Campbell, *Royal Marriages*; and Erickson, *Lilibet*.
16. Bradford, *Elizabeth*, pp. 131–32.
17. Crawford, *Little Princesses*, p. 216.
18. According to Kitty Kelley's *The Royals*, Philip complained to friends that his new wife was sexually voracious. This account might be put down to vicious gossip,

especially since one of Kelley's sources was a gossip columnist. There is no dispute, however, that Philip and Lilibet had a passionate early marriage.

19. Parker, *Prince Philip*, p. 148.

CHAPTER 7: MRS. MOUNTBATTEN ASCENDS

1. Duff, *Elizabeth of Glamis*, p. 326.
2. Bradford, *Elizabeth*, p. 173.
3. Ibid., p. 169.
4. Ibid., p. 174.
5. Pearson, *The Selling of the Royal Family*, pp. 110–12.
6. Bradford, *Elizabeth*, pp. 176–77.
7. Ibid., pp. 178–79.
8. Lilian Bailey was a famous medium whose clients were said to include Mae West, Mary Pickford, and Merle Oberon. In *Death Is Her Life*, a biography by W. F. Neech (London: Psychic Press, 1957), the following incident is recounted: "One night Lilian was approached by a lady who asked her if she would give a consultation 'to a group of VIPs' in London. She agreed, even though she had to be blindfolded in the limousine, and then secretly driven to a mystery venue. Lilian was ushered into a building and invited to sit down. She thought she heard a rustling of skirts at this time; then, still unable to see, she fell into a trance. After the séance, upon removing the blindfold she discovered that she was seated in an elegant drawing-room before Queen Elizabeth, the Queen Mother, and other immediate members of the British Royal Family. Lilian learned that during her deep-trance state, the late King George VI had controlled her and spoken again to his devoted Queen Consort, Elizabeth—and this was to be the first of many such séances by royal command." Anne Morrow also writes about Lilian Bailey in her book *Queen Mother*.
9. Duff, *Elizabeth of Glamis*.
10. Parker, *Prince Philip*, p. 163.
11. Pope-Hennessy, *Queen Mary*.
12. Bradford, *Elizabeth*, p. 184.
13. Shawcross, *Queen & Country*, pp. 50–52.

CHAPTER 8: SISTER DEAREST

1. There are many written accounts, but the most reliable are found in Barrymaine, *Peter Townsend Story*; and Warwick, *Princess Margaret*.
2. Bradford, *Elizabeth*, p. 196.
3. Pearson, *The Selling of the Royal Family*, p. 120.

4. Warwick, *Princess Margaret,* p. 166.

5. Barrymaine, *Peter Townsend Story,* p. 96.

6. Ibid., p. 167.

7. Forbes, *Elizabeth,* p. 106.

8. This question would turn out to have great significance, as we will see in chapter 16 of this book.

9. Pearson, *The Selling of the Royal Family,* p. 134.

10. Warwick, *Princess Margaret,* p. 203.

11. Barrymaine, *Peter Townsend Story,* p. 214.

12. According to Bradford, *Elizabeth,* p. 214, Princess Margaret felt a great responsibility to share her sister's burdens.

13. Warwick, *Princess Margaret,* p. 166.

14. Barrymaine, *Peter Townsend Story,* p. 231.

15. Ibid., p. 239.

16. Brough, *Margaret,* pp. 235–36.

CHAPTER 9: ROYAL FAMILY VALUES

1. *Time,* Woman of the Year issue, January 5, 1953.

2. Davies, *Queen Elizabeth II,* p. 218.

3. Pearson, *The Selling of the Royal Family,* p. 85.

4. Roosevelt, *On My Own,* p. 36.

5. Davies, *Queen Elizabeth II,* p. 282.

6. Parker, *Prince Philip,* p. 156.

7. *Time,* February 18, 1957.

8. Davies, *Queen Elizabeth II,* p. 178.

9. Philip, speaking in an interview with Fiametta Rocco of the *Independent on Sunday,* December 13, 1992.

10. His given name was John Grigg, which he returned to in 1963 when he gave up his title.

11. Lacey, *Majesty,* pp. 153–54.

12. Duff, *Elizabeth of Glamis,* p. 343.

13. When Anne married Captain Mark Phillips, she signed the register "Anne Elizabeth Alice Louise Mountbatten-Windsor."

14. There are other reasons to suspect that Andrew was not a reconciliation baby. In his most shocking revelations, Nicholas Davies, in *Queen Elizabeth II,* puts forward the possibility that the queen's two youngest sons were fathered by other men to whom the queen was extremely close. Davies suggests that Andrew is the son of Lord Porchester, and Edward is the son of Baron Patrick Plunket, the former Deputy Master of the Royal Household. "Get ahold of a picture of Prince An-

drew and then one of Lord Porchester at the same age," he writes. "You'll see that Prince Philip could never have been Andrew's father." It is true that the queen was extremely close to both men. Porchester shared her passion for racing, advised her on horse breeding, and became a confidant. Plunket was her closest aide, and they shared the same worldview and sense of humor. She was said to be inconsolable when he died prematurely in 1975. However, to believe that the queen would engage in extramarital affairs is to *dis*believe nearly everything else we know about her strict morality, devotion to duty, and her lifelong sublimation of self in adherence to her role—not to mention the fact that, in spite of his straying, she has always been deeply in love with her husband.

15. Brendon and Whitehead, *The Windsors,* p. 198.
16. Pearson, *The Selling of the Royal Family,* p. 191.
17. Ibid, p. 194.
18. Barry, *Royal Secrets,* p. 3.

CHAPTER 10: BEING ANNE

1. Forbes, *Elizabeth,* p. 116.
2. Hoey, *Anne,* p. 29.
3. Forbes, *Elizabeth,* p. 114.
4. Courtney, *Princess Anne,* p. 60.
5. HRH Princess Anne, *Riding Through My Life.*
6. Ibid.
7. Campbell, *Royal Marriages,* p. 215.
8. There are various accounts of the kidnapping attempt. The most detailed is in Parker, *Princess Royal,* pp. 124–40.
9. Ibid., p. 162.
10. Ibid., p. 183.
11. Hoey, *Anne,* p. 70.
12. Campbell, *Royal Marriages.* However, according to Nicholas Davies, Anne's affair with Cross continued after Zara was born, until Cross broke it off for another woman.
13. Campbell, *Royal Marriages,* p. 230; and Davies, *Queen Elizabeth II,* pp. 254–55.

CHAPTER 11: ALWAYS A ROSEBUD, NEVER A ROSE

1. Lacey, *The Queen Mother's Century,* p. 31.
2. Brough, *Margaret,* p. 256.
3. Ibid., p. 239.
4. Warwick, *Princess Margaret,* p. 247.
5. Ibid., pp. 271–73.

6. Margaret's affair with Robin Douglas-Home lasted only a month. She ended it, purportedly to save her marriage, and he committed suicide eighteen months later. It remained secret for thirty years until the author Noel Botham reproduced Margaret's letters in his 2002 book, *Margaret: The Last Real Princess.*

7. Bradford, *Elizabeth,* p. 404.

8. Pearson, *The Selling of the Royal Family.* p. 268.

9. Hamilton, *My Queen & I.*

10. Lacey, *Majesty,* p. 284.

CHAPTER 12: CRASH OF SYMBOLS

1. Bradford, *Elizabeth,* p. 446.

2. By most accounts, the queen and Philip had not slept in the same bed for years at this point, so the gleeful speculation was somewhat cruel.

3. Press accounts.

4. Wilson, *Rise and Fall.* However, Thatcher mostly kept her views of the queen to herself. Damning her with faint praise in her memoirs, *Downing Street Years,* Thatcher wrote, "I always found the Queen's attitudes toward the work of the government absolutely correct."

5. Pearson, *The Selling of the Royal Family,* p. 323.

6. Press accounts.

7. Erickson, *Lilibet,* p. 242.

8. Strober and Hart, *The Monarchy,* p. 242.

9. Ibid., pp. 207–17.

10. Wilson, *Rise and Fall,* p. 173.

11. The heir apparent has, since the institution of the title by King Edward I in 1301, usually been "created" Prince of Wales. Edward I led the conquest of independent Wales between 1277 and 1283. He subsequently proclaimed his infant son Edward, born at Caernarvon in Wales in 1284, the Prince of Wales. There is no succession to the title, which is only renewed at the sovereign's pleasure. Prince Charles was created Prince of Wales at Caernarvon Castle on July 1, 1969.

12. Bradford, *Elizabeth,* p. 425.

13. Ibid., p. 426.

14. According to *War of the Windsors,* it is highly questionable that the IRA would have chosen to target Mountbatten directly. However, he had many enemies and there is speculation that the IRA was subcontracted for the hit, perhaps by the KGB.

CHAPTER 13: TO DI FOR

1. Or what he *thought* was genuine sympathy. This is the moment Diana describes on the Settelen tape, and her perception is quite different: "He leapt upon me and

started kissing me and everything. And I thought, 'Waaaaah, you know. This is not what people do.' And he was all over me for the rest of the evening, following me everywhere . . . (like) a puppy."

2. According to Morton, *Diana: Her True Story*, p. 12, Diana's parents were so convinced she would be a boy that they hadn't chosen a girl's name, and it took them a week after the birth to think of one.

3. Bradford, *Elizabeth*, p. 432.

4. Ibid., p. 437.

5. Biographical accounts disagree about whether Lady Fermoy was for or against the marriage. Dimbleby, Charles's biographer, states in *The Prince of Wales: A Biography* that she approved of the marriage, but Morton, in *Diana: Her True Story*, has Diana saying she was against it.

6. Press accounts.

7. It was true. Camilla's great-grandmother Alice, the Honorable Mrs. George Keppel, had been the mistress of King Edward VII.

8. Forbes, *Elizabeth*, p. 122.

9. Barry, *Royal Secrets*.

10. Erickson, *Lilibet*, p. 249.

11. Burrell, *A Royal Duty*, p. 448.

12. Ibid., p. 80.

13. This is disputed by official biographers. Charles's recollections, recounted by Dimbleby in *The Prince of Wales: A Biography*, are of spending a reflective evening alone. Barry, in *Royal Secrets*, says the prince was definitely with Mrs. Parker Bowles that night.

14. Morton, *Diana*, pp. 96–98.

15. Dimbleby, *The Prince of Wales*, p. 331.

16. Seward, *The Queen & Di*, p. 60.

17. Diana, Princess of Wales, interview by Martin Bashir, *Panorama*, November 20, 1995, BBC.

18. Taped conversation with Dr. Colthurst for Andrew Morton.

19. Dimbleby, *The Prince of Wales*, p. 331.

20. Seward, *The Queen & Di*, pp. 118–19.

21. Taped conversations with Dr. Colthurst for Andrew Morton.

22. Campbell, *Royal Marriages*, pp. 232–33.

CHAPTER 14: THE PRINCESS OF WAILS

1. Morton, *Diana: Her True Story*.

2. Morton, *Diana: In Pursuit of Love*, p. 34.

3. According to Morton, a fierce rivalry developed between Charles and Diana over who was on top in the charity circuit. They didn't like to share kudos. On one

occasion, after the couple made a joint visit to Canada, Diana wrote thank-you letters to various charities and government agencies who had arranged the trip. When the letters were passed on to Charles for approval, he went through each letter, crossed out "we" and inserted "I" before signing it (*Diana: Her True Story*, p. 191).

4. Various accounts, including that of Wharfe, *Diana: Closely Guarded Secret*.
5. Diana, Princess of Wales, interview by Peter Settelen. Videotape aired by NBC News, December 2004.
6. Ibid. Diana's suspicions are also discussed by Burrell in *A Royal Duty*.
7. Dimbleby, *The Prince of Wales*, p. 395.
8. Wilson, *Windsor Knot*, p. 322.
9. Seward, *The Queen & Di*, pp. 192–94.
10. Bradford, *Elizabeth*, p. 468.
11. Seward, *The Queen & Di*, pp. 195–96.
12. Morton, *Diana*, pp. 148–49.
13. In the Settelen interview, Diana recalls the prince's words in this way. However, Bradford recounts them in *Elizabeth*, p. 477, as "I'm not the first Prince of Wales who's had a mistress."
14. Burrell, *A Royal Duty*, pp. 167–68.
15. Ibid., p. 171.
16. Seward, *The Queen & Di*, pp. 174–75.
17. Diana, Princess of Wales, interview by Peter Settelen.
18. According to Morton, in *Diana: Her True Story*, p. 200, "The Queen Mother exercised an enormous influence over the Prince of Wales. It was a mutual adoration society from which Diana was effectively excluded."
19. Campbell, *Royal Marriages*, pp. 156–58.

CHAPTER 15: THE QUEEN'S HORRIBLE YEAR

1. Brendon and Whitehead, *The Windsors*, p. 235.
2. Text from Queen Elizabeth's speech on the occasion of her fortieth anniversary on the throne, November 23, 1992.
3. Interview with Anthony Holden, p. 213; Brendon and Whitehead, *The Windsors*.
4. Wilson, *Windsor Knot*, pp. 228–30.
5. Ibid.
6. The transcript was first published by the Australian weekly women's magazine *New Idea*, in January 1993.
7. Seward, *The Queen & Di*, pp. 4–5.
8. Dimbleby, *The Prince of Wales*.
9. Pasternak, *Princess in Love*, tells Hewitt's story. Hewitt has been a subject of extreme interest over the years. Prince Harry bears an uncanny resemblance to

Hewitt—not just the red hair, which he might have inherited from the Spencers, but the cut of his jaw. The resemblance becomes stronger as Harry grows older. Over the years Hewitt has made public denials, stating he didn't even meet the princess until 1986, but this, too, is in dispute.

10. Seward, *The Queen & Di*, pp. 223–25.

11. According to Seward, *The Queen & Di*, p. 233, it was not Diana's wailing about the family to Bashir, or even her revelation about an affair, that most disturbed the queen. "What was inexcusable and unforgivable was the way Diana . . . accused the Palace of Machiavellian conspiracy and questioned the wisdom of allowing her estranged husband to ascend the throne."

12. The following day Diana received a second letter, this one from Charles, asking for a divorce. She was convinced that the queen and Charles had colluded. Burrell, *A Royal Duty*, p. 238.

13. Ibid.

CHAPTER 16: PALACE COUP

1. Burrell, *A Royal Duty*, pp. 243–44.

2. Seward, *The Queen & Di*, p. 240.

3. Burrell, *A Royal Duty*, p. 254.

4. Seward, *The Queen & Di*, p. 218.

5. Wilson, *Windsor Knot*, p. 288.

6. Under royal protocol, the queen's flag cannot fly at Buckingham Palace unless she is there. It is never flown at half-staff, because it represents the institution of the monarchy. At the time of the outcry, the queen was five hundred miles away, in Balmoral, Scotland, with Prince Charles and his children.

7. The contrast between Mother Teresa and Diana is sharply drawn in a commentary by Richard Rongstad's special to Sun Tzu's Newswire, September 5, 1997: "Today, the world's news media was distracted momentarily from the biggest media circus event of 1997. The media circus event I'm talking about is the death of Diana, Princess of Wales. That momentary distraction was the death of a diminutive Roman Catholic woman ending a life of service to the poor. Mother Teresa was 87. Early in her life, Mother Teresa made four vows—one, a vow of poverty, she gave away all her possessions. Two, a vow of chastity, she was the Bride of Christ. Three, she took a vow of obedience to her church, her Christ and her God. Her fourth vow was to serve the poor. By contrast, Princess Diana made one holy vow that I know of, that of Holy Matrimony. She couldn't even keep that vow."

8. Correspondence between Diana and her brother, which was made public during Paul Burrell's trial, showed that Spencer was not the loving and protective brother he made himself out to be. When Diana asked if she could live on his estate after

her divorce, the earl responded, "I am sorry but I have decided that the Garden House is not a possible move. There are many reasons, most of which centre on the inevitable police and press interference that will follow. . . . In theory it would be lovely to help you out and I am sorry I can't do that."

9. *The Sun* and other newspaper reports.

10. Fayed has been the mostly discredited source behind the biggest rumors—that Diana had "last words," that Diana was pregnant with Dodi's child, etc. He has spent millions pursuing various avenues of investigation, to no avail.

11. Burrell, *A Royal Duty,* pp. 411–13.

12. The 1955 Downing Street file also revealed that the lord chancellor said the Royal Marriages Act 1772 was out of date and an embarrassment that should be repealed. He told Prime Minister Anthony Eden that he was not even sure it applied to the princess. The files showed that the queen was also prepared to reform the 1772 act so that it was restricted to the marriages of her children or grandchildren and those of the heir presumptive. It would have meant that Margaret could marry without seeking her sister's formal consent.

CHAPTER 17: ROYAL IS AS ROYAL DOES

1. Press accounts of the Queen Mother's death, in Erickson, *Lilibet.* The full funeral service is detailed on the official website of the Royal Family, www.royal.gov.uk.

3. Press accounts.

3. Burrell, *A Royal Duty.*

BIBLIOGRAPHY

Allen, Martin. *Hidden Agenda: How the Duke of Windsor Betrayed the Allies*. New York: Macmillan, 2000.

Barry, Stephen B. *Royal Service: My Twelve Years as Valet to Prince Charles*. New York: Macmillan, 1983.

———. *Royal Secrets: The View from Downstairs*. New York: Villard, 1985.

Barrymaine, Norman. *The Peter Townsend Story: The True Facts by His Friend*. New York: E. P. Dutton, 1958.

Botham, Noel. *Margaret: The Last Real Princess*. London: Blake Publishing, 2002.

Bradford, Sarah. *The Reluctant King: The Life and Reign of George VI 1895–1952*. New York: St. Martin's Press, 1989.

———. *Elizabeth*. London: William Heinemann, 1996.

Brandreth, Gyles. *Philip & Elizabeth: Portrait of a Marriage*. London: Arrow, 2004.

Brendon, Piers, and Phillip Whitehead. *The Windsors: A Dynasty Revealed*. London: Hodder & Stoughton, 1994.

Brody, Iles. *Gone with the Windsors*. Philadelphia-Toronto: John C. Winston, 1953.

Brough, James. *Margaret: The Tragic Princess*. New York: G. P. Putnam's Sons, 1978.

Bryan, J., III, and Charles V. Murphy. *The Windsor Story: An Intimate Portrait of Edward VIII and Mrs. Simpson by the Authors Who Knew Them Best*. New York: William Morrow, 1979.

Burrell, Paul. *A Royal Duty*. London: Penguin Books, 2003.

Campbell, Lady Colin. *The Royal Marriages*. New York: St. Martin's Press, 1993.

Cathcart, Helen. *The Married Life of the Queen*. London: W. H. Allen, 1970.

Courtney, Nicholas. *Princess Anne: A Biography*. London: George W. Weidenfeld & Nicolson Ltd., 1986.

Cozens-Hardy, H. T. *The Glorious Years*. London: Robert Hale, 1953.

Crawford, Marion. *The Little Princesses: The Story of the Queen's Childhood*. London: Cassell, 1950.

Davies, Nicholas. *A Princess and Her Troubled Marriage*. New York: Birch Lane Press, 1992.

———. *Queen Elizabeth II: A Woman Who Is Not Amused*. New York: Citadel Press, 1996.

———. *Diana: Secrets & Lies*. New York: AMI Books, 2003.

Dimbleby, Jonathan. *The Prince of Wales: A Biography*. New York: William Morrow, 1994.

Douglas-Home, Charles, and Saul Kelly. *Dignified and Efficient: The British Monarchy in the Twentieth Century*. Brinkworth: Claridge Press, 2001.

Duff, David. *Elizabeth of Glamis: The Story of the Queen Mother*. London: Frederick Muller, 1973.

Duncan, Andrew. *The Queen's Year: The Reality of the Monarchy*. New York: Doubleday, 1970.

Edwards, Anne. *Royal Sisters: Queen Elizabeth II and Princess Margaret*. New York: William Morrow, 1990.

Ellis, Jennifer, ed. *Thatched with Gold: The Memoirs of Mabell, Countess of Airlie*. London: Hutchinson, 1962.

Erickson, Carolly. *Lilibet: An Intimate Portrait of Elizabeth II*. New York: St. Martin's Press, 2004.

Ferguson, Sarah. *My Story*. New York: Simon & Schuster, 1996.

Forbes, Grania. *Elizabeth The Queen Mother: A Celebration of a Remarkable Life*. London: Pavilion Books, 1999.

Fox, James. "The Oddest Couple." *Vanity Fair,* September 2003.

Godfrey, Rupert. *Letters from a Prince: Edward Prince of Wales to Mrs. Freda Dudley Ward, March 1918–January 1921*. London: Little Brown, 1998.

Hamilton, Alan. *The Times Royal Handbook*. London: Judy Piakus, 2002.

Hamilton, Willie. *My Queen & I*. London: Quartet Books, 1975.

Hari, Johann. *God Save the Queen*. Cambridge: Icon Books, 2002.

Haseler, Stephen. *The End of the House of Windsor: Birth of a British Republic*. London: I. B. Tauris, 1993.

Hoey, Brian. *Anne The Princess Royal*. London: Grafton Books, 1989.

Kelley, Kitty. *The Royals*. New York: Warner Books, 1997.

Lacey, Robert. *Majesty: Elizabeth II and the House of Windsor*. London, New York: Harcourt Brace Jovanovich, 1977.

———. *The Queen Mother's Century*. London: Little, Brown, 1991.

Lewis, Roger. *Life & Death of Peter Sellers*. New York: Applause Books, 2000.

Longford, Elizabeth. *The Royal House of Windsor*. New York: Alfred A. Knopf, 1977.

———. *The Queen Mother: A Biography*. New York: William Morrow, 1981.

———. *Elizabeth R*. London: George Weidenfeld & Nicolson, 1983.

Matheson, Anne, and Reginald Davis. *Princess Anne: A Royal Girl of Our Time*. London: Frederick Muller, 1973.

Morgan, Janet, ed. *The Backbench Diaries of Richard Crossman*. New York: H. M. Holmes & Meier, 1981.

Morrow, Anne. *The Queen Mother*. New York: Stein & Day, 1985.

Morton, Andrew. *Diana: Her True Story*. New York: Simon & Schuster, 1992.

———. *Diana: In Pursuit of Love*. London: Michael O'Mara Books, 2004.

Parker, John. *The Princess Royal*. London: Hamish Hamilton, 1989.

———. *Prince Philip: His Secret Life*. London: Sidgwick & Jackson, 1990.

Pasternak, Anna. *Princess in Love*. New York: Dutton, 1994.

Pearson, John. *The Selling of the Royal Family: The Mystique of the British Monarchy*. New York: Simon & Schuster, 1986.

Picknett, Lynn, Clive Prince, and Stephen Prior. *War of the Windsors: A Century of Unconstitutional Monarchy*. Edinburgh and London: Mainstream, 2002.

Pope-Hennessy, James. *Queen Mary, 1867–1963*. London: George Allen & Unwin, 1959.

Pritchard, Myron T., ed. *Poetry of Niagara*. Boston: Lothrop Publishing, 1901.

Roosevelt, Eleanor. *On My Own*. New York: Harper & Brothers, 1958.

Seward, Ingrid. *William & Harry*. New York: Arcade, 1993.

———. *The Queen & Di: The Untold Story*. London: HarperCollins, 2000.

Shawcross, William. *Queen & Country: The Fifty Year Reign of Elizabeth II*. New York: Simon & Schuster, 2002.

Starkie, Allan. *Fergie: Her Secret Life*. London: Michael O'Mara Books, 1996.

Strober, Deborah, and Gerald S. Hart. *The Monarchy: An Oral Biography of Elizabeth II.* New York: Broadway Books, 2002.

Swift, Will. *The Roosevelts and the Royals: Franklin and Eleanor, the King and Queen of England, and the Friendship That Changed History.* New York: John Wiley & Sons, 2004.

Thatcher, Margaret. *Downing Street Years.* New York: HarperCollins, 1993.

Thornton, Michael. *Royal Feud: The Dark Side of the Love Story of the Century.* New York: Simon & Schuster, 1985.

Vickers, Hugo. *Alice: Princess Andrew of Greece.* New York: Simon & Schuster, 2000.

Warwick, Christopher. *Princess Margaret: A Life of Contrasts.* London: Andre Deutsch, 2000.

Wharfe, Ken, with Robert Johnson. *Diana: Closely Guarded Secret.* London: Michael O'Mara Books, 2002.

Wilson, A. N. *The Rise and Fall of the House of Windsor.* New York: W. W. Norton, 1993.

Wilson, Christopher. *The Windsor Knot: Charles, Camilla and the Legacy of Diana.* New York: Citadel Press, 2002.

Windsor, Duke of. *A King's Story: The Memoirs of the Duke of Windsor.* London: Prion Books, 1951, 1998.

Ziegler, Philip. *Crown & People.* London: William Collins, 1978.

———. *Mountbatten.* London: William Collins, 1985.

———. *King Edward VIII: A Biography.* London: William Collins, 1991.

INDEX